Fins de Siècle

FINS DE SIÈCLE

How Centuries End
1400 – 2000

Edited by Asa Briggs and Daniel Snowman

Yale University Press
New Haven and London

Set in Garamond Simoncini by SX Composing
Printed in United States

Library of Congress Cataloging-in-Publication Data

Fins de siècle/edited by Asa Briggs and Daniel Snowman.
    Includes bibliographical references and index.
    Contents: The 1390s: the empty throne/Paul Strohm — The 1490s: continuities and
    contrasts/Malcolm Vale — The 1590s: apotheosis or nemesis of the Elizabethan
regime?/Ian Archer — The 1690s: finance, fashion and frivolity/Peter Earle — The
1790s: "visions of unsullied bliss"/Roy Porter — The 1890s: past, present, and future in
headlines/Asa Briggs — The 1990s: the final chapter/Asa Briggs.
    ISBN 0–300–06687–2 (alk. paper)
    1. Great Britain — History — Periodization. I. Briggs, Asa. II Snowman, Daniel.
DA44.F56 1996
941—dc20
    96–19885
    CIP

A catalogue record for this book is available from the British Library.

10 9 8 7 6 5 4 3 2 1

Contents

Notes on the Contributors

Ian Archer is Fellow and Tutor in Early Modern History at Keble College, Oxford, and the author of *The Pursuit of Stability: Social Relations in Elizabethan London* (1991).

Asa Briggs is an internationally-known historian and President of the English Social History Society. He has been Professor of History at the University of Leeds, Vice-Chancellor of the University of Sussex, Provost of Worcester College, Oxford and Chancellor of the Open University. Among his books are *The Age of Improvement, 1783–1867* (1979), *Victorian People* (1975), *A Social History of England* (1985) and *Victorian Things* (1988).

Peter Earle is Reader Emeritus in Economic History at the University of London. Among his books are *The Making of the English Middle Class* (1989) and *A City Full of People: Men and Women of London, 1650-1750* (1994).

Roy Porter is Professor in the Social History of Medicine at the Wellcome Institute for the History of Medicine, London. He is a frequent reviewer and broadcaster, and among his many books are *A Social History of Madness* (1987) and *English Society in the Eighteenth Century* (1990).

Daniel Snowman has written several books on twentieth-century social and cultural history (including a comparative study of British and American values), as well as on such diverse topics as the polar regions and Placido Domingo. For many years he was Chief Producer, Features, at the BBC.

Paul Strohm is Professor of English at Indiana University. He has published widely on Chaucer and his age, and is the author of *Hochon's Arrow: the Social Imagination of Fourteenth-Century Texts* (1992).

Malcolm Vale is Fellow and Tutor in Medieval History at St John's College, Oxford. Among his books are *War and Chivalry* (1981) and *The Angevin Legacy and the Hundred Years War* (1990).

Illustration Acknowledgments

British Library: 1 (Harley 1319 f57), 2 (Egerton 1894 f2v), 6 (Roy 15 D III f526), 10 (Cotton Nero D VII f106), 15 (Harley 4380 f186v), 17 (Roy 18 E f175), 18 (Egerton 615 f57v), 25 (Add. 59899 f98), 27 (Roy 16 F II f210v), 28 (Cotton Nero D VII f105v), 36, 41, 45, 67, 71, 81, 89, 94; The Bodleian Library, Oxford: 3 (MS Rawl. D. 939), 5 (MS Douce 104 f104), 12 (MS Douce 104 f35), 13 (MS Douce 104 f 72), 50 (Douce Prints a 53 (2)), 53 (Douce b 1 f3); President and Scholars of Corpus Christi Collge, Oxford: 4 (MS 67); Württemburgerische Landesbibliothek (photo Joachim Siener): 7; Niedersächsisches Landesgalerie, Hannover: 8; by permission of the Syndics of Cambridge University Library: 9; The Dean and Chapter of Durham: 11; National Gallery, London: 14; The Master and Fellows of Corpus Christi College, Cambridge: 19; The Royal Collection © 1996 Her Majesty the Queen: 20, Ashmolean Museum, Oxford: 21; Bibliothèque Municipale d'Arras: 22; Bibliothèque Nationale, Paris: 23; Hulton Getty Picture Collection: 24, 87, 90, 95, 96, 98, 100; private collection: 29, 38; photo RCHME © Crown copyright: 31, 62; reproduced by permission of the Huntington Library, San Marino, California: 32; Alinari: 33; Victoria and Albert Museum, London: 34, 39, 60, 63, 64, 66, 97; A. F. Kersting: 37; British Museum, London: 40, 47, 51, 52, 56, 57, 58, 72, 76, 77, 119; reproduced by permission of the Marquess of Bath, Longleat House, Warminster, Wiltshire, Great Britain: 42; Guildhall Library, Corporation of London: 43, 70, 74; Society of Antiquaries, London: 44; National Portrait Gallery, London: 49; Science Museum/Science and Society Picture Library: 54, 65; The Governor and Company of the Bank of England: 59, 99; Christie's Images: 61; Bridgeman Art Library/ Guildhall Library: 73; Bedford County Record Office: 78; Board of Trustees of the National Museums and Galleries on Merseyside (Walker Art Gallery, Liverpool): 79; Derby Museum and Art Gallery: 80; photo Courtauld Institute of Art: 81; Ann Ronan at Image Select: 83; The Illustrated London News Picture Library: 84; photo Bulloz: 86; Scottish National Gallery of Modern Art: 101; British Airways Millennium Wheel conceived and designed by David Marks Julia Barfield Architects. The Engineers are Ove Arup & Partners. Picture Nick Wood/Hayes Davidson: 102; John Sturrock/Network: 104; AFP/PA News: 105; Associated Press Ltd: 106, 107; Rainforest Action Nework: 108; Mike Goldwater/Network: 111; Dennis Doran/Network: 113; Neil Libbert/Network: 116.

Introduction

Asa Briggs and Daniel Snowman

'Tis well an old age is out
Time to begin anew.
(*Dryden, 'The Secular Masque', 1700*)

'Millennium' is an old word that carries with it heavy historical, religious and anthropological freight. But the word 'century' (*siècle* in French) is modern both in conception and in use. It is a quite different kind of time unit from the season, the reign or even the era. It was in the seventeenth century that the present and previous centuries began to be compared with each other, but it was not until the nineteenth that the phrase *fin de siècle* was first used. This was the period when history developed as a subject of research and of daily reference. Its time span was lengthened and its range broadened to cover economics and politics, society and culture.

At the end of our own twentieth century, which has defied most nineteenth-century forecasting of what it would be like, there is more concern about a new millennium than about a new century: in Britain, there is even a Millennium Fund looking for imaginative projects to support. In many quarters the arrival of a new millennium is awaited less with eager expectation than with a sense of resigned and even fatalistic inevitability, yet there have been strident warnings of imminent cataclysm. 'The End of the World!' was one of the headlines in November 1992 as sober scientists identified a comet, dubbed Swift-Tuttle, that looked set to collide with the Earth in August 2016. Some observers, anticipating an insupportably large global population, have talked of eventual devastation on an undreamed-of scale by such neo-Malthusian forces as AIDS, by global warming or by nuclear annihilation.

There is an inclination to look backwards, too, with a combination of nostalgia, pride and guilt, in an attempt to assess the nature and quality of our own century: how did we reach the point where we are now? How well equipped are we, the inheritors of a civilisation responsible for Auschwitz and Hiroshima – or heart transplants and interplanetary travel – to cope with the history that awaits us? There was a similar inclination to look backwards in the last decade of the nineteenth century before looking forwards; and it is fascinating to compare the assessments and forecasts made. H. G. Wells said later of his book *Anticipations*, which appeared in 1902, that he was 'already alive to the incompatibility of the great world order foreshadowed by scientific and industrial progress with existing political and social structures'.

The idea of the present book, which invites the reader to travel further back in time than the nineteenth century and to revisit the ends of previous centuries before the term 'century' came into general use, first took shape as a BBC radio project. This was brought to fruition by Daniel Snowman in 1994, although it had been simmering in the editors' minds since the 1960s, when interest in possible 'futures' beyond 2001 began to quicken and deepen. How did ends of centuries compare and contrast? Already there was a sense then that the twentieth century had a shape, although – and it is a warning to 'futurologists' – there was little intimation of the surprises that were to come before the century ended, despite talk of the 'end of history'.

During the 1990s echoes of history, sometimes accompanied by gunfire, have been heard in all parts of the world; and since we are now more aware than ever that we all inhabit the same planet, the widely divergent opinions about the future of our world have their origin in divergent opinions about its past. The forty leading historians whose reflections were recorded for the BBC project each had his or her particular perspectives. The result was a kaleidoscope of views about earlier ends of centuries, inviting perceptive listeners to look for possible clues to the nature of our own. These clues are scattered through distant centuries and not merely through the period immediately preceding our own. As we stumble towards and beyond the year 2000 we may find it instructive to revisit some of the *fins de siècle* of earlier history: *reculer pour mieux sauter*.

All the contributors to this book were among the historians interviewed for the BBC project; and now in print, as on radio, their knowledge and expertise prompt basic questions about what is common to the various *fins de siècle* they discuss and what is distinctive about each. They have approached the particular ends of the centuries with which they are concerned in different ways, aware that at all times and in all places people have certain basic common needs and common reactions, obvious when survival is threatened. Just how people have reacted – and they have had to show resilience – has varied from one place and time to another and has depended on the influence of (for example) current attitudes towards religion, science and technology.

In all centuries there has been stratification, based mainly on property and income: some people have enjoyed better standards of housing, furnishings, dress, food and drink, education and health, than others less privileged. But fortune – and ambition – make for movement. Who is climbing up and who is falling off economic and social ladders largely determines what gives any period of history its own particular quality. The balance between continuity and change itself changes, as do perceptions of it in different sections of society – especially, perhaps, when people perceive themselves to be undergoing a period of transition.

The nature of historical change can be expressed in many ways: in words, above all, but also in statistics, in pictures and in music. Statistics are easier to communicate in print than on radio, while words are common to both. On radio, however, it was easier to communicate the music of the past, a fundamental and evocative ingredient in programmes produced as carefully structured sound montages with no scripted narration. Comparison between one *fin de siècle* and another – and, by implication, with our own – was unstated but powerfully suggested in the radio series.

In the book, the music of the past is essentially absent, except by reference. But we can add pictures – not to decorate but to express and to explain. Nor is it only individual pictures that achieve this purpose, for the iconographies of the various 'ends of centuries' illustrated in this book invite comparison.

In planning the radio series and the book the first intention was to travel back a thousand years and consider England before the Norman conquest and on the eve of the first millennium; popular imagination now turns back not a hundred but a thousand years. Nonetheless, there was little sense in the 990s of the beginning of a new millennium: it was not until the sixteenth century that stories of tenth-century apprehension, even terror, began to circulate. Rumour came late. The volume now begins, therefore, as did the radio series, with the end of the fourteenth century, when there were already signs of what has been called a 'new time consciousness'. The last essay ends where we now are, with our contemporary consciousness both of time and of space, qualified by the fact that, despite clocks and railways, aeroplanes and satellites and journeys to the moon, most people in the world are still largely tied to their own time and place.

The aim of the volume is essentially modest. It does not claim that there is a special significance, metaphysical or otherwise, in the ends of centuries as compared with their middles or their beginnings. The calendar is man-made (as the French revolutionaries stridently reminded the world in the 1790s by reinventing it) and in earlier times people tended to regard time as cyclical and seasonal and to date events by religious and regnal references. But if calendrical time is in part mere artifice, there seems little doubt that in recent centuries it has fed back into the consciousness of those adopting it and that this in turn has had a marked effect upon the way people perceive their own place in history. From our perspective it is impossible not to note how frequently a 'sense of ending' seems to have pervaded each of the periods considered in this book.

One only has to look, for example, at the political leadership. Richard II was ousted in 1399 and killed by the first of the Lancastrians in 1400; Henry VII acquired the throne of England in 1485, putting down firm roots for his new regime (and the subsequent Tudor dynasty) over the next twenty years; Elizabeth I died in 1603 to be succeeded by the first of the Stuarts; William and Mary ousted James II and became joint monarchs in his place in 1689;

George III 'went mad' and political power fell to his prime minister (William Pitt the younger) in the 1790s when the French invented a new calendar; and Queen Victoria died after the longest reign in British history in 1901. Virtually every 'end of century' thus saw the end and/or the beginning of effective power for a monarch, minister, regime or dynasty.

Many other great public landmarks stand out during these periods. The last fifteen years of Elizabeth's reign, for example, were darkened by the shadow of successive armadas from Spain and recurrent wars in Ireland and the Low Countries, while the longest and bloodiest wars in English history were those that erupted in the 1690s and 1790s. Many important social and cultural transitions, too, appear to have occurred as one century gave way to the next: the English rather than the French language seems finally to have been adopted as the tongue of daily discourse at court and in the Church as well as among merchants and yeomen farmers between about 1380 and 1410, while the first infiltration into England of Renaissance humanist ideas occurred during the reign of Henry VII. Between the 1680s and 1720s, a society that had long believed in the magic of the monarch's touch and had burned people for heresy or witchcraft underwent a rapid conversion (if that is the right word) to a more tolerant, rational – or cynical – set of values that vigorously embraced the stock exchange, the political pamphlet and the newspapers.

Clearly, there are some striking parallels   not only between events at the ends of earlier centuries but also with those of our own times. And attitudes, or *mentalités*, then and now, also have their parallels. Euroscepticism is not a phenomenon that began with Norman Tebbit. A sense of insularity, mental as well as physical, is a theme that recurs at various times and in a multiplicity of often mythologised guises throughout both English and British history. 'The English are great lovers of themselves and of everything belonging to them,' wrote an Italian ambassador to England at the end of the fifteenth century: 'Whenever they see a handsome foreigner, they say that "he looks like an Englishman"; and when they partake of any delicacy with a foreigner, they ask him "whether such a thing is made in *their* country?"' Just a century later, Shakespeare's John of Gaunt talked of England in some of the most frequently quoted words in the language as a:

> precious stone set in the silver sea,
> Which serves it in the office of a wall,
> Or as a moat defensive to a house,
> Against the envy of less happier lands

– while a popular novel of 1901 portrayed the fanatical French secretly thrusting their 'steel tube' beneath the Channel across into Britain in an act of international rape.

There are many other cross-century reverberations. Complaints about vagrants and travellers were widespread in late Elizabethan England. A sense of the overwhelming dominance of London and of the magnitude of its problems was common currency at the end of the seventeenth century. Tabloid preoccupation with peccadillos and scandals among the great had its parallels in the later years both of Elizabeth I and Victoria. 'She's fine,' people were wont to say of the latter just as most people do now of Elizabeth II; 'but it will be chaos once she finally goes.'

All the essays focus on Britain, although Ireland can never be omitted from English (or Scottish) history. Nor can continental Europe be left out of British history – or, in more recent periods, the empire or North America. For this reason the study of changing conceptions of space as well as of time is a necessary part of any historical investigation that covers different centuries, each of which had its own changing map. The great voyages of Columbus, which opened up a 'new world' and the explosive repercussions of the French Revolution on the map of Europe are two of the more spectacular examples of *fin-de-siècle* geographical change, to be set alongside the break-up of the Soviet Union in our own decade. Comparisons are often illuminating, and, for example, any survey of London at the end of each century invites comparisons with surveys of other cities, like Florence in the 1490s with its extraordinarily rich, probing cultural life, Amsterdam in the 1690s, Paris in the 1790s or Vienna in the 1890s, the world of Freud, Mahler and Klimt.

Each chapter in this volume is self-contained, and while each is structured in such a way as to reveal something of the texture of daily life during one brief period of history, each too is concerned with retrospect and prospect. No discussion of English attitudes in the 1390s, for example, the theme of Paul Strohm's essay, could avoid looking back (as people did at the time) to the great victories over the French earlier in the century, or to the Black Death which decimated the population of England. Malcolm Vale's chapter places Henry VII's somewhat insular England alongside the more cosmopolitan, thrusting Renaissance culture of continental Europe which did not finally take root in England for another century. Ian Archer's takes account of the shift from pre- to post-Reformation Christianity as Elizabeth's courtiers tried to contain (or foment) potential revolt, while Peter Earle's looks forward to the commercial and industrial changes of the eighteenth century which are picked up by Roy Porter. He, in turn, sets the scene for a century which bequeathed a cluster of unresolved problems which are described in the essay on the 1890s, the first real *fin de siècle*.

Each chapter reveals the particular interests and values of its author, and equally each reader will doubtless draw different conclusions from the historical sequence that unfolds across the seven chapters. Yet authors and readers alike start from the same vantage point in time, if not in space. We are all involved in the same voyage of discovery as we navigate the unknown oceans of the future.

1. An empty throne awaiting the king who would occupy it: Richard II lost his throne in 1399. From a French manuscript *Histoire du Roi d'Angleterre Richard II*, 1400–25.

The 1390s

The Empty Throne

Paul Strohm

The king's seat, with cloths of gold and estate royally apparelled, [was] empty, without anyone presiding or occupying it.[1]

People living in England in the 1390s may not have thought much about the century's approaching end. This unawareness had nothing to do with the state of bovine ignorance sometimes attributed to the middle ages. Nor did it result from any tampering on the part of the much maligned 'medieval Church' – an institution often regarded from our vantage point as narrow and oppressive, but in fact highly varied internally and diffuse in impact. Rather, the great majority of medieval people, including a good many educated ones, simply understood time differently than how we do today. It was perceived not as a continuous flow from the birth of Christ to the present, but as being divided into discontinuous units according to the reigns of kings and the seasons of the liturgical year.

Rather than considering the present as a year in a sequence – 1399, for example – the medieval person would have dated the year in terms of the present king's reign; in this case, the twenty-third year of King Richard, second of that name since the conquest. The battle of Crécy was, by this standard, fought not in 1346 but in the twentieth year of Edward, now king, third of his name since the conquest. Similarly interruptive to a sense of consecutive time were the reckonings of days and hours. Weeks and days were normally measured by the liturgical calendar. Henry IV's deposition of Richard II occurred on Monday of the feast of St Michael the Archangel (rather than on 29 September), and Henry IV's coronation was (symbolically) held on the day of the translation of St Edward, king and confessor (rather than on 13 October). Clocks were a rarity, and most of those in existence were astrological, measuring the movements of the heavens rather than the hours of the day.[2] Thus people were as likely to identify the time of day by an adjacent liturgical service, such as prime or lauds, as by a particular hour.

The practice of framing time within a king's reign or a sacred holiday or a liturgical ceremony disposed the medieval English to consider historical correspondences and repetitions rather than to assess the rate of progress to an unknown future. To be sure, a handful of learned people – mostly literate clerics and theologians – operated within a sense of the calendar year. The practice of dating from the birth (or, alternatively, the incarnation) of Christ was devised by a Scythian monk in Rome during what would be known by his calculations as the sixth century.[3] So some ecclesiastically oriented chroniclers and historians knew the last year of Richard II and the first year of Henry IV as 1399 in a sequence dating from the birth of Christ, and were aware that a new century was impending. This knowledge was undoubtedly shared, but very unevenly, among some segments of the populace as a whole.

Supposing that few and scattered residents of England would have paused to mark the passing of 1399 into 1400, a remarkable paradox remains. Even if few knew of the century's passing, most of them *acted* as if they did. In 1399 a king who had reigned for twenty-three years, son of the revered Black Prince and last direct heir of the Plantagenets, was deposed and replaced. Rival popes – one in Rome supported by the English and Germans and another under French protection in the 'sinful city of Avignon' – vied for control of the Church and branded each other supporters or incarnations of the Antichrist. Bogged down at the midpoint of its fruitless Hundred Years' War with France, England faced active military pressure from the kingdom of Scotland, insurgence in English-dominated sections of Ireland, and the imminence of a bloody and decade-long rising in Wales.

Domestic religious conflict, previously muted in England even as it raged on the continent, sprang to prominence with the emergence of the reformist Lollard movement in the 1380s and 1390s (see p. 31) and the first burning for heresy in 1401. The Rising (or Peasants' Revolt) of 1381 had enlisted large numbers of disgruntled city-dwellers as well as serfs and free agricultural

2. A woman at the loom, depicted in a late fourteenth-century illuminated manuscript.

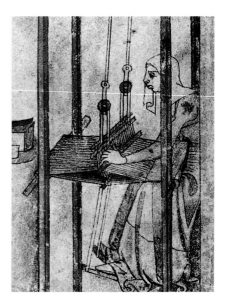

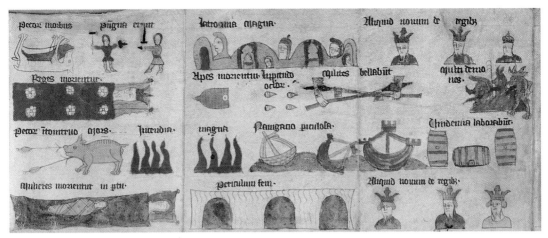

3. An ecclesiastical and astrological almanac from the end of the fourteenth century, packed with current information and predictions for the year ahead.

workers, and its aftershocks continued to perturb social relations. Bondsmen or serfs, other rural workers and apprentices and journeymen of the cities and towns continued to press their landlords and their guild masters for exemption from traditional duties and for the right to sell their labour on more advantageous terms. Women (often widows, but occasionally wives) tentatively entered the world of small production, via brewing and aspects of the cloth trades, in a temporary and short-lived expansion of economic influence. In a variety of ways, therefore, those living in the last years of the fourteenth century might have sensed that a decisive moment was at hand. But what sort of moment, and what was about to be decided?

Few contemporaries would have regarded the last decade of the fourteenth century as a moment of 'progress'. Rather, this decade would (like all medieval decades) have been understood primarily as a way-station in a pattern of drastic, irremediable and inevitable decline. That all time was running downhill from the creation to a final and inevitable Day of Doom (literally 'Judgment Day') was a matter of generally shared conviction. The only question was when that judgment would occur. Fourteenth-century people, anxiously scanning the historical record and signs of deterioration in their immediate surroundings, generally agreed that the moment was near.

The baleful conclusion that 'the day of vengeance is nigh' was, for example, central to one of the most famous and widely circulated of sermons in the English tongue, that delivered by Thomas Wimbledon before St Paul's in 1388. Wimbledon reports a number of popular computational schemes, including Joachim of Fiore's contention that 'from the year of our Lord a thousand and two hundred all times are suspect to me' (accompanied by the ominous observation that 'we are past this suspect time nearly two hundred years'), and Hildegard of Bingen's conviction that the world should endure 7000 years of which 6600 had elapsed, and the near-universal belief that the world should enjoy seven ages (concurrently figured by seven seals) of which the seventh and final was well advanced. Then, in a further refinement of Joachim, Wimbledon argued that 'the great antichrist should come in the fourteen hundredth year from the birth of Christ, of which the number of years is now fulfilled with not fully twelve and a half lacking'.[4]

Ever a poet of educated consensus, John Gower begins his *Confessio Amantis*, written in 1390–4, with a gloomy iteration that,

> the world shall change
> and wax less and yet less,
> till it to nought shall overpass.[5]

His authority is Daniel's interpretation of Nebuchadnezzar's dream, in which the beast of gold, silver, iron and clay betokens the kingdoms of the world and the beast's feet of clay the state of the world in the final age which succeeded the fall of Rome:

4. *Confessio Amantis* (q.v. 1390), the poet John Gower's collection of love stories linked within a narrative framework. In this illumination a lover is shown confessing his sins.

> upon us is fallen
> the end of the world; so we may know,
> this image is near overthrown,
> by which this world was signified,
> that onetime was so magnified,
> and now is old and feeble and vile,
> full of mischief and peril,
> and stands divided now also.

Examining the contemporary scene for signs that the end is near, Gower finds them in profusion. With society threatened by dissolution of customary hierarchies, Gower, who had earlier written a Latin poem denouncing the Rising of 1381, laments that 'now stands the crop under the root', even as the members of the social body refuse to subordinate themselves to its rightful head. The state of the Church concerns him even more, as the contest of rival popes drags on undecided, giving rise to additional and emulative forms of schism:

> Schism causes forth to spring
> this new sect of Lollardy,
> and also many a heresy
> among the clerics in themselves.
> It were better to dig and delve
> and stand upon the right faith,
> than know all that the Bible says
> and err – as some clerics do.

The Lollards might be considered retrospectively as a kind of 'proto-Protestant' movement within the later fourteenth and early fifteenth centuries. Within the context of their own time, they may be seen as they saw themselves, as one of many currents of reformation and dissent within the Church. Whether intrinsic or extrinsic to Catholicism, however, the Lollards represented a doctrinal pluralism that seemed to contemporaries a clear sign of dissolution and decay. Gower wishes that, in the face of such divergent tendencies, his poem may function like the music of Arion's harp, reconciling discord. Finally, though, his review of the world's many sources of division leads him to conclude that 'no world's thing may last / till it be driven to the last'. The only permanence will be the end of time itself.

If topicality and externalisation of assumptions were the mark of a major poet, Gower would be the only literary source requiring examination in this contest. Chaucer, certainly, is a good deal more elliptical about any time-related anxieties he might entertain. Yet a certain shadowed and uneasy undertone rests within Harry Bailly's anxious injunction to tell what seems to be Chaucer's final tale: 'but hasten you, the sun will a-down'.[6] And the

12

5. An image of Reason, one of many images of Langland's *Piers Plowman*, written between 1360 and 1399. Reason wears riding gloves, having travelled to court with Conscience.

Parson, his final story-teller, has much to say of the necessity for contrition in view of 'the day of doom and of the horrible pains of hell': 'For, as St. Jerome says, "At every time that I remember the day of doom I quake; for when I eat or drink, or what soever I do, it ever seems to me that the trumpet sounds in my ear: Rise up, you who are dead, and come to the judgment."' The *Canterbury Tales* ends with a sense that the long-deferred day of judgment is at hand, for the individual whose soul will be summoned before the final tribunal, and for society as a whole.

Resulting from the view of a world in terminal decline and rushing towards judgment was an anxious search for signs that the end might be near. Remote history and immediate surroundings were canvassed for clues of divine intent. In this spirit William Langland causes Reason, a speaker in his allegorical poem *The Vision Concerning Piers the Plowman*, to interpret the recent pestilence and a more recent storm of wind as signs of God's anger and the impending end of the world:

> He proved that pestilences were for pure sin,
> And the south-western wind on Saturday at evening
> Was openly for pride and no other reason.
> Pear- and plum-trees were puffed to the earth
> Beeches and broad oaks were blown to the ground
> And turned their tails upward in token of dread,
> That deadly sin before doomsday shall destroy them all.[7]

And so, at the end of Langland's poem, Antichrist is actively abroad in the world, attracting hordes to his banner and ruling nations with the help of his confederates the false friars, even as plague-death assails the nations' pride.

An understanding of world history as inevitable decline would seem to leave little room for dreams of amelioration or social improvement. Yet certain small spaces did exist for a vision of progress – or at least temporary stabilisation within decline. One such imaginative space rests within the idea of apocalypse itself, in the belief that a millennium or period of spiritual refreshment and grace will intervene between the coming of Antichrist and the final end of time. Associated variously with Joachimite and Sibylline prophetic traditions, the notion of the millennium varied widely with respect to its timing (either after or before the coming of Antichrist) and duration (from the thousand-year kingdom of Revelation to the mere forty-five days unaccounted for in Daniel 12 or virtually any timespan between). Whatever

6. Alpha and Omega, a late fourteenth-century representation of the Apocalypse.

the timing, the notion gave a stimulus to reveries or fantastic projections of earthly betterment and spiritual development.[8]

Often deliberately inscrutable and evasive in final import, but always representing an affront to established arrangements and kingly powers, millennial prophecies waxed and waned from late Antiquity until the Reformation, especially in continental Europe, cresting in such movements as the sect of Fra Dolcino in the early fourteenth century, the rising of the Taborites in 1419–20 and the sixteenth-century German Peasant Wars. The end of the fourteenth century was not, by such standards, a high point of millennial speculation. But such speculation rests constantly at the fringes of more orthodox discourse. Langland's Conscience can, for example, imagine an impending time when,

> One Christian king shall rule us each one.
> Meed [reward] shall no more be master as she is now,
> But love and lowness and loyalty together –
> These shall be masters on earth true men to save.
>   . . . Such love will arise
> And such peace among the people and a perfect truth . . .
> Each who bears dagger, broadsword, or lance,
> Axe or hatchet or any weapon at all,
> Shall be judged to death unless he have it hammered
> Into a sickle or a scythe, a share or a coulter . . .
> And ere this fortune befall, men shall find the worst,
> By six suns and a ship and half a sheaf of arrows;
> And the middle of a moon shall make the Jews convert,
> And Saracens at that sight shall sing *Gloria in excelsis*.[9]

The gnomic refrains of the rebels of 1381 – 'God bring a cure, for now is the time' – would seem to depend on such hoped-for relief, on the view that God might offer worldly redress at that low point of worldly fortune, just before the end of time.[10]

Hope for the future was, however, an insubstantial and unreliable consolation. Rationales for reform were more commonly sought in the past, in an effort to reinstitute inherently superior past practice, however briefly, within present time. Thus history and precedent were ransacked by devotees of present reform. Although frequently accused of destroying tax rolls and other records bearing on their oppression, the rebels of 1381 also invaded muniment rooms in search of old deeds and charters with which they hoped to bolster their claims. The chronicler Walsingham, for example, complained that the St Albans rebels 'asked for all records in the abbey which might be of help to them or to the detriment of the monastery', including a demand 'to restore to them the liberties and rights held by their fathers and ancestors in the days of King Henry',[11] in fact, they briefly

7. Blind Fortune's wheel, a recurring medieval image: here a king rises, a beggar descends (*c.* 1425).

succeeded in extracting from King Richard a letter (soon to be disavowed) instructing the abbot to deliver 'certain charters in your custody which were made by our ancestor, King Henry . . . concerning common, pasture, fishing rights and several other commodities'.[12]

The other potentially transformative social movement of the time, the Lollard critique of the established Church and its theological superstructure, was similarly grounded upon an attempted return to an earlier and simpler form of Church organisation and theology. A contemporary life of Henry V, praising him for combating heresy in the realm, accuses John Wyclif of deriving his malevolent ideas by 'dressing in new terms errors and heresies summoned up from ancient paganism', and depicts the Lollard leader John Oldcastle as arrayed 'cum vetustate et novitate' – with archaisms and innovations.[13] Many Lollard arguments were grounded on the words of the Bible and the early Fathers, especially Augustine, and the simplicity of the apostles and martyrs, and the Lollards regarded subsequent theological and, especially, organisational developments and practices (tithing, cults of relics, administrative hierarchies) with extreme suspicion.

8. Plague victims: prayers for them at the altar. The altar of the Barefoot Carmelites at Göttingen.

Even in the shadow of imminent destruction, life nevertheless had to be lived. From the letters of St Paul onward, the problem of mobilising activity and making choices in the face of ultimacy was a recurring one, and people in the 1390s obviously found functional, as well as theoretical, ways of sustaining their hope for what the world might offer them. The pessimistic Gower, conceding his pleasure that those who preceded him wrote books that remain, expresses his own determination to refresh literary tradition with new materials expressive of his world:

> It is good that we also . . .
> Do write anew some of the material
> Set forth by the old wise ones
> So that it might in the same way,
> When we are dead and gone away,
> Be left to the world's ear
> In times coming after this.[14]

'Times coming'? A rare act of faith on Gower's part. And, even as he insists that the world is going downhill, he yet recognises that his writing must embrace 'the world which neweth every dai'.[15] A certain thoughtful resolve, a decision to make the best of life even while acknowledging its precarious character, pervades medieval literature and especially that of the end of the fourteenth century. All know the Wife of Bath's gallant:

> The flour is gone, there is no more to tell,
> The bran as I best can now must I sell;
> But yet to be right merry will I strive.[16]

Consider in the same vein the sober reflections of the Merchant in Chaucer's 'Shipman's Tale' – not the most profound of his characters, but obviously not the least either:

> For of us chapmen . . .
> Scarcely among twelve will two thrive
> Continually, achieving our full age.
> We must make cheer and good visage,
> And endure the world as it may be,
> And maintain our position privately
> Till we are dead . . .[17]

The brevity of life – if not through apocalypse, then through the personal apocalypse which each must face through illness, violence or age – was freely admitted. Undoubtedly, with the support of a religion that insisted upon ephemerality, it was more broadly acknowledged than today. Yet life's allotted span might be lived with enterprise and verve. Academic medievalists are always cautious about what has been called 'swat-on-the-rump' medievalism, and the tendency is to emphasise the *gravitas* of the period and its state of mind. But, in fact, it is not hard to discern a certain zestful relish in the minutiae of daily living and the material world. To be sure, the English people of 1399 lived with the horrors of plague and famine (and the memory of the mid-century visitation of the plague that had eliminated between one-third and one-half of the populace in one year); recurrent warfare (having broken its temporary truce with France, the England of 1400 had not a single friend in any contiguous or neighbouring state); and social turmoil (including the experience of tens of thousands of rural workers and urban labourers, provoked by a poll tax and other intolerable exactions, up in arms in 1381). Yet the English at the century's end were also excited to discussion by a range of engrossing curiosities – stories such as that of two Londoners who were served eggs containing images of the face of a man, Richard II's reopening of the tomb of Richard Earl of Arundel to demonstrate that his severed head had not rejoined his body, bells that rang unbidden at the shrine of St Edward, Westminster, and a spring in Wales that ran for a day with blood.[18]

The apparent cataclysms of the century underwrote some of the most turbulent excitements and possibilities of late-century life. Yet the very reduction in population through plague and famine from some five million people at the beginning of the century to three million or less at the end meant more sustenance, more movable wealth, and increased vocational and social opportunity for survivors of every rank and class. Although starvation and plague persisted as occasional instances and as imaginative possibilities (and would return with a vengeance in the sixteenth and seventeenth centuries), both were in abeyance at the end of the fourteenth century. Consequent labour shortages and increased opportunity to sell services in rural and urban production hastened the end of serfdom. Migration from the countryside to town or city became an increasingly attractive option. Most people at the turn of the century were still agricultural workers of one sort or another, but their situation also improved. Although the peasant diet was mainly restricted to brown bread, pottage and ale, better farming techniques (including cultivation of legumes) on better land for a smaller populace meant that few actually starved.[19] In merchant and gentle households, in monasteries and religious establishments, and of course in aristocratic households, consumption of foods and luxuries burgeoned. A detailed study published in 1993 suggests that these groups consumed meat

9. Pilgrims at the shrine of the last Saxon king, Edward the Confessor, centuries after his death.

10. Richard de Threton, a priest, from *The Golden Book of St Albans*, compiled in 1380, listing gifts made to St Albans Abbey and including portraits of the benefactors.

and fish at a rate that would be considered shockingly high today.[20] Spices, furs, silverplate, featherbeds, Gascon wine and well-lit homes were also available to the advantaged.

Medieval social theory remained to some degree bound (as the later twentieth-century imagination is still in some respects bound) by the idea of three social classes or estates – in the medieval case, knightly, priestly and agrarian. One can certainly understand how the 1 per cent of the populace enjoying aristocratic or knightly status and the 2 or 3 per cent of the populace in clerical orders might benefit by such a theory, especially since it was couched in the notion of interdependence for the 'common profit' of all. But, in point of fact, English society had never fully adhered to such a system, and its departure in the years after about 1350 was rapid indeed. An exceptionally revealing document is the Anonimalle chronicler's description of the poll tax of 1379, which was governed by a scheme that set different rates for different social groups and was calibrated by a concept of social justice considerably more refined than that of its Thatcher-era counterpart. Its first group included dukes (assessed at £6 6s), counts (£4), barons and knights (40s), bachelors and esquires with means to become knights (20s), esquires of lesser estate (6s 8d), and esquires in service (3s 4d). A second group included sergeants at law (20s) and attorneys (6s 8d), while a third consisted of substantial urban citizens, including the mayor of London (£4), aldermen of London and lesser mayors (40s), grand merchants of the realm (20s), other merchants (13s 4d), lesser merchants and artificers (6s 8d to 2s

6d) and sergeants and franklins (6s 8d to 40d). A fourth group was more miscellaneous: it included pardoners and summoners (3s 4d to 12d), hostellers below the estate of merchant (40d to 12d), and at the base ordinary citizens (4d per household) and 'true mendicants', who were not expected to pay.

Evident in this survey is the rapid development of what might be called the 'middle strata' of the society, consisting of merchants, artificers, and craftsmen below the 'gentle' ranks of aristocrats, knights and esquires. Most of the Canterbury pilgrims so vividly represented by Chaucer in his Prologue to the *Canterbury Tales* belong to this varied occupational grouping. The traditional 'three estates' are present in the persons of the Knight, the Parson and the Plowman – the latter is arguably, and not coincidentally, the most idealised of his pilgrim band – but the ranks of the pilgrims are filled by urban entrepreneurs, including not just the Guildsmen and their Cook but also people like the Merchant, the Physician and the Manciple. Some are Londoners, whereas others, like the Miller and the Reeve, are figures from town life and the countryside.

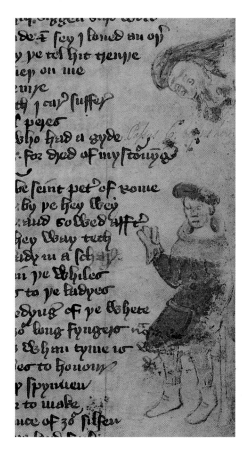

11 (*facing page*) Knightly service. A new knight receives his sword from the king. This ornamented initial letter D is from a late thirteenth-century English Bible.

12 (*left*) Piers Plowman. Although ploughmen were plentiful in the middle ages, only a few representations of them survive. William Langland immortalised them in his *Vision Concerning Piers the Plowman*.

Altogether, the urbanites and town-dwellers pursuing such vocations would have comprised no more than 15 per cent of the population, but they embraced some of its most politically volatile and economically creative members. In his Prologue Chaucer exploited at every turn their penchant for self-definition and display. His authorial purpose was thereby well served, since the broad range of vocations and personal foibles among his tellers assisted him in 'staging' a wide variety of tales. Equally pertinent is the fact that few villeins or ploughmen would have possessed the personal freedom or the means to undertake a pilgrimage in the first place. Nonetheless, whatever its fidelity to the composition of an actual pilgrim-band, Chaucer's assembly is hardly a cross-section of late-century English society. Had demographic accuracy been one of Chaucer's concerns, twenty or more of his thirty-odd pilgrims would have been one or another kind of agricultural worker. As it is, his idealised and politically complacent Plowman stands in for a more diverse and politically unruly band.

Barely hinted at in the Anonimalle account of the 1379 poll tax was a numerous but wholly unofficial and largely untallied category, that of 'true

13. A figure of Poverty, rarely depicted. She is 'feble' and downcast, but patient too (from *Piers Plowman*).

mendicants' (together with its shadow-category, by no means insignificant in its own right, an implied underworld of 'false mendicants'). This turbulent group of people had probably, and somewhat paradoxically, multiplied as a result of expanded opportunities for wage labour resulting from the population shortage prevailing from the mid-century onwards. Despite a series of regulatory statutes of labourers (the first dating from 1351), agricultural workers bound to the land by law and custom deserted in droves throughout the second half of the century, with the object of bettering themselves by marketing their agricultural labour or by seeking employment in the towns. Increasingly severe legislation dictated the arrest of servants or labourers found on highways or in towns without letters of patent sealed under the authority of justices of the peace. Many of these employment-seekers found what they sought, but others ended up as casual labourers, charity-cases or beggars, or in other marginal capacities. The historian Christopher Dyer adds to his inventory of city-dwellers 'vagabonds, beggars, street-entertainers, prostitutes and professional criminals' and his anatomisation of country-dwellers includes those who 'lived precariously from casual labouring, gleaning, begging, prostitution and sheaf-stealing'.[21]

Something of the confused turbulence of the late fourteenth-century social picture is conveyed in William Langland's opening vision of the fair field of folk, in his *Piers Plowman*:

> A fair field of folk found I there:
> All manner of men, the mean and the rich,
> They work and they wander in the way of the world.
> Some put themselves to the plough, playing full seldom,

> Setting and sowing they worked full hard,
> With winnings that gluttons will casually waste.
> Some went in for pride, apparelled them accordingly,
> In countenance of their clothing they come disguised.
> But in prayers and penance many put faith,
> All for the love of our Lord they lived strictly . . .
> Some chose trade; they succeeded the better,
> And it seems to our sight that such men thrive;
> And some to make mirths, as minstrels know how,
> They get gold with their glee – guiltless I think . . .
> Bidders and beggars went fast at their work
> Till their bellies and their bags were brimful of loot,
> Faked it for their food, and then fought over ale.

Scarcely present here (though fleetingly implied) are the ordered social hierarchy and devout humility which figure so prominently in many later accounts of the middle ages, especially those of Victorian sentimentalists and neo-traditionalists. The world described by Langland is marked by a bewildering variety of personal choices, as expressed through vocation, whether it is pursued for personal gain or for social good, for present or for future reward.

Some of our earliest narrative sources are already stories of confused loyalty and betrayal, like the *Song of Roland* and the various tellings of *Tristan and Isolde*. Chaucer can imagine a simpler time when 'man's word was obligation' ('Lack of Steadfastness'), but common sense suggests that such retrospective imaginings were tactical in nature, meant like most versions of the past to carry a present-day point. Moreover, while the ideal of durable personal loyalty had been widely celebrated in the earlier middle ages, in the later climate of the 1390s drastic alterations in the *forms* of social relation were leading to the abandonment of durability even as an abstract ideal. During earlier medieval centuries, personal indebtedness had been understood in terms of the relationship between social superior and social inferior – lord and vassal, master and apprentice, prelate and parishioner – a relationship which was often bound by formal oath, and consequently sanctified or divinely sanctioned; and it was often understood to endure (or at least aspired to endure) 'for the term of life'. Beginning in the thirteenth century, however, and rampant after the middle of the fourteenth century, was a new and more opportunistic kind of social relation, bound not by timeless personal oath but by expedient contract enduring only for the term of the agreement, expressed in legal language and motivated by personal advantage rather than by a presumed ideal.[22] Such contractual relations represent a considerable slackening of social obligations and bonds. The loyal vassal of high medieval conception (and possible occasional practice) was now rapidly becoming something like a 'salaryman', knit in less savoury

14. An icon of kingship: Richard II shown as a boy king at prayer in the Wilton Diptych (*c.* 1395–9). Note the heraldic emblems including the white hart.

relation to a group of temporary confederates for extortionary purposes. As Chaucer laments of his own time in 'Lack of Steadfastness':

> Among us now a man is held unable
> Unless he can, by some collusion,
> Do his neighbour wrong or oppression.

However slight their evidence for a former, better time, many people in the 1390s plainly understood themselves to live in a benighted and degraded society, when enduring ties of loyalty had given way to more temporary, legalistic and self-interested arrangements.

The influential social metaphors of the earlier middle ages had been corporate or organic, emphasising the existence of a social 'body' whose limbs were inextricably (and beneficially) interdependent.[23] Ideas of mutuality persisted in the later fourteenth century, in theories of the 'common good' or, in the dialect of the day, 'common profit'. But such slogans were often the first resort of the self-interested scoundrel. Increasingly, social discourse of the day exhibited a shift from a 'corporate' to a 'conflict' model of social interaction, in which different groups vied with one another to realise sectional interests.

The central and unavoidable sign of social contention was, of course, Henry Bolingbroke's forcible supplanting of his cousin Richard II, last of the Plantagenets, in 1399 – especially after the symbolic affront was sealed by Richard's murder in captivity in February 1400. The extent of Richard's unpopularity at the time of his deposition remains open to debate. Certainly, he had attempted in the earlier 1390s to overawe the City of London, and in fact had succeeded in extorting immense contributions and gifts from Londoners as the price of the City's return to favour. He had adopted an increasingly imperial style in his latter years, fancying himself a candidate for Holy Roman Emperor, surrounding himself with a picked guard of Cheshire archers, and even (according to one chronicler) adopting the habit of seating himself on his throne after dinner and casting his eye about the room, anyone who fell under his gaze being expected to kneel. In addition, Richard's dispossession of Henry of Derby, his cousin and soon-to-be rival, from the extensive Lancastrian estates upon the death of his father John of Gaunt must have been very unsettling to his most influential subjects' sense of aristocratic privilege. Even so, the ease with which Henry seized control of the kingdom – progressing rapidly from his landing in July 1399 to his capture of Richard outside Conway Castle in August, his self-proclamation in Westminster at the end of September and his coronation on 13 October – might seem in retrospect to have arisen as much from Richard's ill-timed absence in Ireland and certain shifts of loyalty among a handful of aristocrats as from any abiding sense of Richard's unfitness for the throne.[24]

15. Henry Bolingbroke becomes Henry IV after the deposition of Richard II. He carries the Sword of State.

Whatever the circumstances surrounding the seizure of the throne, the spectacle of a king's displacement and of the throne itself briefly standing empty could only have been extremely unsettling for those who beheld or knew of it. The throne was, of course, the seat from which the king exercised his royal *dignitas* and will, and even its temporary voidance seriously fissured the concept of majesty and divine sanction upon which later medieval society relied with a mixture of ardent belief and growing unease.

The ceremony of Richard's deposition and Henry's elevation was designed to provide as much reassurance as a symbolic enactment of harmony, orderly succession and divine election can afford. It occurred before a gathering of dignitaries and citizens in Westminster Hall on 30 September 1399. There, in the presence of Richard (who, according to Lancastrian accounts, had already agreed 'with cheerful countenance' to resign the throne) and Henry (who occupied only his position as Duke of Lancaster), all gathered about the vacant throne: 'the king's seat, with cloths of gold and estate royally apparelled, empty, without anyone presiding or occupying it'.[25] Richard's renunciation was read in Latin and in English. For good measure he was accused and convicted of numerous failings and misdeeds, including disrespect for the laws of the land.

Richard convicted and the throne declared formally void, Duke Henry rose from his seat ('marking himself meekly with the sign of the cross on his forehead, and his breast, naming the name of Christ'), and issued this challenge for the throne, speaking in the English tongue:

I, Harry of Lancaster, claim the realm of England, and the crown with all the members and appurtenances. As I that am descended by right line of blood, coming from the good lord King Harry the third. And through that right, that God of his grace hath sent to me, with the help of my kin and of my friends to recover it; the which realm was in point to be undone for default of governance and good law.

Following this carefully orchestrated and publicised succession of events, Henry had himself crowned king in an imaginatively choreographed coronation ceremony. But the void briefly revealed in those summer and autumn months of 1399 was not quickly to be filled.

Richard, imprisoned at Pontefract Castle as the year 1399 ended and the year 1400 began, remained a problem. Stripped of his crown and allies and sequestered from his friends, he was not a hard man to kill. A belated and

16. A royal tomb. Richard II's remains were returned to Westminster soon after the coronation of Henry V in 1413.

not very authoritative-seeming account of his death, from John Capgrave's mid-fifteenth-century chronicle, might be the best we will ever have: 'Some men said that he refused sustenance ['peyned himself'] and died from hunger. Some others say that he was kept from meat and drink while a knight rode to London and came again.'[26] Might this business of a knight riding to London and back constitute what Americans call 'a smoking gun', linking Henry to Richard's death? Very probably so. The issue rolls of the Exchequer for March 1400 contain several items related to travel to and from Pontefract castle, including: 'To a certain valet of Thomas Swinford, knight, coming from Pontefract Castle to London, in order to certify to the Council about certain related matters convenient to the king.'[27] And a closely following item adds, 'To a certain other valet sent from London by the Council to Pontefract Castle for the protection and custody of the body of Richard the Second, late king of England.' Other items relate to the body's transport to London, and display and burial at Langley Abbey. But, if Richard was easy to kill, in other ways he died hard. At the turn of the century and well beyond it his unappeased spirit walked the land; rumours of Richard alive and well in Scotland, and even sightings of Richard in England, persisted through the first two decades of the new century, unimpeded even by Henry V's ostentatious translation of Richard's remains to his tomb in Westminster soon after his coronation in 1413.

Strife at the top was amplified by every kind of sectional hostility. Border skirmishes between representatives of the royal court (in Westminster) and the City of London were endemic. Richard II had conducted his own highly visible 'quarrel' with the City in and after 1392, but relations between Westminster and London had never been smooth.[28] Open spaces – and often a barge-ride – separated Westminster from the City at the end of the fourteenth century, and a more than metaphorical distance can frequently be seen. Officers of the king and court both tyrannised the City and suffered as its victims. Plea rolls and other City records abound in accounts of scuffles between City-dwellers and members of royal retinues, and such quarrels often involved the City elite. A representative 1396 treason case involved the murder of a horn-maker who had been recruiting workers on royal commission – allegedly at the hands of his urban rivals, the elite of the Goldsmiths of London.[29]

Cities constantly recruited new residents from the country (since high mortality in the cities typically resulted in the extinction of many families within a generation or at most two). Once urbanised, however, the city-dweller found ways to ignore even the closest family origins, as well as the more complex economic interdependencies uniting city and country, and to embrace a view of country-dwellers as ignorant and threatening rustics. The city-dweller venturing into the country was likely to traverse it with all possible speed, on relays of horses, until reaching the sanctuary of another city or a country estate. Those entering into country dealings were likely to end up 'marked' – as when the subtle clerk Alain of Chaucer's 'Reeve's Tale' tangled with the canny miller of Trumpington and bore away a broken nose (squashed down to the 'camus' or pugged silhouette attributed to country folk by tradition) as an emblem of his ill-judged involvement.[30] Urban unease was also engendered by any country influx to the city that escaped the closest regulation. Citified chroniclers of Westminster and elsewhere described the peasants of Essex and Kent who entered the City of London in 1381 as raving yokels, bent on orgies of drunken destruction, and barely human (if human at all) in their animalistic excess.

Yet the city was itself hardly a paradigm of social order; constant tension informed the relations between the different urban vocations and groups. The fault lines ran between citizens and non-citizens, merchant-capitalists (often trading on a grand scale in goods and other commodities) and ordinary guildsmen; monopolists in the victualling trades and artificers in

17. Wat Tyler led what came to be called the Peasants' Revolt of 1381. The scene is described in formalised fashion in Froissart's illuminated *Chronicles*, which tells tales of medieval chivalry.

the more usual sense; city-dwellers and suburbanites (the suburbs being at that time places of extreme disrepute); natives and aliens; guild masters and apprentices; persons with a future in a craft or trade and journeymen and casual workers; the employed and unemployed and beggars; property-owning men and legally vulnerable women (including the most vulnerable of all, the *femmes couvertes* or women who relinquished rights to their husbands in marriage).

Emblematic of social unrest in late fourteenth-century London were the constant efforts of journeymen–labourers to organise to protect themselves against monopolising guildsmen – sometimes employing such novel forms as parish religious associations in an effort to further their aims – and, on the other side, the constant vigilance of city leaders in ferreting out and proscribing their meetings. Consider the observation of the Westminster chronicler who, noting the passivity of London's upper classes during the invasion of the City by country-dwelling rebels in 1381, concluded that the essential strategy was to keep the rebels and disaffected City-dwellers from joining hands: 'It was feared that, if the ever-stronger serfs should be resisted, commons of the city might rise as their accomplices against the rest of the citizens, and that the whole city should be lost as a result of its internal divisions.'[31] Even so, unknown sympathisers opened the City gates to the rebels, and many (if not most) of the rioters within the City consisted of disgruntled journeymen, impatient apprentices and casual workers from Southwark and adjacent areas.

The prevailing xenophobia of the period, sharpened by urban economic competition, also surged to the fore in the rising of 1381, when Londoners seized upon the turmoil to settle scores with the community of resident Flemish cloth-workers. The Westminster chronicler says that rebels (undoubtedly, in this case, of the urban variety) 'proceeded to the area along the banks of the Thames where the greatest number of Flemings live, and they beheaded without judgment and without trial all the Flemings found there, so that you could see thrown in the streets and elsewhere heaps of corpses and headless bodies of those killed'.[32] Nor were Flemings the only sufferers. Lombards were said to have been slain too. The growing importance of Florentine and other north Italian financiers (in the wake of the expropriation and expulsion of the Jews in the later thirteenth century) and the inevitability of tension between Genoese and other north Italians and London capitalists over control of the wool trade guaranteed periodic outbreaks of anti-Lombard feeling between the mid-fourteenth and mid-fifteenth centuries. In 1379 the London mercantile establishment was scandalously involved in the effectively unpunished death of Janus Imperial, a Genoese ambassador engaged in direct trading negotiations with the Royal Council. This crime was subject to repetition with minor variations, with the growth of the trading share and economic leverage of the great Italian carracks (landing at Southampton rather than London and frequently arranging with the king to bypass the tariffs and restrictions of the Calais wool staple).

Mistrust of the foreign merchants and workers in the capital centred on their 'otherness' with respect to language and custom and economic interests. Other differences of culture and political concerns, linked with territorial ambition and the manifestation of an early form of colonialism guaranteed continuing antipathy between the English and the 'wild Irish', the unruly Welsh and the marauding Scots. But a more surprising, or at least longer delayed, sort of 'othering' went on at the end of the fourteenth century and beginning of the fifteenth – this time not of an alien group but of a distinctly English stratum involving artisans and petty tradesmen, lesser clergy and a handful of gentlepersons: the Lollards. The origin of their name is uncertain; it may derive from the Latin *lolium*, or 'cockle', thought to adulterate the good grain of orthodoxy, or it may have implied in English that its followers were slackers or loiterers. In any event, it had the effect of such terms of derision as quakers or ranters or shakers, by which dissenting groups of later centuries were known before they themselves defiantly adopted the hostile term. The Lollards' self-conception was, however, as an elect or true Church within the falsity of the established Church, as a 'sect' striving to set a truthful and more virtuous standard for itself. Their views, derived in part from the writings of Wyclif and his followers, seem somewhat less controversial today, focusing on ecclesiastical poverty, mistrust of images and – especially – the consecrated host of the eucharist as possessed of a continuing material (as well as spiritual) identity.

Although certain churchmen throughout the reign of Richard II had opposed Wyclif, seeking expulsion of his educated followers from their university posts and deploring the early spread of Lollardy, Richard never much interested himself in persecuting Lollards – in fact, the emergent sect may have enjoyed some support among members of his inner circle, and some of his other courtiers might have been intrigued by the possible financial windfall to be realised through divestment of ecclesiastical property.[33] It remained for Henry IV, in concert with the fervently anti-Lollard archbishop Arundel, to emulate continental anti-heretical practice by escalating the persecution of Lollards to a new and more active stage soon after his coronation in 1399.[34]

The opening months of 1401 saw the coincidence in time of an ecclesiastical convocation headed by Arundel as Archbishop of Canterbury and the Hilary session of Parliament at Westminster, each of them formally concerning themselves with the Lollard threat. The convocation convicted William Sawtry, a previously accused and recanted priest, of Lollard views (including his insistence that the consecrated host possessed a material residue), degraded him from his priesthood, and turned him over to the

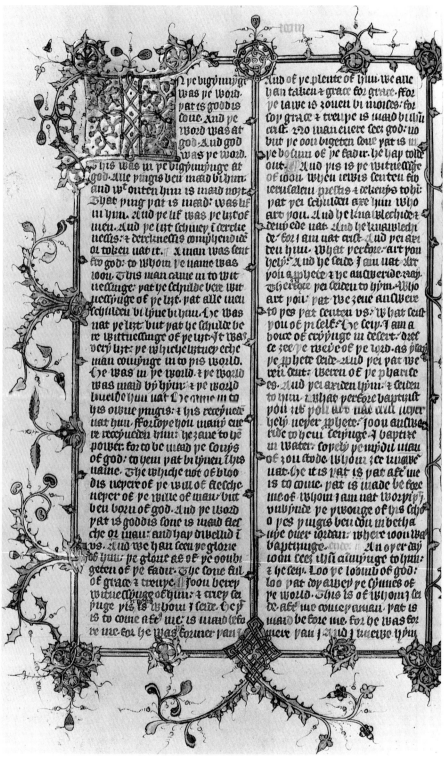

18. Wyclif's Bible: the beginning of St John's Gospel. The first six words link the centuries and are all still featured in the text of the King James Bible, read in the twentieth century.

secular arm for punishment. Parliament, meanwhile, was in the process of framing its terrible statute 'On the necessity of burning heretics', but Henry IV was so impatient for execution that he arranged for Sawtry to be burned by royal decree, several weeks before final approval of the statute.

Sawtry, naturally enough, received a bad press in the orthodox chronicles, among which the *Annales Ricardi* turns the final encounter between Sawtry and Arundel into a bad joke on the doomed priest. Learning of his degradation,

> the debauchee [Sawtry], in the height of his pride, responded, 'And so your malice has achieved its end. What more malice will you be able to do to me?' And Arundel said to the military marshal, 'Take him with you and punish him according to your law.' And he was led to Smithfield, and there, with many watching, was burnt.[35]

Other descriptions are more vividly detailed. Adam of Usk, possibly an eye-witness, says that Sawtry was 'chained standing to a post in a barrel, surrounded with burning faggots, and reduced to ashes'. Thus the English burned their first heretic. Accounts of Sawtry's death imply that many Lollards were chastened by the example made of him, but the burnings were not to cease. It would appear that the usurping Lancastrians, eager by all available means to portray themselves as champions and enforcers of orthodox and established institutions, *needed* a heresy – and were of no mind to let this one pass from public view.

As the fourteenth century passed to the fifteenth, the English tongue began to enter the written record, not only in literary works by Chaucer and others, but also in the sphere of public life, through official proclamations and records. Emphasis on a shared language might be a source of social solidarity, as Henry IV well understood in his spoken and written 'challenge' for the English throne and as his son Henry V acknowledged in letters written in English describing the achievements of his French campaigns. More often, however, English enters the written record as a language of contention and conflict. One of the first books written in English, Thomas Usk's *Testament of Love* (c. 1384), boldly declares an intent (here we preserve the form of the original English) to 'shewe our fantasyes in suche wordes as we lerneden of our dames tonge' – and goes on to make a political and factional argument designed to illustrate the author's loyalty to the City of London's Mayor Brembre and his wish to serve the king.[36] Mayor Nicholas Brembre himself, upon his 1383 election over his rival John Northampton, sought to secure the grip of his faction and to quell civil unrest with the first proclamation in English to appear alongside the Latin and French of the London City records:

19. Medieval Romance. The
poet Geoffrey Chaucer talks to
a group of lords and ladies
(from *Troilus and Criseyde*,
early fifteenth-century).

> The mayor, sheriffs and aldermen . . . command on the king's behalf and our
> own also that no man make any congregations, meetings or assemblies of
> people, privately or openly, any more of craft guilds than of other men, with-
> out leave of the mayor. Nor overmore in any manner make alliances,
> confederacies, conspiracies or obligations to bind men together, to sustain
> any quarrels by living and dying together, upon pain of imprisonment.[37]

Others, Brembre's factional rivals, complained that this law-maker was
actually the arch law-breaker; in 1385–6, for example, the rival guild of
Mercers complained in English to the Royal Council that Brembre had
actually stolen the election:

> And in the night [before the election] he carried great quantities of armour to
> the Guildhall, with which strangers from the countryside as well as others

from within were armed on the morrow . . . and certain ambushes were laid, that, when free men of the City came to choose their Mayor, they broke out armed crying with a loud voice, 'slay! slay!' Wherethrough the people for fear fled to houses and other hiding-places as in time of war, afraid to be dead in common.[38]

And so, increasingly in English, the debate moved on.

From time to time, usually in court records or in some other potentially altered form, something approximating a 'common voice' is heard. And, when it is heard, it seldom contains much of comfort to the status quo. Disapproving chroniclers have preserved some rebel communiqués, thought to have circulated on the eve of 1381, such as: 'Jack Truman doth you to understand that falseness and guile have reigned too long, and truth has been set under a lock, and falseness reigns in every flock . . . God do cure, for now is the time.'[39] And, by virtue of their controversial content, other more domestic voices of complaint surface within court records. Summarised in English is the late-century tabletalk of Thomas Austin, mercer, and Mrs Austin, about Richard II: 'At diverse times his wife said that the king was certainly never the prince's son and she also said that his mother was never anything but a strong whore and that same Thomas was never the man that once would bid her hold her words, but cherished her in her malice.'[40]

Nor did his successor, Henry IV, always fare any better. In legal records of 1402, we read (this time translated from French) that one John Sparrowhawk fell into casual conversation with the wife of a tailor:

> The tailor's wife said to John: 'See how wet it is and what dreadful weather there is these days and has been all the time of the present king, for there has not been seven days' good and seasonable weather all this time.' And she further said that the present king was not the rightful king but that the earl of .March is king by right, and that the present king was not son to the very noble prince John, duke of Lancaster . . . but that he was born son to a butcher of Ghent.[41]

Sparrowhawk made the mistake of repeating these and other calumnies to one John Taylor and to a beggar and his wife in the village of Morden, and lost his head for his words. It was displayed outside Newgate as a warning to others.

But Sparrowhawk's trial record preserves for our attention a current of casual conversation. Always present at the fringe of official reports is a barely hinted ocean of unofficial talk – often introduced in everyday exchanges about 'what's new?' between neighbours or in the local alehouse or during a journey or in a tradesman's workshop or in a manorial field. Such talk, swelling to a certain volume, could change history and topple kings.

Notes

1. Manuscript Julius B II, in *Chronicles of London*, ed. C. L. Kingsford (Oxford, 1905).
2. See Jean Gimpel, *The Medieval Machine: The Industrial Revolution of the Middle Ages* (Harmondsworth, 1976), pp. 147–70.
3. Reginald L. Poole, *Medieval Reckonings of Time* (London, 1918).
4. Nancy H. Owen, 'Thomas of Wimbledon's Sermon: "Redde racionem villacionis tue"', *Medieval Studies*, xxviii (1966), 175–97.
5. Adapted from G. C. Macaulay, *The Complete Works of John Gower*, 4 vols (Oxford, 1899), vol. 3, II. 882–9.
6. Adapted from *The Riverside Chaucer*, ed. Larry D. Benson, 3rd edn (Boston, 1987), 'Parson's Prologue', X, 70.
7. Adapted from William Langland, *The Vision of Piers Plowman*, ed. A. V. C. Schmidt (London, 1978), V, 13–20.
8. See Marjorie E. Reeves, 'History and Prophecy in Medieval Thought', *Medievalia et Humanistica*, n.s. v (1974), 51–75; Robert Lerner, 'Refreshment of the Saints: The Time after Antichrist as a Station for Earthly Progress in Medieval Thought', *Traditio*, xxxii (1976), 97–144.
9. *Piers Plowman*, III, 289–92, 200–1, 305–8, 325–8.
10. Texts available in R. B. Dobson (ed.), *The Peasants' Revolt of 1381* (London, 1970), pp. 381–3.
11. Ibid., pp. 270–1.
12. Ibid., p. 275.
13. Frank Taylor and John S. Roskell (eds), *Gesta Henrici Quinti* (Oxford, 1975), p. 9.
14. Gower, *Confessio Amantis*, ll. 4, 6–10.
15. Ibid., l. 59.
16. Chaucer, 'Wife of Bath's Tale', III, 183–5.
17. Chaucer, 'Shipman's Tale', VII, 226, 228–36.
18. These examples are all drawn from Adam of Usk, *Chronicon*, ed. E. M. Thompson (London, 1904).
19. For a detailed review of material conditions see Christopher Dyer, *Standards of Living in the Later Middle Ages: Social Change in England c. 1200–1520* (Cambridge, 1989).
20. Barbara F. Harvey, *Living and Dying in England, 1100–1540: The Monastic Experience* (Oxford, 1993).
21. Dyer, *Standards of Living*, pp. 25, 181.
22. The crucial essay on this subject – now often modified but not fully supplanted – is K. B. McFarlane, 'Bastard Feudalism', *Bulletin of the Institute of Historical Research*, xx (1943–5), 161–80. Representative of the best recent studies of this issue are Simon Walker, *The Lancastrian Affinity, 1361–1399* (Oxford, 1990) and Christine Carpenter, *Locality and Polity: A Study of Warwickshire Landed Society, 1401–1499* (Cambridge, 1992).
23. See John of Salisbury, *Polycraticus*, ed. Clemens C. J. Webb, 2 vols (Oxford, 1909), book 6, ch. 25.
24. A provocative argument along these lines has recently been made by Caroline M. Barron, 'The Deposition of Richard II', in *Politics and Crisis in Fourteenth-Century England*, ed. John Taylor and Wendy Childs (Gloucester, 1990).
25. Manuscript Julius B II, in *Chronicles of London*.
26. John Capgrave, *Chronicle of England*, ed. F. C. Hingeston, Rolls series, no. 1 (London, 1858), p. 276.
27. Public Record Office MS E403/564.
28. Caroline M. Barron, 'The Quarrel of Richard II with London 1392–7', in F. R. H. DuBoulay and C. Barron (eds), *The Reign of Richard II* (London, 1971).
29. Unpublished manuscript, delivered by Andrew Prescott to the Medieval Economic History Seminar, Institute of Historical Research, 1993.
30. Argued by David Wallace in *Chaucerian Polity* (Stanford, 1996).

31. *The Westminster Chronicle, 1381–1394*, ed. L. C. Hector and Barbara Harvey (Oxford, 1966), p. 8.
32. Ibid., p. 6.
33. See K. B. McFarlane, *Lancastrian Kings and Lollard Knights* (Oxford, 1972).
34. These events are admirably surveyed by Peter McNiven, *Heresy and Politics in the Reign of Henry IV* (Woodbridge, Suffolk, 1987).
35. Ed. H. T. Riley, Rolls Series, vol. 28, pt 3 (London, 1866), p. 336.
36. Paul Strohm, 'Politics and Poetics: Usk and Chaucer in the 1380s', in Lee Patterson (ed.), *Literary Practice and Social Change in Britain, 1380–1530* (Berkeley, 1990).
37. Adapted from R. W. Chambers and M. Daunt (eds), *A Book of London English, 1384–1425* (Oxford, 1931), p. 31.
38. Ibid., p. 34.
39. Dobson, *The Peasants' Revolt*, p. 382.
40. Adapted from Andrew Prescott, appendix to *Hochon's Arrow* (Princeton, 1992).
41. G. O. Sayles (ed.), *Select Cases in the Court of King's Bench*, Seldon Society, vol. 88 (London, 1971), p. 124.

20. Lineage: myth and fact. Henry VII, his queen and their seven children kneel. Above, St George slays the dragon to protect Princess Cleodolinde. Thought to have been painted in 1492 as an altarpiece for the royal palace at Sheen.

THE 1490s
Continuities and Contrasts

Malcolm Vale

At nine o'clock on the evening of 30 December 1497, Henry VII's Christmas revels were cut short by 'an huge fyre withyn the kyngis lodgyng' at Sheen Palace.[1] King and court fled from the scene and within three hours the entire palace had been gutted. But Henry's previous experiences had made him well acquainted with adversity and, undeterred by this setback, he proceeded to build the most magnificent royal residence of his time on the ruins of Sheen. In February 1501 he named it 'Richmond', after the earldom which he had held before his accession. It was a Rich Mount indeed, costing a vast sum, and was also seen by contemporaries as an expression of the cult of magnificence which the new Tudor dynasty had made its own.

Our view of the 1490s is to some degree dominated by paradox. How can we explain the apparent contradiction between the display and magnificence (exemplified by Richmond Palace) to which Henry was apparently devoted and his legendary frugality as a miser–king? Why did Erasmus, the humanist scholar and scourge of what he considered to be 'superstitious' practices in the Church, make a pilgrimage to the shrine of Our Lady at Walsingham and compose an affecting prayer on the subject? How did exponents of 'new' learning and 'new' devotion manage to reconcile their views with the demands and expectations of older institutions? The period around 1500 appears, on the surface, to be fraught with near-schizophrenic contrasts: between outward forms and inner meanings, between chivalric fantasy and harsh reality, between intense personal devotion and routine religious observance. The questions posed by the great Dutch cultural historian Johan Huizinga (1872–1945) could well be applied to England in the 1490s. Are we witnessing the 'decline' of the middle ages or the emergence of 'Renaissance' values? Was this a backward- or forward-looking period?[2] Was there a sense of impending fundamental change in the Church, the state and social life? Polarisations such as these can be misleading, because they often assume a degree of unity and homogeneity which few cultures possess. They also tend

RICHEMONT

21. Richmond (Richemont) was Henry VII's imposing main new residence. It was built on the site of the ancient royal manor of Sheen. The earlier palace there had been destroyed by fire in 1497.

to be loaded with value-judgments about the quality of the artistic and literary manifestations of a given culture. Yet it is undeniable that the end of the fifteenth century saw dynastic, political and cultural changes in England which coexisted with, rather than entirely superseded, the legacy of the past.

The accession of Henry Tudor, Earl of Richmond, to the English throne as a result of his victory over the Yorkist Richard III at Bosworth on 22 August 1485 was to put an end to civil war in England. But the conflict could not be said finally to have ended until the battle of Stoke on 16 June 1487. Even then, there were persistent outbreaks of discontent and rebellion, and despite the reconciliation of the houses of York and Lancaster through Henry's marriage to Elizabeth of York, the new Tudor dynasty was not truly secure until quite late in his reign. The appearance of Yorkist pretenders still haunted the Crown in 1497, when the Flemish puppet Perkin Warbeck, supported by James IV of Scotland, made his last attempt on the throne. By November 1499, with the executions of both Warbeck and the last remaining symbol of Yorkist claims – Edward, Earl of Warwick – Henry could at last sleep more easily.

Here was a king who had come to the crown without much support, with virtually no experience of government, with a period of exile in France and Brittany behind him, and with a desperate need for loyalty and assistance from his subjects, above all from the factious nobility and gentry. In May 1487, as the pretender Lambert Simnel's forces assembled in Ireland to invade England, the loyal Earl of Oxford wrote to Sir Edmund Bedingfield of Oxburgh in Norfolk:

> Whereas I understand by your late writing unto me that ye have right well endeavoured you to th'execution of the king's commission and command-ment, in preparing yourself with the gentlemen and other of the country, to be ready to do the king [Henry VII] service, which I have shewed unto the king's highness, so that his Grace is right well content and right thankfully accepteth the same, understanding the right good minds and disposition of you and of other gentlemen there towards his Grace.[3]

Henry was indeed grateful for any support that he could obtain from the 'gentlemen' of Norfolk and other shires. Unlike some of his continental contemporaries, he had no standing army and, apart from some contingents of foreign mercenaries, he was totally dependent for military aid on the retinues of his lords and the commissions of array executed by men such as Bedingfield in the counties. As in 1399, 1461 and 1470–71, when crowned monarchs had been toppled from their thrones, dynastic insecurity simply added another dimension to the existing uncertainties of life at this time. The wills and testaments of the period speak constantly of these fundamental uncertainties. In his will of November 1459, the aged soldier Sir John Fastolf pondered: 'How, among all earthly things that is present or for to come,

22. Perkin Warbeck, son of a boatman on the River Scheldt, claimed to be Duke of York, the younger of the two Princes in the Tower. After the failure of his rebellion he was executed in 1499.

23. Plague added to the hazards of life and could strike great and small. Little was known about either cause or treatment. *Danse macabre* from a late fourteenth-century French manuscript.

there is no thing in this unstable world so certain to creature of mankind as is departing out of this world by death, the soul from the wretched body; and no thing earthly so uncertain as the hour and time of death . . .'[4]

The very instability of the visible world thus provided a spur to piety and devotion, and the unknown hour at which the inevitable might strike moved men and women, as we shall see, to affecting expressions of personal conviction. Abrupt and unexpected turns of political events prompted comments such as the Franciscan friar Brackley's observation, 'By my faith, here is a coysy werd [an unsettled world].'[5] The tumultuous events of the early months of 1477, set in train by the violent death in battle of Charles the Bold, Duke of Burgundy, drew forth the remark from Sir John Paston that 'it seemeth that the world is all quavering'.[6] These uncertainties were made more acute by the threat, and fear, of epidemics. In 1499–1500, the plague in London was so severe that Henry and his court decamped to Calais to escape contagion. An age in which medical science was relatively primitive and in which diagnosis could often be determined by factors apparently (to modern thinking) irrelevant to a patient's symptoms and condition offered very few defences against the

Januarius

Februarius

Marcius

Aprilis

Maius

Junius

Julius

Augustus

September

October

Nouember

December

24. The new year: time ahead. A broadside almanac, 1495.

onset of disease and sudden death. Political instability threw another factor into the equation, causing men to resort to astrology to ascertain their future, as well as trusting in God's will.

Could the new dynasty bring the stability that so many apparently desired to a political society weary of civil strife? For the first decade of his reign, Henry VII's style of kingship was conventional. He was resistant to the adoption of Yorkist methods in, for example, finance, and tended to look back to his Lancastrian predecessors. The expedients of decentralised Chamber finance, whereby the Yorkists had attempted to bypass the medieval Exchequer by diverting revenues into the Chamber, were not adopted until later in the reign. Such methods had enabled the Crown to raise money quickly but at the expense of accountability, bypassing the slower but safer procedures of the Exchequer.

Concentrating upon income from the Crown lands and the process of 'living of his own', Henry was nevertheless faced with the problem of securing baronial loyalty, and one means of obtaining this was to wage a foreign war. In February 1492, William Paston wrote from London to his brother that the king already:

sendeth ordnance daily to the sea side, and his tents and pavilions be a-making fast, and many of them be made; and there is also great provision made by gentlemen that should go with his Grace, [f]or horse, armour, tents, pavilions, baggage, carts and other things that should serve them for this journey that the king intendeth to take on hand, so that by likelihood his Grace will be going soon upon Easter . . .[7]

In the event the expedition was delayed until October and resulted only in a treaty. Yet Henry, like his Yorkist predecessor Edward IV, came back from France with a large annual pension from the French Crown.

The threat of English invasion remained a useful weapon in the armoury of the Tudor dynasty against their French rivals. But wars demanded taxation, and the tax revolts which broke out in the west country demonstrated the hazards of such a course. When further Yorkist pretenders, backed by dissidents operating from relative security in Scotland or overseas (including Edward IV's sister Margaret of York, who had married Charles the Bold in 1468), also appeared on the scene, Henry felt still more

25. Royal accounts. Henry VII, a careful accountant, personally and vigilantly checked all the entries in the receipts book of Sir Thomas Lovell, Treasurer of the King's Chamber.

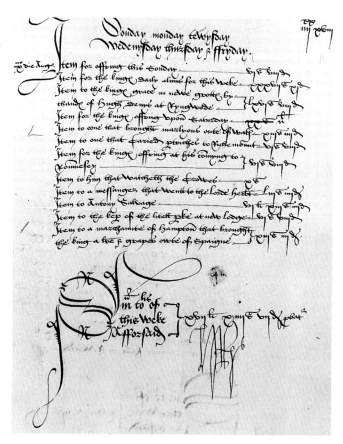

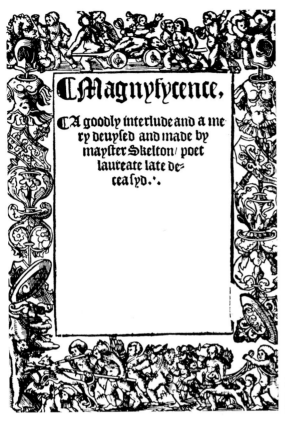

26. Cult of Magnificence. Title-page of *Magnificence* by the poet John Skelton, *c.* 1532.

threatened. He was betrayed even by members of his own household, and a certain change of direction in the reign can be observed after 1495–7. Traitors, and those suspected of treason, were treated with greater harshness, and a cult of magnificence was added to the attributes of a monarchy which had until then been marked more for its relative austerity than for conspicuous consumption and display.

Miserly Henry may have been – and it is this picture of him that has come down to us, largely through the famous seventeenth-century biography by Francis Bacon – but his accumulated wealth was to be spent in unstinted fashion on 'bearing the port, dignity and estate of majesty'. It was abundantly clear that the new dynasty needed its own propaganda. Princely magnificence was adopted on the model provided by the Valois dukes of Burgundy and their Habsburg successors. This was not unknown to England before the 1490s, for Edward IV had modelled his court and (to some degree) his household on Burgundian examples. Henry, however, added a new dimension. In this process of image-making, external display was all-important. Continuity with his predecessors was emphasised by his commissioning of a series of portraits of his ancestors in the great hall of

27. Arthur, Henry's eldest son, born in 1486, shown twice, once at prayer. He died in 1502, leaving the throne and Catherine of Aragon to Henry VIII.

Richmond Palace. These included such heroes as Brutus, Hengist, Arthur, Richard I and Edward III, and at the focal point above the throne was painted:

> the seemly picture and personage of our most excellent and high sovereign now reigning upon us, his liege people, King Henry the VIIth, as worthy [of] room and place with those glorious princes as any king that ever reigned in this land, that with his great manhood and wisdom hath continued nobly and victorious unto this now the eighteenth year of his reign.[8]

By 1502–3, when the cycle of historical portraits was completed, Henry could be said to have established himself securely upon the throne, by dint of harsh penalties against errant magnates (such as execution, attainder and forfeiture) as well as by the creation of what might be called a Tudor ideology. His Welsh ancestry gave him certain natural advantages: a connection with Henry V through the (admittedly controversial) marriage of that king's widow to Henry's grandfather, Owen Tudor; and a 'British' pedigree which could be exploited, especially within the context of the Arthurian legend and the 'matter of Britain'. In the 1490s it is these elements of his image-making which stand out: his eldest son (born 1486) had been baptised Arthur, and the insecure monarch began to bolster his title with myth. The subject matter of court drama (the early masques or 'disguisings') often drew upon Arthurian stories. Henry refurbished the surviving late thirteenth-century Round Table which was preserved as Arthur's own at Winchester, repainting the segments of the table with the names of Arthur's knights, and adding a Tudor rose to its centre.

Henry's personal frugality, therefore, was offset by lavish expenditure on building projects and on ceremonial occasions, ranging from the creation of knights of the Garter and the Bath to receptions for foreign princes. The Garter celebrations could provide opportunities to impress. In May 1488,

28. Knights of the Garter were created ceremonially as they still are today. Here, Sir Nigel Loring (d. 1386) wears the original Garter robes.

29. Arthur's betrothal, 1501, a grand occasion (with unforeseen consequences) commemorated in a Flemish tapestry.

William Paston reported that the Earl of Oxford 'hath been with the King in Windsor at St George's feast, and there at the same feast were both the ambassadors of Brittany and Flanders, as well from the king of the Romans [Maximilian I] as from the young duke [Philip the Handsome, Duke of Burgundy]'.[9] This was at a particularly sensitive time, as English aid was being sought by the Duke of Brittany during the revolt and civil war that had broken out in that duchy. Henry's munificence went further. His chapel at Westminster Abbey is a perfect example of late Gothic, with elaborate fan-vaulting and huge pendant bosses adorned with heraldic display. It was this miser-king who completed Edward IV's great works at Windsor and gave us St George's Chapel as we know it today.

The celebrations devised by Henry for the marriage of Prince Arthur to Catherine of Aragon in October–November 1501 were among the most elaborate ever seen in London. Both courtly and civic resources were brought to bear, and the festivities took place with a complete apparatus of pageant-cars and pageant-fountains (from which wine flowed) on the Burgundian pattern. Although the king himself was wont to dress simply when not exposed to public gaze, he could adopt the style of majesty when appropriate. An account of his meeting with Philip the Handsome, by then King of Castile as well as Duke of Burgundy, near Windsor in January 1506 tells us that Henry rode a bay horse, its trappings covered with embroidery, and wore a purple velvet gown, a gold chain around his neck with an image of St George in diamonds as a pendant, and a purple velvet hood, with hat and bonnet.[10] Philip was entertained at Windsor with true regal magnificence. The same contemporary observer spoke of 'the king of Castile's chamber, which is the richestly hanged that ever I saw: seven chambers together hanged with cloth of Arras wrought with gold as thick as could be; and as for the three beds of state, no Christian king can show such a three'.[11] It is known that Henry had in his possession tapestries, such as the *History of Troy* and the *Siege of Jerusalem*, which had formerly belonged to Charles the Bold, Duke of Burgundy. The insecure king was determined to rival, if not outshine, his European peers.

From the 1490s onwards England was in a strong position to hold the balance of power in north-west Europe between the Habsburg rulers of Spain and the Netherlands and the kings of France. Watchful diplomacy rather than aggressive military action (despite Henry's abortive French invasion of 1492) now became the norm and the benefits of peace were soon apparent. Economic interests were furthered by treaties such as the *Magnus Intercursus* (1496) with the Netherlands, and England's maritime commerce was regulated and protected by 'Navigation' Acts (1485, 1489) which prohibited the import of Gascon wines in foreign ships. A staple for English wool passing to north-west Europe was maintained at Calais (which had been captured by Edward III in 1347), and the Company of Staplers was responsible for the customs and garrison there, Calais remaining an English 'colony' – with its own English mayor and aldermen – until 1558. By 1500, however, the Company of Merchant Adventurers was already the Staplers' major rival, with depots at Antwerp, London, and other English ports, and the influence of the Company meant that England's foreign trade was now directed towards the Low Countries, the Baltic, north Germany, the Rhineland, Iceland and (to a lesser degree) the Iberian peninsula. English cloth, as well as raw wool, found buyers throughout Europe.

The kingdom over which Henry VII ruled was experiencing greater prosperity than it had seen a century earlier, and its population, although never achieving its pre-Black Death figure, was beginning to recover after the epidemics of the second half of the fourteenth century. A total population of something over three million is a reasonable estimate for the 1490s, with one large city, London, accounting for between 50,000 and 80,000 people. The next largest towns – York, Norwich, Bristol – housed a mere 5000 or 6000. Urbanisation in England was far less dense, therefore, than in the Low Countries or northern Italy, the areas of what has been called the highest 'urban potential', measured in terms of size and spread of the city, the proximity of other large towns, and the ease of travelling between them. Only in south-east England were there levels of urbanisation that corresponded to those across the Channel in the Paris region, the northern Netherlands or the Rhineland. Towns acted as magnets, drawing towards them labour and goods for sale, and in England by far the greatest of these magnets was London. Nonetheless, the large number of relatively small market towns was a prominent feature of fifteenth- and sixteenth-century England.

Outside the urban concentrations, the countryside was sparsely populated, although standards of living among the rural inhabitants were high when compared with those of their continental neighbours. Indeed, English wealth was derived from the country's agrarian base. Rural England was not populated by serfs, and it could be argued that the English 'peasantry' was not a peasantry at all by 1500. A high proportion were in effect tenant farmers, enjoying the profits of pastoral agriculture, unhindered by excessive levels of seigneurial rent. Both foreign observers and English witnesses, like the lawyer Sir John Fortescue, commented upon the relative prosperity of rural life and on the quantities of meat eaten by the lower orders; its freehold and copyhold tenants formed the basis of a yeomanry which (especially in southern England) was remarkably independent of feudal and manorial lordship on the French or German pattern. With fewer servile constraints, they were more mobile than their continental counterparts, often moving around on horseback, carrying produce to markets and sometimes swelling the ranks of the urban

30. London, 1510, the earliest
view in print. In the centre is the
spire of Old St Paul's, with
London Bridge and the Tower of
London to the right, and
Ludgate Arch in front.

population by immigration into the towns. There was a substantial turnover
in families, often well over 50 per cent in many villages between 1400 and
1500. This was caused not only by the extinction of families through failure
of heirs but by ease of mobility, so that people would seek employment and
marry outside their own village.

An impression of general prosperity was also given by the housing of many
of England's inhabitants. The single-storey 'long' house, often timber-
framed, was giving way to the two-storey house, a type which spread from
East Anglia to other parts of the country in the fifteenth century. No longer
did families coexist with their animals in single-storey houses; they could
now sleep upstairs. A separation between the communal hall and the private
chamber, which had already begun to take place in aristocratic households,
now became more widespread. Upstairs rooms gave greater privacy and also
contributed to higher levels of hygiene. Chimneys, fireplaces, glazed

31. Paycocks House, *c.* 1500, a characteristic Tudor two-storey house at Coggeshall, Essex.

windows and better latrines are found even in yeomen's, as well as gentlemen's, houses by the end of the century. But social distinctions could still be observed to the extent that inventories of possessions would refer to 'gentlemen's bedsheets' and 'yeomen's bedsheets'.

Although the domestic market accounted for much of the country's production, England was well placed to act as a net exporter and supplier to the European market of essential commodities such as wool, cloth, tin and leather, while importing wine, fabrics (such as Italian silks, Netherlandish cloth and tapestries), dyestuffs, spices and a host of luxury goods for the upper end of the market. The coinage was sound, and to maintain her accustomed level of prosperity easy networks of communication with her neighbours were necessary. The sea passages had to be kept open and protected for the benefit of all. London merchants and their agents were well used to constant toing and froing across the Channel and the North Sea, most often to Calais or Antwerp. Other regions, such as East Anglia and the north-east, were closely linked to the Low Countries and the Baltic. Active and extensive sea-faring made the English an essentially maritime people, increasingly dependent upon foreign trade for their livelihood.

Not only were such mercantile contacts with Europe of paramount importance at this time, but cultural and religious influences also tended to flow from the continent. In both England and Scotland, some of the devotional cults of the age – such as that of the Holy Blood, already venerated at Hailes Abbey in Gloucestershire – had Netherlandish origins. And in the visual arts the dominance of Netherlandish and French models reigned more or less supreme. The king's painter was one Maynard (or Meynnaert), almost certainly a Fleming or Walloon, who painted portraits of Henry and his court, and is best remembered today for his striking full-length representation of Lady Margaret Beaufort, the king's mother. It was only in architecture, where English Perpendicular offered a peculiarly indigenous style, that a truly 'English' art-form dominated.

The king and his court commissioned and owned Netherlandish illuminated manuscripts and French printed books, as well as panel paintings and tapestries from Brussels and Arras, and in 1492 Henry appointed as his court librarian Quentin Poulet, from Lille in French-speaking Flanders. His court poet was the blind Bernard André from Toulouse. The dominant literary culture at the early Tudor court was therefore French, or – when vernacular works were produced – much influenced by both French and Burgundian models. The poet John Skelton was to adopt many of the features of the Burgundian *rhétoriqueurs* in his English works. A royal library of both manuscripts and printed books was established under Poulet's supervision at the new palace of Richmond, and Henry's collection was much admired by foreign visitors. Its contents were largely French – translations of Latin works, or original texts in the French language – with a small admixture of books in English.

William Caxton (d. 1491) was already printing and selling books at Westminster as well as Bruges on Henry's accession, and was well placed to become stationer (that is, supplier of books and writing materials) to the king, an office which was created in December 1485. But he was passed over in favour of the Savoyard Pierre Actoris, perhaps because of too close an association with Edward IV and Margaret of York. The impact of printing was beginning to be more generally felt at this time, although (with the important exception of Caxton) the book trade was largely in foreign hands. The publishers' lists of the 1490s tended to be conventional, with a clear emphasis upon chivalric romances, devotional manuals and tracts, and well-established works of moral philosophy or pastoral theology. Much of the printed material which circulated was in a single-leaf format, cheap, accessible and short lived. The *de luxe* market was catered for by lavishly illustrated volumes on parchment which were made to look as far as possible like illuminated manuscripts. It was these that Henry VII showed to his visitors at Richmond, and their subject matter was almost identical to books

32. William Caxton presents
one of his books to Margaret
of York, 1474.

in the Burgundian ducal library or that of great Flemish noblemen such as
Louis de Bruges, Lord of Gruuthuse.

Such evidence as we possess for the dissemination of Italian humanistic
literature to king and court came through the filter of French and English
translation: it was men such as John Tiptoft, Earl of Worcester (executed in
1470) who had had more direct contacts with the new humanism across
the Alps. Besides his own translations of Cicero (*Of Friendship*) and
Buonaccorso da Pistoia (*The Declamation of Noblesse*), Tiptoft was the
author of rules for the conduct of tournaments.

Such eclectic tendencies in secular culture were paralleled in religious life
and practice, where there was evidently a wide diversity and plurality of
beliefs, observances and devotional habits. Few, if any, of these (outside the
cells of surviving Wyclifites or Lollards) were in any sense unorthodox or
heretical, and it is difficult to discern the emergence of anything which
resembled Protestant attitudes at this time. Nevertheless, the emphasis upon

33. Humanism was – and is –
best represented by Erasmus
of Rotterdam (*c.* 1466–1536),
a key figure in the cultural
history of Europe.

the individual soul and on a personal relationship with God, albeit mediated through the saints and guided by the priesthood, was not totally alien to the more introspective attitudes which the reformers were soon to encourage.

The idea of God's immanence in all things, even the most mundane and everyday, which characterised some of the new devotional movements, may also have contributed something to the rise of new forms of piety. But all this was contained within the framework of Catholic doctrine. The centrality of the mass, the saints and the doctrine of the Incarnation went unchallenged by the great body of believers. One of the most significant effects of the invention of printing was to enable the fundamental tenets of the faith to be more widely disseminated. Although no formally approved English Bible was yet in circulation, many portions of the Gospels, psalms and other scriptural texts had appeared in the vernacular language as well as sermons, homilies and prayers. Thus the Church's mission was no longer confined to the Latin of the mass and the other liturgical offices by the 1490s, but was attempting to reach out to a wider public than ever before.

Criticism there was: but it did not move very far beyond what the Lollards had been asserting since the later fourteenth century. Pilgrimages, images, relics, processions, saints' cults and so on had all come under attack. Questions such as 'how many pieces of the True Cross were there?' or 'how many thorns from the Crown of Thorns were there?' were not new. The quasi-scepticism which maintained that if all the relics of the True Cross were put together they would form a forest was not a product of the age of Erasmus. Veneration of the saints was embodied, as before, in fraternities and guilds which formed important social mechanisms in both urban and rural communities at this time. Normally associated with parish, collegiate or cathedral churches, these religious and devotional fraternities had an important social and charitable role to play. No craft was without its patron saint, and many crafts, trades and professions could be brought together in such bodies as the confraternities of Corpus Christi.

The functions of these collective expressions of identification with the saints and their lives ranged from charitable works to drinking bouts, and from the production of mystery and miracle plays to mutual help in times of need. Some guilds had their own chantry chapels within their local church, and these can still be seen at King's Lynn, Norwich or Bristol. In many ways the 'old' religion provided a coherent belief-system in which the performance of good works, the saying or singing of masses and the administration of the sacraments were thought to lead to the soul's redemption. The celebration of masses for the dead kept open a link between this world and the next, as souls were remitted from the pains of purgatory by investment in chantries. The living were thereby kept perpetually in touch with the dead.

There can be little question of the continued vitality of such traditional beliefs in the 1490s. What was new, perhaps, was the extent to which ordinary people were laying claim to what had formerly been the preserve of the clergy. The popularity of such cults as that of the Seven Works of Mercy, or the Five Wounds of Christ, although ultimately based upon scriptural truth, demonstrated the extent to which the laity had appropriated doctrines which, under clerical guidance, they shaped to meet their own needs. The Church could do little to stem the tide of devotional fashion and lay religiosity. It was as if the laity were asserting a proprietary interest in their churches. Space was found for chapels within the church, new aisles and bell-towers were built, and even the monastic and mendicant orders – whose fortunes had been declining in the fourteenth century – were recipients of renewed patronage. They had begun to put their houses in order during the fifteenth century, and the reform and observant movements within the Cistercians, Carmelites and, above all, the Carthusians met with lay support and subsequent endowment.

Throughout these movements in both lay and clerical piety there was a common theme: the Incarnation of God's Son and its implications for man. Although more abstruse doctrines, such as that of the Trinity, undoubtedly

34. Life is short: prepare for eternity. In fifteenth-century wills endowments for providing masses for the dead were common. Thomas and Joan Smyth ask us in this embroidered tapestry to pray for their souls.

continued to exercise their power over the minds of men and women, their hearts were won by the human aspect of the Christian story. It was a tragedy that ended in triumph; from the Annunciation to the Virgin, through the Nativity to the Passion and Resurrection of Christ, there unfolded a timeless, continuous narrative that could be told and retold in both word and image. But the forms in which those words and those images were presented had changed. By 1500, the advent of more naturalistic depictions of the life of Christ and the saints, and of a body of vernacular literature – both written and oral – on the same theme, had enabled ordinary men and women to experience their faith in a more vivid, immediate and perhaps more profound manner.

Of course, the more mechanical and routine aspects of later medieval piety – repetitious prayer and mass-saying in a language understood by few, the almost commercial mentality behind investment in chantries and so forth – must raise some doubts about the true depth of the 'people's faith'. Yet the intensity of personal religious conviction (or lack of it) is difficult to measure in any age. Parallels with contemporary Poland or southern Italy suggest that when devotional religion is so integral a part of the daily life of a people it makes little sense to speak censoriously of 'over-familiarity' with the sacred or of its 'profanation'. The religious climate of late fifteenth-century England favoured a higher degree of lay participation in the non-sacramental aspects of the institutional Church, which were closely guarded by the clergy. The doctrine of salvation through good works informed many of the laity's activities – the Works of Mercy invited men and women to observe Christ's injunctions in St Matthew's Gospel more or less to the letter. Feeding and clothing the hungry, visiting the sick and those in prison, found expression in both the individual and collective acts of charity which fill their wills, testaments, registers of fraternities and act books of devotional guilds. Luther's doctrine of justification by faith alone seems remote from this world.

The Church was sustained therefore not only by its own resources – landed endowment, tithes and rents – but by the gifts of the faithful. The fabric and liturgical apparatus of parish churches and chantries attracted substantial sums. In the prosperous regions – above all in the west country and East Anglia – new porches, towers, roofs and chapels abounded, bearing witness to a strong sense of local identity. The provision of vestments, communion plate and liturgical banners, often bearing the images of patron saints, the Virgin and the Five Wounds of Christ, was also of concern to the laity, and gifts of such items feature in their wills. Reflection upon Christ's Passion was prompted by images of anguish and pain, and by contemplation of the attributes of his mocking, scourging and crucifixion.

Shrines, votive offerings, talismans, relics and the supernatural attributes of the mass look like magic and superstition to us. But these aspects of the Church's activities were often inseparable from its devotional and pastoral functions. As Keith Thomas has pointed out, the attitude of the higher clergy to such practices was that:

> If a belief in the magical efficacy of the Host served to enhance respect for the clergy and to make the laity more regular church-goers, then why should it not be tacitly tolerated? Such practices as the recitation of prayers, or the wearing of talismans and amulets, could all be taken to excess, but what did it matter so long as their effect was to bind the people closer to the true Church and the true God? It was the intention of the worshipper, not the means employed, which counted.[12]

The adoration of images, rather than their veneration, stressing the role of the saints as intercessors and mediators between God and man, could lead to excesses; but no harm necessarily came of it. Close identification with the saints could anchor religious sentiments in a concrete, localised context. The enormous popularity of works such as the *Fifteen Oes*, printed by Caxton in 1491, is revealing. This was a collection of prayers attributed to the mystic St Bridget of Sweden (d. 1373), beginning with the vocative 'O', such as: 'O Jhesu endles swetnes of lovyng soules / O Jhesu gostly joye passing and excedyng all gladness and desires. O Jhesu helthe and tendre lover of al

The art and craft of printing.

35. (*left*) Woodcut of a printing press, dating from *c*. 1500.

36. (*below*) *The Fifteen Oes*, 1491, a collection of prayers printed by William Caxton.

repentaunt sinners that likest to dwelle as thou saydest thy selfe with the children of men . . .'[13]

The mutual love of Christ and the believer runs through much of this literature, stemming from the mystical tradition of the fourteenth century, now more readily available in Middle English and in printed form. A personal relationship with the Godhead, made possible by the Incarnation, could assume many forms: from ardent love to reverential and respectful acquaintance or the fitful encounter of little depth. So much might depend upon individual needs and responses. Women appear to have been especially moved by these sentiments, and the very different forms of piety espoused by the burgess's wife and religious writer Margerie Kempe, or by the noblewomen Margaret of York and Lady Cecily Neville, showed that this ran through a wide spectrum of English society.

From our perspective, it is easy to see the 1490s as a time in which Christian believers felt that they were living on the eve of some great seismic eruption which was to lead to the post-Reformation rift in western Christendom. Yet the evidence suggests that they themselves did not, and that it was changing political and dynastic considerations which, in the first instance, were to lead to the English Reformation. Although there was (and had been) vociferous opposition to the Roman papacy, targeting papal provisions to English benefices or the sale of indulgences, few coherent doctrinal alternatives had emerged. Those that had, including Lollardy, had been condemned through their equation with sedition in the minds of both secular and ecclesiastical authorities. Such desire as there was for reform came from inside the Church, from men with ideas, and from pious laymen who found that they had no monastic or clerical vocation. The circle which grew up in the 1490s around the young Thomas More, John Colet and William Grocyn represented a new generation of humanist-inspired lawyers and educators who saw orthodox reform from within the Church as their end.

From about 1500, More lived either in or very close to the London Charterhouse, uncertain whether he had a vocation for the monastic life. He 'gave himselfe to devotion and prayer . . . religiously lyvinge there, without vow, about iiijer years'.[14] Carthusian austerity, and the strict observance of the order's rule, deeply impressed many contemporaries. Houses such as Mountgrace in Yorkshire (founded in 1398) attracted lay benefaction, and testators frequently willed that 'the brothers there . . . have my soul especially recommended in their prayers'.[15] For many in the upper and middle ranks of English society, including those bent on reform, the Carthusians were meeting needs which had been met in the twelfth century by the austere Cistercians. Thus the overthrow of the Church was completely alien to their thinking.

A further characteristic of the pious and intellectual elite of the period was a concern for education and for the living of the Christian life. The

37. The Henry VII Chapel (erected from *c.* 1503) in Westminster Abbey is a great memorial to a king who, for all his frugal reputation, loved grandeur where appropriate.

foundation statutes of Colet's St Paul's School (placed by him under the supervision of the Mercers' Company in 1512) laid down that its purpose was to increase 'knowledge and worshipping of God and oure lorde Jesu, and good Cristen lyff and maners in the Children'.[16] They were to read 'good litterature both laten and greke', and Colet specifically banned such 'fylthynesse and al suche abusyon' as was found in more recent books. Yet both kinds of literature – the good and the bad – were now more accessible to a wider public through higher levels of basic literacy and through the art of printing. Through the use of the vernacular language – English rather than French or Latin – much that had previously been inaccessible was made more readily available. When Wynkyn de Worde printed his edition of the *Martiloge* (a collection of martyrs' lives) he said that it was intended for those who, although they used the Latin texts in Church, could not understand what they read.

This was the case even among some of those who had chosen a religious vocation. The Brigittine nuns of Syon at Isleworth (founded by Henry V in 1414) were clearly not all expected to know Latin. Hence Wynkyn produced an English edition of the *Martiloge* 'as it is read in Syon'. The sisters' lack of Latinity was also exemplified in the practice whereby the priest-brothers of the house read the Gospel to them in English on certain feast days. Increasing evidence for the ownership of English books, and the drawing up of wills and other documents in the vernacular, also attest to the cultural shifts that were taking place. Although the court and higher aristocracy might still mark themselves off from the rest of society by their knowledge of French, the 'maternal tongue' of the majority of English men and women was spoken and written English. Henry VIII was to acknowledge this fact when he commissioned John Bourchier, Lord Berners, to translate Froissart's *Chroniques* into English. Secular as well as religious literature now chose the vernacular language for a larger and socially broader audience.

The picture of England in the 1490s which has been drawn here is one of relative prosperity, cultural richness (though often of a derivative kind) and religious orthodoxy. Religious life in particular presents an image composed of many intersecting circles and overlapping layers of piety, devotion and magic which cannot easily be prised apart. Reformers and intellectuals were certainly disturbed by the proliferation of saints' and martyrs' cults and by quasi-superstitious practices among the body of the people. But, by and large, they let sleeping dogs lie. There was little fear of a renewed upsurge of the kind of heretical movement which the 1390s had witnessed. Beneath the surface of English society in the 1490s scant sign of a boiling cauldron of doctrinal radicalism, millenarianism or dissent was visible. There was, after all, no English Savonarola.

Notes

1. A. H. Thomas and I. D. Thornley (eds), *The Great Chronicle of London* (London, 1938), p. 286.
2. See J. Huizinga, *The Waning of the Middle Ages* (London, 1924), passim.
3. J. Gairdner (ed.), *The Paston Letters* (Edinburgh, 1910), iii, pp. 335–6.
4. Ibid., i, p. 446.
5. Ibid., p. 497.
6. Ibid., iii, p. 174.
7. Ibid., pp. 375–6.
8. G. Kipling, *The Triumph of Honour* (Leiden, 1977), p. 59, quoting College of Arms, MS Ist M 13, fo. 62v.
9. Gairdner, *Paston Letters*, iii, p. 343.
10. Ibid., pp. 404–5.
11. Ibid., p. 405.
12. Keith Thomas, *Religion and the Decline of Magic* (Harmondsworth, 1971), p. 56.
13. See G. Holmes (ed.), *The Oxford Illustrated History of Medieval Europe* (Oxford, 1988), plate on p. 339.
14. See J. B. Trapp and H. S. Herbrüggen (eds), *The King's Good Servant: Sir Thomas More, 1477/8–1535* (London, 1977), p. 21, quoting Roper's *Life* of More.
15. For one example see M. G. A. Vale, *Piety, Charity and Literacy among the Yorkshire Gentry, 1370–1480* (York, 1976), pp. 21–2.
16. See Trapp and Herbrüggen, *King's Good Servant*, pp. 26–7, no. 14.

38. The Queen on High: Elizabeth I in courtly procession (attributed to Robert Peake the Elder, *c.* 1600).

THE 1590s

Apotheosis or Nemesis of the Elizabethan Regime?

Ian Archer

One of the most arresting images of the closing years of the reign of Elizabeth I is that of the queen represented in the manner of a victorious general in a Roman triumph. Resplendent in her bejewelled dress, she is being carried on a chair on wheels, a decorated canopy above her. She is accompanied by the knights of the Garter and her gentlemen pensioners, and at the centre of the picture in front of the queen stands her last master of the horse, Edward Somerset, fourth Earl of Worcester, by whom the painting was probably commissioned. Here is Elizabeth supreme in her authority, fêted by her loyal subjects.[1] And yet the closing years of Elizabeth's reign in reality saw her authority increasingly flouted by her generals, her courtiers at loggerheads with each other, and everyone nervously looking to her expected but unnamed successor north of the border. The painting itself probably celebrates the appointment in 1601 of Worcester to the office of master of the horse, formerly held by Robert Devereux, Second Earl of Essex, Elizabeth's favourite of her declining years, who had died ignominiously on the scaffold after an attempted *coup d'état* earlier in the year. There was in fact little to celebrate in the last decade of Elizabeth's rule. Harvest failures spelt impoverishment for the mass of the people, and crime soared; taxation soared too, with few military gains to show for it; and standards of public administration deteriorated as ravening courtiers battened on to the economy. There was an enormous gulf between the image of the monarchy projected in paintings like *Eliza Triumphans* and the real views of the Crown held by its subjects.

There is not much sign in the 1590s that the English people, who continued to reckon time in terms of the passing of reigns, were conscious of a century drawing to a close. But living under an ageing virgin queen they were acutely conscious of the end of an era, and they were deeply anxious as they contemplated the future. There was a possibility that the succession, that 'main point and straightly forbidden to Englishmen to discuss', would be contested. Surveying the potential candidates in 1600, Thomas Wilson

39. Behind the myth: an
unflattering portrait of Elizabeth I,
c. 1592, painted by Isaac Oliver
before it was decided that the
queen should always be depicted as
eternally youthful.

listed no fewer than twelve claimants, both home-grown and foreign, that 'gape for the death of that good old Princess the now Queen. . ...Thus you see this crown is not like to fall for want of heads that claim to wear it, but upon whose head it will fall is by many doubted.' Some feared that James VI of Scotland, the most plausible candidate, would 'attempt to gather fruit before it is ripe', pre-empting other claimants by invasion, while ministers sought to insure themselves against the dangers of a possible Stuart succession by opening up correspondence with Edinburgh. As John Harrington, the queen's godson, put it in December 1602, 'I find some less mindful of what they are soon to lose than of what they may perchance hereafter get.'[2]

The queen's obsession with her image in these closing years betokens an underlying unease about the way she was regarded by her subjects. In 1596 she sent out a proclamation ordering the destruction of all unseemly portraits of herself. Woodcuts showing a shrivelled old woman inspired by Isaac Oliver's all-too-frank miniatures were to be replaced by the officially approved images of an eternally youthful queen. Her jealousy of the proliferation of images of some of her leading peers (especially Essex, Cumberland and Mountjoy) cast in the role of military heroes led to a proclamation banning their production in 1600. Elizabeth's anxieties about the embarrassing parallels it was possible to draw between her rule and that of Richard II resulted in June 1599 in a ban on the production of history chronicles without conciliar approval. 'I am Richard II, know ye not that?' Elizabeth told the Kentish antiquary William Lambarde in 1601, a few months after Essex's rebellion, which itself had been preceded by a performance of the play *Richard II.*[3] Nor were all Elizabeth's subjects as persuaded by the myth-makers as later generations. Elizabeth herself told the French ambassador in 1597 that although the people 'made great demonstration of love towards her, nevertheless [they] were fickle and inconstant, and she had to fear everything'. Over their pots of ale her subjects expressed sentiments very much at odds with the official line. 'This is no good government which we now live under, and it was merry England when there was better government, and if the queen die there will be a change,' opined an Essex labourer in 1592.[4]

The rot was manifest at the core. The 1590s witnessed a dangerous narrowing in the basis of the regime. Familiar faces disappeared one after another, Leicester in 1588, Mildmay in 1589, Walsingham in 1590, Hatton in 1591. Elizabeth came to lean more on that great survivor, William Cecil, Lord Burghley: 'old Saturnus is a melancholy and wayward planet but yet predominant here and if you have thus to do it must be done that way and whatsoever hope you have of any other believe it not'. Burghley's ambitions became more concentrated on passing on his political influence intact to his hunchbacked son Robert, who enjoyed a steady ascent through the decade. As the Cecilian grip tightened, the Privy Council contracted in size. Whereas the Council appointed at the beginning of the reign had twenty members, by 1597 there were only eleven, the majority of them officials dependent on the queen rather than territorial magnates, and representing three or four dominant families.[5]

At the same time as control over patronage slipped into an ever narrower clique, demand for royal favour was increasing. The gentry class, benefiting from a fluid land market and rising agricultural prices, underwent a remarkable numerical expansion during the sixteenth century. The failure of family lines, political miscalculations by individual nobles and the long-term decline of the military power of the Crown's leading subjects contributed to an erosion of the independent territorial power of the traditional magnates and caused the ambitions of the gentry to be ever more focused on the court. Through its landed resources the Crown could grant leases at below-market rents; through its control over the honour system it could grant titles; through its power to regulate the economy it could grant lucrative monopolies and licences; and through its control over an incipient bureaucracy it could grant profitable offices. In an intensely competitive environment access to these favours depended on intermediaries at court. As one of the Manners family unctuously explained to Robert Cecil, seeking to retain the

The most noble ROBERT
Earle of Eſſex and Ewe, Earle
Marſhall of England, Vicount He-
reford and Bourgcher, Lord Ferres
of Chartley, L. Bourgcher and
Louayn, and her Maieſties
lieutenant, and Governour generall
of the Kingdome of Irland. 1601.

40. Robert Devereux, Earl of
Essex, leader of the unsuccessful
rebellion which was preceded by
a performance of William
Shakespeare's *Richard II*.
Pronounced a traitor, Essex met
his death on the scaffold in 1601.

favour he had enjoyed with the secretary's father, 'my desire . . . is to be
protected under the shadow of your wings as I was by his Lordship'. The
patron benefited from the prestige that accrued from the demonstration of
his power, from the creation of a debt which might be called in at a later date,
and sometimes from cash bribes. It was a game played for high stakes, as
failure with the monarch would lead to a falling away of supporters: 'Who
will be desirous to come under a roof that threateneth ruin?' wailed the Earl
of Essex as his fortunes waned.[6]

As competition for patronage increased in a climate of war-induced
economy allied to the queen's natural parsimony, standards of political
morality deteriorated. 'I will forbear to mention the great and unusual fees
exacted lately by reason of buying and selling offices, both judicial and
ministerial, as also the privileges granted unto private persons to the great

prejudice and grievance of the common people,' noted a contemporary. Lord Keeper Puckering trafficked in offices and accepted bribes, selling the office of *custos rotulorum* in Devon for £300, and taking £100 from the Brewers' Company of London to suppress a parliamentary bill directed against their pricing policy. The greatest resentment was engendered by the monopolists and other patentees. Monopolies had originally been granted with the object of encouraging enterprise and innovation, but now they were simply devices by which greedy courtiers battened on the economy; patents gave individuals the right to profit from enforcing certain penal statutes or granting exemptions therefrom. Richard Drake, for example, enjoyed a monopoly of vinegar production, while Sir Edward Darcy enjoyed successively a patent for sealing leather and a monopoly of the production of playing cards. By 1601 there was a loud outcry in Parliament against these 'bloodsuckers of the commonwealth'. As a list of commodities subject to monopolies was read out, one wag shouted, 'What? Is not bread there?' The sense of corruption, venality and disintegrating public virtue in the 1590s was palpable, contributing to the literary vogue for Tacitus, whose accounts of the servility and flattery of imperial Rome under Tiberius offered chilling contemporary parallels. The high hopes entertained of James in 1603, that he would put an end to 'base and guilty' bribery, testify to the growing disillusionment with Elizabeth.[7]

The Earl of Essex came to be the focus for those discontented with the Cecilian monopoly. He sought to take on the mantle of the queen's late favourite, Robert Dudley, Earl of Leicester, posing as the champion of an aggressive foreign policy and building up a clientele of a markedly military nature. Lacking a strong territorial base, Essex could only build his power on such a foundation; hence his desperate quest for command, and his repeated flouting of royal orders and consequent confrontations with the queen. He sailed with Drake and Norris for Portugal in 1589 in direct contravention of the queen's orders; in 1591 he ignored her instructions on the disposition of his troops in Normandy, falling into a fit when she threatened to strip him of the command; in 1596 he turned what had been intended by Elizabeth as the disruption of Spanish naval preparations into an attempt to establish a base on the Iberian mainland; and, most fatally, in Ireland in 1599, he failed to confront the rebel Tyrone directly as the queen had ordered and, when at length he did march into Ulster, it was not to fight but to parley with him.[8]

Essex's relationship with his mistress was exacerbated by the way in which war exposed one of the key problems of female rule, namely that the feat of arms was emphatically masculine, and that it was therefore difficult for the queen to retain the respect of her commanders. As the historian Mervyn James writes, 'a woman's nature could only partially and imperfectly embody the spectrum of virtues appropriate to a prince. Female rule could be

41. Sir Philip Sidney's funeral roll, 1587. The men shown were suspected of complicity in Essex's revolt.

expected to be strong in humility, mildness, and courtesy, all princely qualities which were natural to women; but also lacking in courage, open-handedness, and constancy of fixed purpose, these being male, not female characteristics.' In an extraordinary outburst in 1592 her lord deputy in Ireland exclaimed, 'this fiddling woman troubles me out of measure . . . God's wounds, this it is to serve a base, bastard, pissing kitchen woman.' Essex explained that the vacillating character of English foreign policy during the 1590s 'proceeded chiefly from the sex of the Queen'. The queen's mounting frustration with his persistent lack of respect for royal orders burst forth in the disastrous episode in July 1598 when, in a dramatic reversal of gender roles, Elizabeth struck the earl and told him go hang for having turned his back on her in the course of a Council meeting.[9]

Essex increasingly came to see his ambitions as being thwarted by the pacifically inclined Cecils, with whom he sought confrontation, making every appointment a matter of personal honour. As he foolishly told Robert Cecil in the course of his quest for the office of attorney general in 1594 for Francis Bacon, 'The attorneyship for Francis is that I must have; and in that I will spend all my power, might, authority, and amity, and with tooth and nail defend and procure the same for him against whom whatsoever; and whosoever getteth this office out of my hands for any other, before he have it, it shall cost him the coming by.' His constant petulance and lack of military success hardly enhanced his standing with the queen, and his patronage suits were regularly, as on this occasion, rebuffed. The last straw was his behaviour in Ireland; when he deserted his post, bursting un-announced into the queen's bedchamber, he was detained, and subsequently stripped of most of his offices. His position deteriorated over the course of 1600 as the Cecilians planned treason charges, and in September the queen spelled out financial ruin for him by her refusal to allow the renewal of a lucrative customs farm. Essex came to see a court putsch as the only solution to his problems as it would remove those who were poisoning the queen's mind against him. But when on 8 February 1601 the earl with his 100 followers attempted to raise the City of London, no one stirred, he was declared a traitor, and surrendered to the forces besieging Essex House. Within three weeks he had mounted the scaffold to die a traitor's death.[10]

While the politicians bickered, the majority of Elizabeth's subjects suffered an appalling fall in living standards. There had been a long-term decline over the century because of the failure of the economy to respond adequately to the demands of a population which still stood at around three million or less in the 1540s but had grown to some four million by the end of Elizabeth's reign. But the situation was exacerbated during the 1590s by a succession of climatic disasters which sent prices spiralling upwards. Poor harvests in 1594 and 1595 were followed by two years of dearth in 1596 and 1597. Even before the nadir of suffering was reached, George Abbot preached in December 1596: 'Behold what a famine [God] hath brought into our land . . . One year there hath been hunger; the second year there was a dearth, and a third, which is this year, there is great cleanness of teeth . . . our years are turned upside down; our summers are no summers; our harvests are no harvests; our seed times are no seed times . . .' The effects on living standards were dramatic as flour prices tripled and real wages fell by about 20 per cent during the mid-1590s. Domestic demand collapsed as consumption perforce concentrated on foodstuffs, while overseas demand was disrupted by warfare; the resultant difficulties of the textile industry are reflected in the precipitous drop in the yield of tolls on cloth sales at Blackwell Hall, the main market for cloth in the capital.[11]

It is notoriously difficult to get an idea of the reality of what life at the time would have been like for the poor, but the diet given to the inmates of Bridewell (the London house of correction) tells us something about what was thought to be appropriate sustenance. The hospital's allowances varied according to whether the inmate worked or not: non-workers received 12 ounces of bread and a quart of beef each day together with 6.5 ounces of beef on non-fast days, and 4 ounces of cheese or 2 ounces of butter on fast days; while those at hard labour in the hemphouse received a daily allowance of 24 ounces of bread and four pints of beer, with the same quantities of beef or dairy products. Such a diet was severely deficient in vitamins, despite the presence of meat. The Bridewell diet suggests minimum daily requirements for food of 1.25d in the early 1580s, but by the mid-1590s this had risen to 2d, which would have been well beyond the reach of many poorer consumers.[12] William Harrison, vicar of Radwinter in Essex, indicated that the poor could survive by switching their consumption to inferior grains: '[they are] enforced to content themselves with rye or barley, yea, and in time of dearth, with bread made . . . of beans, peas, or oats'. And yet in areas of poor pastoral economies the poor undoubtedly starved during the mid-1590s. In Cheshire, we are told, 'great sickness by famine ensued and many poor died thereof'; at Tamworth 'divers died of the bloody flux'; at Shrewsbury it was noted in late 1596 that without corn imports the town's poor would 'perish . . . as many in all counties in England die'. Such impressions are confirmed by the work of the historical demographers; in 1597–8 the national death rate was 25 per cent above trend, and probably about one parish in five experienced crisis mortality.[13]

The suffering of the 1590s was not shared by all. On the contrary the decade may have contributed to the polarisation of society as the rich got richer and the poor got poorer. One of the most influential accounts of social change remains that of William Harrison, who testified to rising standards of domestic comfort. Among the things 'marvellously altered', according to his older parishioners, were 'the multitude of chimneys lately erected . . . the great amendment of lodging . . . and the exchange of treen platters into pewter, and wood spoons into silver or tin'. Harrison was writing in the 1560s, but the process of growing wealth among the middling sections of society he describes continued to be applicable in the closing years of Elizabeth's reign. The degree to which men were able to profit from the economic changes of the period depended crucially on how much land they possessed. If they farmed for the market, they were in a position to benefit from rising agricultural prices, whereas if they farmed for subsistence they were likely to find that the harvest failures of the 1590s forced them to consume their seed corn and to become indebted. Successive harvest failures would compromise the viability of their holdings and force them to sell up. Thus, in the corn producing parish of Chippenham, Cambridgeshire, the dearth of the 1590s seems to have contributed to the mounting difficulties of those with medium-sized holdings (between 15 and 45 acres) who were gradually forced to sell up to the engrossing yeomen, the beneficiaries of the growing commercialisation of agriculture.[14]

The misery of the commons was made more acute by the relentless demands of the government for money to finance its military campaigns. The defeat of the Armada in 1588 settled nothing; rather, in the years which followed Elizabeth's commitments widened. Not only did she have to continue supporting the English forces in the Low Countries, but the Spanish determination to unseat Henri IV, King of France, brought more hostile armies to the Channel coastline and necessitated further continental expeditionary forces. To add to her woes the bungling of cash-starved agents in Ireland provoked a revolt which took nine years to suppress. The total cost of war between 1585 and 1603 was approximately £4.5 million, of which £1.42 million was consumed by the Dutch theatre, £0.424 million in the support of Henri IV, and a staggering £1.924 million by Ireland, Elizabeth's Vietnam.

42. The Tudor family rested on male authority. It was the building block of society. This was the well-ordered aristocratic family of Henry Brooke, Lord Cobham, depicted in an anonymous portrait of 1567.

These costs were borne by a government whose ordinary revenues amounted to just £0.36 million per year. Even the queen's legendary parsimony could not produce a surplus on the ordinary account of more than £100,000, so that the war had to be financed largely by parliamentary taxation, which yielded £1.8 million during the war years. Multiple subsidies became the norm: used for the first time in 1589 with the proviso that the double subsidy granted that year should not be drawn into a precedent, they were repeated in 1593 and 1597 when three subsidies were granted, and again in 1601 when at the time of the Spanish landing at Kinsale in Ireland no fewer than four were granted. Such relentless subsidies doubtless felt still more burdensome because they were levied after a period of relatively low taxation: whereas parliamentary taxation was running at about £35,000 per year in the 1570s, by the 1590s it was £100,000 per year. They were also accompanied by a rising burden of military rates as the Crown shuffled off responsibility for the equipment and apparelling of troops onto the local community, and as port towns were required to provide ships for the various naval expeditions against Spain. These additional levies were often equivalent to the volume of parliamentary taxation.[15]

It is not surprising that the 1590s should have witnessed a swelling chorus of complaint about the pressures of the war effort. Although MPs did not call into question the legitimacy of the Crown's demands, considerable anxiety was expressed about their distribution. Thus in the Parliament of 1593 Fulke Greville asserted the commonplace that 'the poor are grieved by being overcharged', and warned of the threat of disorder in an image which must have chilled many gentlemen: 'it is to be feared if the feet knew their strength as we do their highness they would not bear it as they do'. Local authorities became increasingly reluctant to co-operate as taxation coincided with economic depression. Londoners, confronted by another request for shipping in December 1596, complained of 'the great dearth of victual which hath been continued now these three years, besides three years plague before, which so hath impoverished the general estate of the whole city, that many persons, before known to be of good wealth, are greatly decayed and utterly disabled for all public service, being hardly able to their uttermost endeavours to maintain the charges of their families in very mean sort'. The aldermen went on to warn that the citizens were beginning to question the legality of some of the impositions. At about the same time the Privy Council was locked in an exhausting conflict with the Suffolk magistrates over their refusal to levy ship money in the shire to assist Ipswich, 'dissuading the people by perilous arguments, meeter to move the people to discontentment than to concur in Her Majesty's service'. Conciliar reprimands to recalcitrant local authorities were issued with increasing frequency as the war dragged on.[16]

43. The plague strikes at the heart of London. From an early seventeenth-century broadside.

The widespread misery caused by the combination of dearth and heavy taxation resulted in increasing social tension. We should not be deluded by the pervasive ideology of an order based on hierarchy into thinking that relations between commoners and their social superiors were characterised by unquestioning deference. The very insistence with which the authorities pedalled the theory of obligation through catechisms, sermons and proclamations suggests its fragility. That the poor often adopted a humble petitioning stance does not mean that they shared the values of their superiors. Rather such a rhetoric may be seen as merely tactical, the poorer sort paying lip-service to the gentry as a means of securing concessions. It did not rule out the possibility of other forms of behaviour should the gentry fail to live up to popular expectations or fail to fulfil their social obligations. The principle of the unequal distribution of wealth might be accepted, but on condition that the obligations of paternalistic lordship were fulfilled. Hence the double-edged comments on their social superiors pronounced by the disaffected. Bartholomew Steer, recruiting among the Oxfordshire commons for a projected rebellion in 1596, declared that 'it would never be merry till some of the gentlemen were knocked down', but also simultaneously suggested that there were wealthy men sympathetic to their cause. The gentry as a class were not beyond redemption; it was when the gentry pressed ahead with aggressive enclosures or enjoyed only attenuated relationships with their tenants that they risked becoming objects of local opprobrium. It was the same in the towns: libels circulating in London in 1595 praised Alderman Sir Richard Martin, architect of projects for the relief of the poor, at the expense of the notoriously tight-fisted lord mayor, Sir John Spencer, victim of a spate of rioting.[17]

The pressures of the 1590s undoubtedly nourished social tensions. It is difficult to get behind the façade of deferential exchanges to the 'hidden transcripts' of the poor, but the libels which littered the streets of many communities are one point of entry. In Norwich, a libel of 1595 complained of the greed of the rich who have been licensed 'to set open shop to sell poor men's skins'. But the hour of reckoning was at hand, for there were 60,000 craftsmen in London and elsewhere who would no longer bear the exploitation of the rich and the corruption of their magistrates. The rich would be made to drink to the dregs a draught from the cup of the Lord. They were warned that 'some barbarous and unmerciful soldier shall lay open your hedges, reap your fields, rifle your coffers, and level your houses to the ground'. The proliferation of cases of seditious words provides another index of rising tension: in 1596 a weaver from Ardleigh, Essex, urged a large crowd 'to cut the throats of the rich churls and the rich cornmongers'.[18]

44. The pulpit was used for royal as well as for divine messages: two versions of authority. The famous pulpit at St Paul's Cross was also sometimes used for dissenting messages which might challenge those in authority. The scene depicted here is from the right-hand panel of a diptych painted by John Gipken, *c.* 1616.

A rash of disorders fed officialdom's fears that an overturning was at hand, and the response was often fierce. Perhaps the most pathetic event of the decade was the abortive rising at Enslow Hill in Oxfordshire in November 1596 when just four men turned up. Their intention had been to lead a rising against leading local enclosers and they had planned to join up with disaffected apprentices in the capital. In the event, in spite of widespread grievances, they were unable to generate the critical mass necessary to precipitate a general rising, but the government was convinced of the gravity of the threat, hanging two of the conspirators on an extremely dubious interpretation of the treason legislation for compassing to levy war against the queen. The authorities had responded with a similar lack of proportion to disorders in London the previous year. The failure of traditional sanctions to allay a spate of food rioting and restore respect for the dignity of the mayoral office panicked the authorities into an exaggerated response to a riot in the vicinity of the Tower of London: five apprentices were subsequently hanged.[19]

The excessive response of the government to these disturbances is hardly surprising when one considers the reports flowing in to Whitehall from the Crown's agents in the localities. Edward Hext, justice of the peace in Somerset, in a letter to Burghley in 1596 depicted a society on the point of collapse. Hext was convinced that his county was being overwhelmed by a crime wave of enormous proportions. Bands of vagrants up to sixty strong terrorised the local population and paralysed the apparatus of law enforcement. They stirred up the poor to 'all contempt both of noble men and gentlemen, continually buzzing into their ears that the rich men have gotten all into their hands and will starve the poor'. In his opinion they lay behind the seizure of a cart of cheese by a crowd of eighty, an outrage which he feared presaged further disorders. Hext undoubtedly had things out of proportion, but his views are important for the light they shed on the central government's perception of problems in the realm.[20]

Another symptom of the excessive fears among the governing classes of the 1590s is the popularity at the time of 'rogue' literature – lurid tales of thievery, immorality and conmanship. 'These cony-catchers . . . putrify with their infections this flourishing state of England,' warned Robert Greene in 1591. Rogues and vagabonds were widely depicted as a kind of anti-society with its own internal hierarchies inverting all the values of respectable society. The stereotype of the criminal vagabond was further popularised through countless sermons. Typical was Dod and Cleaver's denunciation of 'rogues and runagates . . . these filthy persons and unprofitable generation, this refuse and off-scouring of the world . . . [who] fill the land with sin, making their life nothing else but a continual practice of filthiness, theft and idleness (which are sins of Sodom), that live without calling, without magistracy, without ministry, without God in the world'.[21]

45. Title-page of Robert Greene's
Notable Discovery of Coosnage which
describes the methods used by the
confidence tricksters of London's
underworld. Tricksters were key
figures in Ben Jonson's plays.

Commentators like Hext, the rogue pamphleteers and other moral
entrepreneurs were not incorrect in their identification of a crime wave in the
1590s. The surviving assize files for the home counties all reveal a surge in
indicted property crime in the years 1596–8: to take the example of Essex,
indictments were 60 per cent above trend in 1596, 114 per cent in 1597, and
60 per cent in 1598. They misled, however, in exaggerating the degree to
which a criminal underworld existed. Contrary to the impression created,
vagrants generally travelled in small groups and their crime was casual and
opportunistic. Typical was the Middlesex man interrogated by a
Hertfordshire justice to account for goods found suspiciously in his
possession who confessed that he had taken his cloak from a house in which
he had lodged, six horseshoes from an adjacent stable, and a goose he had
simply come across while walking.[22]

The stereotypes were important because they contributed to another
significant development of the 1590s – an increasing criminalisation of the
poor. Poor travellers in search of work were likely to be harassed as vagrants;
migrants newly arrived in towns might find themselves the object of scrutiny
by local officials. In the parish of St Saviour, Southwark, surveyors of
inmates snooped on the morals of the poor, keeping a particularly vigilant
eye on single women. Once the statute of 1598 had devolved responsibility

46. Vagrancy, urban and rural, was a major Tudor problem. Different types of vagrancy were distinguished from each other; punishment could be the gallows.

for punishing vagrants on to the local constables – a dramatic mushrooming of their discretionary power – the penalties were probably more consistently applied, if the proliferation of newly painted whipping posts in towns is anything to go by. Meanwhile, key ways in which the poor might make a living were becoming the object of hostile attention by the elites. Fishwives and the petty traders who hawked goods about city streets were assimilated to the vagrant stereotype and, if not licensed, subjected to the discipline of the house of correction. Key elements of the economy of makeshifts by which the poor scraped together a living were being attacked. In 1601 a statute provided for the summary punishment of those caught cutting growing corn and robbing orchards and gardens. Other ambivalent but customarily tolerated practices such as gleaning were being redefined as theft in some areas. The assault on alehouses, although motivated by a concern to limit the consumption of grain and to prevent poor families falling on the rates through the improvidence of the parents, actually had the consequence of depriving the poor of yet another means of making a living in that the keeping of an alehouse was often an essential supplement to their incomes.[23]

Fears of disorder also contributed to the increasingly repressive regulation of sexuality in the 1590s. The closing years of the sixteenth century were characterised by a surge in illegitimacy cases, reflecting 'instability and insecurity in the courtships of the poor'. It was customary for couples to engage in sexual relations after their betrothal but before the formal solemnisation of their marriage in church. Problems arose, however, if in the meantime economic misfortune wiped out the savings the couple had put by with which to establish their new home. The collapse in real wages during the 1590s meant that many couples found their marriage plans unravelling, leaving mothers with unwanted children. Often already dismissed from their employment, such women would find themselves brought before the Church courts and forced to do penance standing before their neighbours in church in a white sheet and confessing their offence. They might also be subject to examination before a justice of the peace who, after an act of 1576, could order that they be whipped.

It seems that these penalties were being applied with greater regularity and escalating severity at the turn of the century. In 1588 the Essex magistrates ordered that the mothers of bastards should be whipped at the cart's tail, but that the strokes should be 'moderately given'; by 1600 they were ordering that the women be whipped until their backs were bloody. Another sign of heightened rigour in the treatment of illicit sexuality was the increasing willingness on the part of parish authorities to present cases of bridal pregnancy to the Church courts. Whatever popular custom might have determined, the authorities were insisting upon solemnisation in church as a precondition of a valid marriage.[24]

It is striking that these moral campaigns were applied in a socially discriminatory manner. Gentlemen were anxious that the reformation of manners should not ascend the social gradient. Edward Glascock opposed a bill against drunkenness in 1601 on the grounds that 'it was a common and usual thing in Lancashire and those parts for gentlemen as they go a hawking to go and take a repast in an alehouse; yea, men sometimes of 500 marks a year'. Whereas twenty years previously the campaigns of the metropolitan godly for a morally reinvigorated society had involved an assault on the misdemeanours of members of the elite who patronised the brothels, by the end of the century the poor bore the full force of the campaigns. 'The wasp breaks through where the little fly is entangled; the poor harlot must be whipped and stripped for the crime that the courtly wanton and city sinner ruffle out, and pass over, and glory in, and count as nothing.'[25]

Another form of discrimination evident in the repression was that it was directed with greater harshness at women. Some historians have gone so far as to argue that the period witnessed a crisis in gender relations. Fear of the headstrong woman who subverted the structures of patriarchal control, it has been argued, was a by-product of the social and economic transformations of the period. As habits of good neighbourliness and social harmony disintegrated in the face of the onward march of capitalism, there was a proliferation of cases of 'scolding', particularly in towns and wood-pasture areas where the greater numbers of poor people were reflected in lower levels of social cohesion. At Southampton, the leet jury complained in 1603 of 'the manifold number of scolding women that be in this town'.

47. (*above*) Gossip was said to be spread largely by women. In fact, it was carried through many different channels (from *Title Tattle*, a broadside, *c.* 1603).

48. (*left*) Witchcraft was associated with women as much as gossip was, and punishment could be severe. The Chelmsford witches, 1589.

Scolds were often prime suspects in cases of witchcraft, another over-whelmingly female offence: Elizabeth Busher of Henton, Somerset, was denounced as being 'of lewd life and conversation, as namely the mother of divers base children, the suspected maintainer of incontinency in her own house, the continual disturber of her neighbours' quietness and threatening mischief against them, and lastly both reputed and feared to be a dangerous witch through the untimely death of men, women, and children'. Some influential people were convinced that the country was being overwhelmed by witchcraft: 'The land is full of witches,' asserted Lord Chief Justice Edmund Anderson in 1602. 'They abound in all places.' And yet it would be unwise to push the notion of a crisis in gender relations too far; it is impossible to prove that there was more concern at the popular level about either witches or scolds, and the records of local jurisdictions suggest intermittent rather than pervasive fear of the headstrong woman. Marginal women were under attack in the 1590s, but they were singled out by virtue of their marginality rather than their femininity.[26]

The social fabric was thus subject to very considerable strain during the 1590s: the mounting difficulties of the poor husbandman and labourer suffering from dearth, a depressed economy and relentless tax demands fed hostility towards rulers who appeared to be benefiting from the changes. The elites responded in turn with increasing repression. These processes may have been reinforced by cultural divisions, especially, perhaps, those arising out of new forms of spiritual adherence.

   One of the most obvious differences between the 1590s and the 1490s was the dramatic remodelling of the people's religion that the Reformation had wrought. Swept away was the bulk of the panoply of comforting rituals and protective magic that traditional religion had provided. Instead of worshipping in richly decorated parish churches adorned with bejewelled images, painted cloths and stained glass, parishioners might now stare at whitewashed walls adorned only with black-letter scriptural texts, the chancel arch dominated by the royal coat of arms, a reminder of who the mistress of the Church now was. In place of a religion in which the intercessory prayers of fraternity members could ease the soul of the departed through the pains of purgatory, Englishmen and women were now offered a direct relationship with God where faith had to be apprehended through biblical instruction. Some parishioners responded: others did not yield to what could be tedious sermons and catechising.[27]

   The new preachers despaired of converting the masses. In 1591 after twenty-one years labouring in an unpromising corner of the Lord's vineyard in Dry Drayton, Cambridgeshire, the model Protestant pastor Richard Greenham left in disgust for a London parish, bemoaning 'the intract-ableness and unteachableness of that people among whom he had taken

such exceeding great pains'. The bulk of the population apparently
remained sunk in a semi-Pelagian theology of good works, failing to
apprehend the central Protestant message of justification by faith alone: 'If a
man say his Lord's Prayer, his Ten Commandments and his Belief, and keep
them, and say no body harm, nor do no body harm and do as he would be
done to, have a good faith in God-ward and be a man of God's belief, no
doubt he shall be saved without all this running to sermons and prattling of
the Scripture.'[28] And yet before we dismiss the Reformation as a failure we
should note the Herculean task that the evangelists were setting themselves
in seeking to achieve levels of religious knowledge that would defeat most
twentieth-century pastors; failure to achieve those heroic goals is not the
same as having had no effect at all. By 1600 they had achieved the
extraordinary feat of providing preachers for half of the 9000-odd parishes
of the kingdom; no less than half a million officially authorised catechisms
were in circulation, supplemented by three-quarters of a million unofficial
ones, catering to differing levels of educational attainment; and an
educational drive sponsored largely by the godly was making considerable
inroads on popular illiteracy. Although the population may not have
apprehended the subtleties of predestinarian theology, a distinctively
Protestant religious culture combining sermons (not necessarily Puritan
ones) and the ceremonies of the prayer book was in the process of
formation.[29]

What cannot be denied is that the process of evangelisation was often a
painful one where the ambitions of the reformers pitted them against a
vigorous traditional festive culture. The godly who stood on a platform of
order ironically often provoked discord in their communities: 'Hath not
Minge brought Ashford from being the quietest town of Kent to be at deadly
hatred and bitter division? . . . What broil and contention hath Fenner made
in Cranbrook, and all the rest likewise in their several cures?' A classic
example is provided by the disturbances in Banbury, soon to be a byword
for godly orthodoxy. In 1589 a group of godly townsmen sought to pull
down the maypoles, but were opposed by another faction. The disorders
reached the attention of the Privy Council, which ruled that maypoles might
remain provided that they were enjoyed in 'due and peaceable manner'. But
within a few years the godly faction had gained control, demolishing
Banbury Cross, and defacing its images with cries of exultation: 'God be
thanked, Dagon the deluder of the people is fallen down.' Some historians
have seen these lines of cultural division as reinforcing those of socio-
economic division discussed earlier, with groups of godly middling people
aligned with the forces of the state against the popular culture. But the
picture is more complex. At Banbury, for example, the proponents of the
maypoles included the crypto-papist sheriff of the county, Sir John Danvers.
The lines of cultural division cut across the divisions of class.[30]

The multiplicity of pressures during the 1590s might tempt us into describing the decade as one of 'crisis'. And yet the transfer of power between Elizabeth and her successor in 1603 was peaceful; by and large, the government succeeded in securing the revenue necessary to wage its campaigns; and there was neither a large-scale popular uprising of the kind experienced in the mid-Tudor decades nor a war of religion of the kind being waged in France and the Low Countries. It might therefore be more accurate to follow Peter Clark, and to talk in terms of 'a crisis contained'. The social fabric was highly flammable, but it failed to ignite – and for a number of reasons.

In the first place, the polity remained stable because of a basic consensus between the local political elites and the Crown. The Tudors had succeeded in cultivating direct relationships with the local gentry, as the power of the territorial aristocracy waned. The Earl of Clare noted in the early Stuart period that 'it was the constant custom of the queen to call out of the counties of the kingdom the gentlemen of greatest hopes and of the best fortunes and families, and with these to fill the most honourable rooms of her household servants, by which she honoured them, obliged their kindred and allegiance, and fortified herself'. The regime thus bound to itself the leading gentle families of the kingdom, and a document of 1598 lists the 54 'principal gentlemen that be of value and service that are usually at court' together with a further list of 272 'principal gentlemen dwelling usually in their counties'. The channels of communication between centre and localities remained open, ensuring that local grievances could receive an airing. It is striking that, although Norfolk politics became bitterly divided over administrative innovations in the 1590s, both sides enjoyed access to the court. Even papists

49. Memorial picture of Sir Henry Unton, *c.* 1596, commemorating scenes in his career. Sir Henry (1557?–96), who was educated at Oxford and the Middle Temple, was a soldier and diplomat, and, for much of his life, a Member of Parliament. He was knighted in 1586.

50. The increasingly busy River Thames which ran through London and gave continuity to the city's daily life and to its identity as the English capital. A detail of Visscher's panorama of London, 1616.

could count on powerful protectors within the Exchequer establishment. Although this consensus was disrupted by the rivalry between Essex and Cecil, few gentlemen were prepared to follow the former into rebellion, because they could not conceive of his role outside the largely shared values which characterised the Elizabethan regime.[31]

The basic identity of interests between centre and locality was reflected in the cautious approach of the Crown to the problems of local government – the relative lightness of the fiscal burdens of the 1590s, for example, as compared to those experienced by other European monarchies. It has been estimated that the Crown was able to extract no more than 3 per cent of national income during this decade, compared with the 8 per cent of Castile's income that was creamed off by Philip II. Moreover, for all her expenditure on war, Elizabeth was levying lower levels of taxation than her father had done during the 1540s: London's tax bill was 40 per cent lower in real terms in the 1590s than in the closing years of Henry VIII's reign. Although the English tax system was becoming more regressive, it did not institutionalise privilege in the way that the tax exemptions for the nobility of France and Spain did, nor did it hit the poorest with the severity of the French *taille*, for the English parliamentary subsidy was probably levied from only the top one-third of the wealth pyramid.[32]

Doubtless late Elizabethans would have given short shrift to statistically minded late twentieth-century historians, for they did not deal in relativities of this kind. But other considerations served to mitigate the perceived burden of taxation in this period. First, there was the critical fact that taxes were being levied for clear purposes which commanded broad assent, at least among the governing elite. Elizabeth's wars were fought for objectives that were more plain than those of her early Stuart successors, whose wars of the 1620s lacked a clearly defined enemy. Lest Englishmen should be in any doubt of the threat represented by Spain, repeated armadas sailed against

England in 1588, 1596 and 1599, and Spanish troops landed in Ireland in 1601. Moreover, there was much common ground between the government and its subjects over the question of taxation, because the ministers' philosophy was essentially a low-tax one. Elizabeth's councillors had reached political maturity during the troubled mid-century decades, scarred by rebellions in which tax grievances had played a major role. Taxation was associated with rebellions and continental tyrants. Among Burghley's arguments for peace was the assertion that 'the nature of the common people of England is inclinable to sedition if they be oppressed with extraordinary payments'. Sir John Fortescue, Chancellor of the Exchequer, opening the subsidy debate in 1597, gloried in 'a government more happy because free from extreme and miserable taxes'. Surveying the 'dangerous impositions' of France, he declared them to be more suitable for 'an austere and strange born conqueror than a mild and natural queen'.[33]

The fact that the government shared the same outlook on taxation as its subjects meant both that councillors often proved responsive to complaints from the localities and that certain obvious fiscal expedients were off the agenda. Far from being an instrument of an incipient royal tyranny, the use of privy councillors as lieutenants to control the local military resources of the Crown provided another level of mediation between centre and locality. Thus the Northamptonshire deputy lieutenants interceded with Sir Christopher Hatton, the lord lieutenant, to secure a reduction in the county quotas for troops and for a forced loan in 1589. The basic hardheadedness of the queen's approach to national finance involved few of the ruinous financial expedients associated with several continental monarchies at the time. Borrowing was minimal; privy seal loans from her subjects were only occasionally resorted to, usually in anticipation of parliamentary taxation, from the proceeds of which almost invariably they were promptly repaid; and there was no debasement of the coinage, and no officially sponsored sale of offices. Even on monopolies, the queen was prepared to compromise, refusing to let Parliament legislate on the matter, but herself withdrawing controversial patents in 1601. The moderation of the Crown's demands and its willingness to compromise meant that such opposition as there was to the taxes of the war years was rarely articulated within a constitutionalist framework, for it was more usually the distribution of the tax burdens rather than its legality that generated objections.[34]

It was also critical to the stability of England in the 1590s that the country, whether through luck or good management, was unperturbed by the kind of religious controversies which rent apart its near neighbours, France and the Low Countries. Elizabeth's religious settlement may have been a fudge, a Church 'but halfly reformed', but it was a fudge which ensured that the conservative silent majority were eventually incorporated successfully in its

51. Elizabethan Parliaments, socially graded, gained in political and social importance.

services. Concessions to conservative feeling were evident in the ambiguous words of administration of the communion, in the retention of the traditional vestments, the 'rags of popery' to which the Puritans so vehemently objected, and in the queen's determination not to surrender to godly scruples on certain key ceremonies such as the sign of the cross in baptism and the ring in the marriage service. By the 1590s the Church of England had succeeded in capturing the loyalties of a basically conservative population through the provision of what has been dubbed 'prayer-book Anglicanism'. Parishioners are regularly encountered demanding that their ministers follow the prayer-book services in full, and, if they were refused, they would vote with their feet and seek out more amenable ministers. In 1598 and 1601, for example, the inhabitants of Leyland in Lancashire complained that their vicar did not use the sign of the cross in baptism, 'wherefore many of the parishioners do cause their children to be baptised at other churches'.[35]

It is true that the Church of England had attracted criticism from what we might call the left. Godly ministers objected to the ceremonies their conservative parishioners often hankered after, and they despaired of the antiquated disciplinary structures of the Church, looking instead for inspiration to the reformed disciplines of continental Churches. Yet by the 1590s Elizabeth had managed to weather the storm of Puritan criticism. The majority of the godly wanted to reform the Church from within; separation was inconceivable, for that would merely open the door to the papist wolves. Therefore, at the point when they were confronted by a stark choice between conforming and abandoning the ministry they were bound in conscience to uphold, they opted to knuckle down. Archbishop Whitgift's campaign to force the Puritans to subscribe to the disputed ceremonies in 1583–5 therefore had the effect of isolating the extremists. It was accompanied by a skilful propaganda campaign which sought to alienate lay sympathisers by pointing out that the implementation of the Puritan programme for a fully preaching ministry would hit the gentry where it hurt most, in their pockets, for a preaching ministry could be created only by getting the gentry to disgorge some of their ill-gotten Reformation gains. Another propaganda coup was the episode in 1590 when the religious visionary William Hacket was hailed in Cheapside as the returned Messiah. Unfortunately for the godly, Hacket turned out to have friends associated with the radical Puritans, who could therefore be depicted as fellow travellers of those dangerous subversives who would realise the Anabaptist nightmare.[36]

There were important 'common and ameliorating bonds' between the Church and its critics. Although conformists and the godly differed over ceremonies, they shared a predestinarian theology. It is true that some avant-garde Cambridge theologians challenged Calvinist orthodoxy in the mid-1590s, but they were stamped upon effectively by Whitgift, who responded with the impeccably Calvinist Lambeth Articles of 1595. A Calvinist monopoly did not exist, but a Calvinist hegemony there certainly was. Anti-popery provided another of these areas of agreement between the establishment and its critics. The godly had still more compelling reasons for conforming once the war broke out with Spain, for this struggle against the Antichrist was one for which they had long been pressing, and it emphasised what Protestants had in common rather than what divided them. Government spokesmen, even those of a less than godly hue such as Elizabeth's dancing chancellor, Sir Christopher Hatton, played the anti-popish card with éclat. Addressing Parliament in 1589 as a prelude to the inevitable request for cash, Hatton recounted the efforts of the pope and Philip II to subdue England, all of which was 'sufficient to show to all

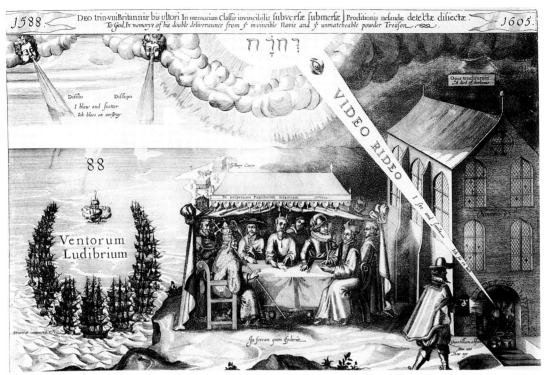

52. The Pope and the Devil were conceived of by many Protestants as enemies both of 'live religion' and of the English monarch. So, too, was Philip II of Spain (sitting on the Devil's left) who was attacked as the 'Devil's agent'. From a broadside of 1621, printed in Protestant Amsterdam.

posterity the unchristian fury, both of the Pope (that wolfish bloodsucker) and of the Spaniard (that insatiable tyrant) in that they never bent themselves with such might and resolution against the very Turk or any other infidel, as they have done against a Virgin Queen, a famous lady, and a country which embraceth without corruption in doctrine the true and sincere religion of Christ'. This sort of stuff was lapped up by the godly.[37]

By the 1590s the Catholic threat was also largely at bay. This was in part because of the Catholics' own strategic errors. The pope's failure to give a lead in excommunicating Elizabeth until 1570 had initially given her Church a critical breathing space in the 1560s; subsequent Catholic missionary efforts had been directed at gentry households in the Thames Valley and the south-east rather than catering to the potentially large constituencies in the north and west. The government's policy of persecution exposed tensions within the Catholic community, many of the secular clergy disagreeing with the Jesuit insistence on the primacy of obligations to the papacy, and seeking some kind of accommodation with the government. Elizabeth could count on the basic loyalty to the dynasty of the Catholic gentry. Things would have been different had Elizabeth died at any point before 1587, for many Catholic gentry would doubtless have mobilised on behalf of Mary, Queen of Scots, whom they regarded as the lawful heir, but the execution of Mary removed their last real hope of achieving their objectives on Elizabeth's demise.[38]

In seeking reasons to account for the lack of large-scale popular disorder in the 1590s we should look more closely at the implications of that process of social polarisation described earlier. Whereas during the reign of Edward VI the middling groups in rural society had been willing to sponsor popular protests, by the 1590s they were too obviously implicated in enclosure to give a lead to those in rural society who wished to reverse the processes of commercialisation. As the beneficiaries of economic change, the yeomanry were unlikely sponsors of movements like the projected Oxfordshire Rising of 1596, 'whose declared aim was', in the words of the social historian John Walter, 'to challenge the agrarian capitalism which underwrote their growing wealth and power'. This meant that risings had to be planned conspiratorially within the village community rather than take the form of revolts of the whole community against some outside force, as the mid-Tudor revolts had been.[39]

The middling groups were increasingly implicated in the structures of state authority as a symbiosis developed between the centre and the local elites. The perceived fragility of the social order caused the state to intrude more into the lives of local communities, while the local elites were often willing partners in the tightening of regulation because of the threat represented by the burgeoning numbers of poor. The central government set the agenda for local officers through circulated articles on which action was demanded, while through the poor laws the yeomen village elites acquired another tool by which they might secure conformist behaviour from their poorer neighbours.[40]

But widespread participation in local government and especially in the legal system meant that popular legalism percolated further down the social scale. Sir Thomas Smith, one of the most perceptive social commentators of the day, although not immune to the prejudices which characterised his class, noted of the 'fourth set of men which doe not rule . . . day labourers, poor husbandmen, yea merchants or retailers which have no free land, copyholders, all artificers, as tailors, shoemakers, carpenters, brickmakers, masons, etc.', that 'they be not altogether neglected. For in cities and corporate towns for default of yeomen, they are fain to make their inquests of such manner of people. And in villages they be commonly made church-wardens, aleconners [inspectors of ale], and many times constables.' Smith's remarks have been borne out by the work of social historians who have pointed to the widespread participation in the criminal law, showing that service on juries extended to husbandmen, artificers and occasionally labourers. Although control over the legal process remained firmly in the hands of the judicial elite (the average length of a criminal trial in England in the 1590s was no more than a quarter of an hour, leaving juries at the mercy of judicial direction), nevertheless participation in the enforcement of the law contributed to an awareness of the law among the lower orders. The courts were not alien institutions: between 70 and 80 per cent of the people who used the court of king's bench in this period came from below the ranks of the gentry, while in borough courts and manorial courts the profile of litigants was even more biased towards the lower orders.[41]

There was a willingness to turn to the law courts to provide solutions to popular grievances, and a belief that legal action might prove more effective than the recourse to violence. Thus, Diarmaid MacCulloch has charted the tenacity of East Anglian communities who, although unsuccessful in the rebellion of 1549, continued to pursue their gentry aggressors through the equity courts and often won. Parliament also acted as a safety-valve, defusing grievances. Much of the popular xenophobia directed at the French and Dutch artisans resident in the capital was channelled through the lobbying efforts of the London craft guilds into the parliamentary arena. Popular legalism was so pervasive that it affected the actions of rioting crowds. In 1595 apprentices in Southwark seized butter and 'took upon them the office of clerk of the market and did abate the price of victuals and sell them at lower rates than they did usually sell them'. In other words, their actions were designed to remind a neglectful magistracy of its duty to activate the machinery of market regulation. Likewise, in the following year rioters in St Dunstan's just outside Canterbury consulted a lawyer's servant before stopping carts of grain: their action was confined to staying the grain 'in her Majesty's behalf'; they would not touch it, nor did they harm anyone. Perhaps this use of the law was instrumental, the poor acting in these ways because they knew that the consequences of not doing so were too dire to contemplate, rather than because they had internalised a legal culture, but it is testimony to the degree to which dense structures of local government were shaping the behaviour patterns of ordinary people.[42]

The spectre of disorder was also kept at bay by the ameliorative social policies pursued by the authorities. Critical to the stability of towns, for example, was the purchase of imported Polish grain by municipal authorities, often for sale to the poor at below-market rates. London led the way, financing the purchase of 10,000 quarters of grain each year, and selling it to the poor at 4d per bushel below the prevailing prices. But the practice was followed by provincial authorities as well: the common council of Shrewsbury, for example, arranged the import of 3200 quarters of corn from the Baltic in 1596. Outside the major towns the Privy Council tried to ensure that markets were kept supplied by implementing the recently codified dearth orders, which required the listing of grain stocks in the hundreds and divisions of the counties.[43]

A poor law was already in existence by the 1590s requiring the setting of rates by parochial authorities to provide pensions for the impotent poor, putting the able-bodied to work on locally provided stocks of wool, flax, hemp or iron, and subjecting rogues to the penalties of ear-boring and hanging. The law was, however, only patchily implemented; the larger towns were levying poor rates, but in the countryside rating seems to have been sporadic, and the poor were relieved by traditional methods of door-to-door begging. Many doubted whether the government should involve itself with the relief of the poor at all. Some of the inhabitants of the West Riding argued against the introduction of rating on 1598 on the grounds that 'many are able to give relief which are not able to give money'; the relief of the poor was best left to the mechanisms of neighbourly support. It is striking that when confronted by crisis conditions the response of the authorities was often to tap these sources of voluntary benevolence and neighbourly support. In 1596 the bishops instructed the wealthy to eat more frugally, observing the required fast days and abstaining from suppers on Wednesdays, donating what they saved to the poor. At Bristol in 1597 the wealthy were urged to give a meal of meat to upwards of eight poor people each. Thomas Minshull, a prosperous Nantwich mercer, noted in 1597 that 'all the gain of my shop was spent but £5, by reason of the dearth and great charges I lived at and giving away to the poor, for corn was at such a very fearful price'. In St Margaret Westminster the bulk of the enormous increase in provision for the poor (expenditure had increased from £36 per year during the 1560s to £223 in the 1590s) came from the benevolences of the wealthier parishioners.[44]

But, once the worst of the crisis had passed, the government sought to tighten the poor laws, with no less than seventeen bills on the subject under consideration by the Parliament of 1597–8. Although the statutes of 1598 and 1601 added little in the way of new principles, they did represent a strengthening of the machinery of control with the introduction of a new tier of administration in the form of the overseers of the poor, sparing justices of the peace much of the burden of implementation. The result seems to have been that rates were more widely implemented and, where they were already in existence, the amounts realised increased substantially; in London, for example, the yield of the poor rate doubled.

The poor law was not the only social legislation of 1598 which reveals a responsiveness to the problems of the past decade. The Oxfordshire Rising encouraged the Council to take tougher administrative action against enclosure. Several prominent enclosers had already been prosecuted, and

53. Charity was one of the public virtues most extolled: it took many forms, including good neighbourliness.

the issue of enclosure was laid before Parliament on the first day of its business by Francis Bacon, who had been involved in the interrogation of Bartholomew Steer and his accomplices. It is a notable testimony to the elites' sense of their own vulnerability in the face of concerted popular action that Parliament should have been willing to reimpose prohibitive enclosure legislation, repealed just four years previously, at a time when attitudes towards enclosure were becoming more permissive.[45]

We have seen how a variety of factors contributed to the stability of the later Elizabethan regime, enabling it to weather the storms of the 1590s. That resilience was demonstrated in the smooth transfer of power from Elizabeth to James VI of Scotland in 1603. It was a transition which surprised many contemporaries. The Venetian ambassador reported that on Elizabeth's death the Crown's ministers, hated by the people, were fearful that masterless men and malcontents would rise; citizens locked away their valuables, and all London was reported to be in arms for fear of Catholics. Elizabeth was now such a familiar figure that her subjects found it difficult to conceive of a world without her. As the pamphleteer Thomas Dekker noted later in 1603:

> the report of her death (like a thunder-clap) was able to kill thousands, it took away the hearts from millions: for having brought up (even under her wing)

a nation that was almost begotten and born under her; that never shouted any *Ave* than for her name, never saw the face of any Prince but herself, never understood what that outlandish word *Change* signified: how was it possible but that her sickness should throw abroad an universal fear, and her death an astonishment?

That James VI should have made a leisurely progress to take possession of his new kingdom without the need for troops indicates the fundamental cohesion of the polity Elizabeth bequeathed to him.[46]

54. The clock ticks. This domestic clock in iron bears the date 1598. Note the prominent display of the mechanism.

Notes

1. R. Strong, *Portraits of Queen Elizabeth I* (London, 1963), pp. 86–7; R. Strong, *The Cult of Elizabeth* (London, 1977), pp. 19–55.
2. T. Wilson, 'The State of England Anno Dom. 1600', *Camden Miscellany XVI* (Camden Society, 3rd series, lii, 1936), pp. 2–5; J. Hurstfield, 'The Succession Struggle in Late Elizabethan England', in S. T. Bindoff et al. (eds), *Elizabethan Government and Society: Essays Presented to Sir John Neale* (London, 1961), pp. 391, 396.
3. J. R. Dasent (ed.), *Acts of the Privy Council of England*, 32 vols (1890–1907), xxx, p. 619; J. J. Manning (ed.), *The First and Second Parts of John Hayward's The Life and Raigne of King Henrie III* (Camden Society, 4th series, xlii, 1991), p. 24; M. E. James, *Society, Politics, and Culture: Studies in Early Modern England* (Cambridge, 1986), pp. 419–20.
4. C. Haigh, *Elizabeth I* (London, 1988), pp. 145, 160–61; F. G. Emmison, *Elizabethan Life: Disorder* (Chelmsford, 1970), p. 58.
5. P. Williams, *The Tudor Regime* (Oxford, 1979), pp. 426–8; Haigh, *Elizabeth I*, pp. 66–7; W. MacCaffrey, *Elizabeth I* (London, 1993), pp. 393–4; A. Collins (ed.), *Letters and Memorials of State*, 2 vols (London, 1746), i, pp. 231, 331–2.
6. E. Ives, *Faction in Tudor England* (London, 1979); J. E. Neale, *Essays in Elizabethan History* (London, 1958), p. 71.
7. Neale, *Essays*, pp. 59–84; P. Williams, 'The Crown and the Counties', in C. Haigh (ed.), *The Reign of Elizabeth I* (London, 1984), pp. 133–6; R. H. Tawney and E. Power (eds), *Tudor Economic Documents*, 3 vols (London, 1924), ii, pp. 269–92; B. Worden, 'Ben Jonson among the Historians', in K. Sharpe and P. Lake (eds), *Culture and Politics in Early Stuart England* (London, 1994), pp. 82–5.
8. MacCaffrey, *Elizabeth I*, pp. 393–416; James, *Society, Politics, and Culture*, pp. 416–65; Haigh, *Elizabeth I*, pp. 134–9.
9. W. Camden, *Historie of Elizabeth* (London, 1630), p. 126; James, *Society, Politics, and Culture*, pp. 443–5; Haigh, *Elizabeth I*, p. 9.
10. T. Birch, *Memoirs of the Reign of Queen Elizabeth*, 2 vols (London, 1754), i, pp. 152–3; J. Guy, *Tudor England* (Oxford, 1988), pp. 447–52.
11. E. A. Wrigley and R. S. Schofield, *The Population History of England, 1541–1871: A Reconstruction* (Cambridge, 1981), p. 528; A. B. Appleby, *Famine in Tudor and Stuart England* (Liverpool, 1978); G. Abbot, *An Exposition upon the Prophet Jonah* (London, 1600), pp. 365–6; S. Rappaport, *Worlds within Worlds: Structures of Life in Sixteenth-Century London* (Cambridge, 1989), pp. 149–50; P. Clark, 'A Crisis Contained? The Condition of English Towns in the 1590s', in P. Clark (ed.), *The European Crisis of the 1590s* (London, 1985), pp. 45–7, 49.
12. I. W. Archer, *The Pursuit of Stability: Social Relations in Elizabethan London* (Cambridge, 1991), pp. 190–92.
13. F. J. Furnivall (ed.), *Harrison's Description of England in Shakspere's Youth*, 4 parts (London, 1877–1908), i, pp. 144, 153; D. M. Palliser, *The Age of Elizabeth: England under the Later Tudors, 1547–1603* (London, 1983), p. 50; Clark, 'A Crisis Contained?', p. 47; Wrigley and Schofield, *Population History*, pp. 653, 670–72.
14. Harrison, *Description*, i, pp. 239–41; K. Wrightson, *English Society, 1580–1680* (London, 1982), pp. 130–42; M. Spufford, *Contrasting Communities: English Villagers in the Sixteenth and Seventeenth Centuries* (Cambridge, 1974), ch. 3.
15. W. MacCaffrey, *Elizabeth I: War and Politics, 1588–1603* (Princeton, 1992), ch. 3; R. B. Outhwaite, 'Studies in Elizabethan Government Finance: Royal Borrowing and the Sales of Crown Lands, 1572–1603' (unpublished PhD thesis, Nottingham University, 1964); Archer, *Pursuit of Stability*, pp. 10–11.
16. Tawney and Power (eds), *Tudor Economic Documents*, ii, pp. 235–43; British Library, Cotton MS Titus F ii, fo. 47; *Historical Manuscripts Commission, Hatfield House*, vi, pp. 534–5; Dasent (ed.), *Acts of the Privy Council*, xxvi, pp. 553–4; Williams, 'Crown and Counties', pp. 129–31.
17. J. Walter, '"A Rising of the People?" The Oxfordshire Rising of 1596', *Past and Present*, cvii (1985), 99; British Library, Lansdowne MS 78/64.

18. *HMC, Hatfield House*, xiii, pp. 168–9; B. Sharp, *In Contempt of All Authority: Rural Artisans and Riot in the West of England, 1586–1660* (London, 1980), p. 37.
19. Walter, 'Oxfordshire Rising'; Archer, *Pursuit of Stability*, pp. 1–2.
20. Tawney and Power (eds), *Tudor Economic Documents*, iii, pp. 339–46.
21. A. V. Judges (ed.), *The Elizabethan Underworld* (London, 1930), esp. pp. 150–51; C. Hill, *Society and Puritanism in Pre-Revolutionary England* (London, 1964), p. 275; P. Slack, *Poverty and Policy in Tudor and Stuart England* (London, 1988), pp. 104–6.
22. J. S. Cockburn, 'The Nature and Incidence of Crime in England, 1559–1625: A Preliminary Survey', in J. S. Cockburn (ed.), *Crime in England, 1550–1800* (London, 1977), pp. 64, 67–9; J. A. Sharpe, *Crime in Early Modern England, 1550–1750* (London, 1984), ch. 5.
23. Archer, *Pursuit of Stability*, pp. 184–5, 244–5; *Statutes of the Realm*, 43 Eliz. I c. 7; P. Clark, *The English Alehouse: A Social History, 1200–1830* (London, 1983), chs 5–8.
24. Wrightson, *English Society*, pp. 84–6, 145–6; A. Fletcher, *Reform in the Provinces: The Government of Stuart England* (London, 1986), p. 256; M. Ingram, *Church Courts, Sex, and Marriage in England, 1570–1640* (Cambridge, 1987), ch. 7.
25. J. Kent, 'Attitudes of Members of the House of Commons to the Regulation of "Personal Conduct" in Late Elizabethan and Early Stuart England', *Bulletin of the Institute of Historical Research*, xlvi (1973), 49; Archer, *Pursuit of Stability*, pp. 232–3, 253–4.
26. D. E. Underdown, 'The Taming of the Scold: The Enforcement of Patriarchal Authority in Early Modern England', in A. Fletcher and J. Stevenson (eds), *Order and Disorder in Early Modern England* (Cambridge, 1985), pp. 117–36, quotes at pp. 119, 120–21; K. V. Thomas, *Religion and the Decline of Magic* (London, 1971), pp. 541–2.
27. E. Duffy, *The Stripping of the Altars: Traditional Religion in England, 1400–1580* (London, 1992).
28. Spufford, *Contrasting Communities*, pp. 327–28; C. Haigh, 'The Church of England, the Catholics, and the People', in Haigh (ed.), *Reign of Elizabeth I*, p. 214.
29. Haigh, 'Church of England', p. 206; D. MacCulloch, *The Later Reformation in England, 1547–1603* (London, 1990), p. 167.
30. P. Collinson, *The Birthpangs of Protestant England: Religious and Cultural Change in the Sixteenth and Seventeenth Centuries* (London, 1988), pp. 56, 137–9; D. Underdown, *Revel, Riot, and Rebellion: Popular Politics and Culture in England, 1603–1660* (Oxford, 1985).
31. P. Williams, 'Court and Polity under Elizabeth I', *Bulletin of the John Rylands Library*, lxv (1982–3), 259–86; A. Hassell-Smith, *County and Court: Government and Politics in Norfolk, 1558–1603* (Oxford, 1974); D. MacCulloch, *Suffolk and the Tudors: Politics and Religion in an English County, 1500–1600* (Oxford, 1986); Williams, 'Crown and Counties', pp. 141–2; James, *Society, Politics, and Culture*, p. 453.
32. I. A. A. Thompson, 'The Impact of War', in Clark (ed.), *European Crisis*, p. 267; Archer, *Pursuit of Stability*, p. 35.
33. Camden, *Historie of Elizabeth*, p. 555; A. F. Pollard and M. Blatcher, 'Hayward Townshend's Journals', *Bulletin of the Institute of Historical Research*, xii (1934–5), 12–13.
34. Williams, 'Crown and Counties', pp. 138–9, 143–6; Outhwaite, 'Studies in Elizabethan Government Finance'.
35. Haigh, 'Church of England', pp. 216–18; J. Maltby, '"By this Book": Parishioners, the Prayer Book, and the Established Church', in K. Fincham (ed.), *The Early Stuart Church, 1603–1642* (London, 1993), pp. 118–19.
36. P. Collinson, *The Elizabethan Puritan Movement* (London, 1967); MacCulloch, *Later Reformation*, pp. 47–61.
37. MacCulloch, *Later Reformation*, ch. 6; J. E. Neale, *Elizabeth I and her Parliaments*, 2 vols (London, 1957), ii, pp. 194–201.
38. Haigh, 'Church of England', pp. 201–5; A. Pritchard, *Catholic Loyalism in Elizabethan England* (London, 1979).
39. Walter, 'Oxfordshire Rising', pp. 119–25.
40. Wrightson, *English Society*, chs 5–6; Fletcher, *Reform in the Provinces*, pp. 137–9.

41. T. Smith, *De Republica Anglorum*, ed. M. Dewar (Cambridge, 1982), pp. 76–7; C. B. Herrup, *The Common Peace: Participation and the Criminal Law in Seventeenth-Century England* (Cambridge, 1987); J. A. Sharpe, 'The People and the Law', in B. Reay (ed.) *Popular Culture in Seventeenth-Century England* (London, 1985), pp. 250–51.
42. MacCulloch, *Suffolk*, ch. 11; Archer, *Pursuit of Stability*, pp. 6, 136–40; P. Clark, 'Popular Protest and Disturbance in Kent, 1558–1640', *Economic History Review*, 2nd series, xxix (1976), 375.
43. Archer, *Pursuit of Stability*, pp. 200–1; Williams, *Tudor Regime*, p. 191.
44. P. Slack, 'Poverty and Social Regulation in Elizabethan England', in Haigh (ed.), *Reign of Elizabeth I*, p. 234; *Acts of the Privy Council*, xxvi, pp. 96–8, 380–82; J. Walter, 'The Social Economy of Dearth in Early Modern England', in J. Walter and R. Schofield (eds), *Famine, Disease and the Social Order in Early Modern Society* (Cambridge, 1989), p. 115; Clark, 'A Crisis Contained?', p. 60.
45. Slack, *Poverty and Policy*, pp. 126–7; Archer, *Pursuit of Stability*, pp. 162–3; Walter, 'Oxfordshire Rising', pp. 130–37.
46. H. F. Brown (ed.), *Calendar of State Papers Venetian*, vol. ix: *1592–1603* (1897), pp. 558, 562; T. Dekker, *The Wonderful Year* (1603).

·LE
JUBILÉ.
DE L'AN 1700,
Chez
NICOLAS CHEVALIER
Marchand Libraire
Sur le Rokin.
1701.

CONC. TRIDEN

DULGENTIA PL

R. de Hooghe

55. The passage of Time: through the mirror the papal Jubilee of 1700 is now mocked. Times have
changed. This is the title-page of an anonymous work published in 1701.

THE 1690s

Finance, Fashion and Frivolity

Peter Earle

Since . . . the Creation of the World   *5696*
The Incarnation of Jesus Christ   *1690*
England received the Christian Faith   *1500*
The horrid design of the Gun-Powder Plot   *85*
Our miraculous Deliverance from Popery by K. William   *2*
(The Protestant Almanack for the Year 1690)[1]

England in 1690 was on the threshold of its period of greatness, just about to become a dominant power, soon to be the first country to undergo an industrial revolution. The population stood at around five million, about a quarter of that of France, and had not grown much in the previous forty years. In the same period the economy had developed quite rapidly and the country was now one of the richest in the world. Agriculture was efficient, second only to that of the Low Countries, and in normal years England was able to feed itself well and still have ample to export. Industry was no longer backward compared to that of its continental neighbours as it had been in 1600, and there was a spirit of inventiveness which manifested itself in an increasing division of labour in many industries, widespread use of waterpower and a growing interest in machines. The seeds of rapid economic development had been sown.

England already had an unusually high proportion of the population living in towns, but nearly half of these urban dwellers lived in London, whose enormous population of over half a million was exceeded in Europe only by Constantinople. London dwarfed all other English towns, the next biggest being Norwich with only 30,000 inhabitants, and as a result the metropolis dominated English society and economy in a way that it had never done before and was never quite to do again. It was the seat of government, the main residence of the court, virtually the only publishing centre and the home of the majority of professional people. The City handled nearly three-quarters of England's foreign trade, dominated inland trade and also had much the largest concentration of industrial workers in the country. London was also the greatest leisure centre in England, particularly in the winter and spring, when wealthy aristocrats and gentry and their ladies came to enjoy themselves in what had become an established social season, so providing employment for hordes of servants and seamstresses, porters and prostitutes and for such specialists as Thomas Forster, who 'lived by my art of drawing faces', or Eleanor Graham, who made 'chocolett cakes for persons of quality'.[2]

London was not just an economic and social capital; it was already an imperial city whose commercial and administrative tentacles stretched across the world. The East India Company had laid the foundations for its later, astonishing adventures with bases in Bombay and Madras, while the small settlement which was to become Calcutta was founded in 1696. The Company celebrated the new decade by going to war with the Great Mogul, an enterprise which the veteran seaman Edward Barlow thought 'an unwise undertaking . . . with a handful of men and money, to go make wars with one of the greatest monarchs in the world who . . . had men enough to have eaten up all the Company's servants for a breakfast.'[3]

There were English settlements too on the west coast of Africa, from which the Royal African Company despatched black slaves to grow sugar and tobacco in the new world, a trade so attractive to Englishmen that the Company struggled in vain to maintain its supposed monopoly to 'barter baubles for the souls of men', as Daniel Defoe put it in one of the few contemporary writings which questioned the morality of the slave trade.[4] But it was in the Americas that English imperialist ambitions had had their greatest successes, with thriving colonies established from New England to the Carolinas, the beginnings of English expansion in Canada, and a cluster of islands large and small in the West Indies, the biggest of which, Jamaica, suffered an earthquake in 1692 which swallowed up Port Royal, the largest town in English America and reputedly the most sinful city in the world. This empire was very small compared with what it was to become, but it already played a significant part in English life, and it was imperial trade, with India and the Americas, that was much the most rapidly growing branch of English commerce at the end of the prosperous 1680s.

A mighty merchant fleet which had nearly doubled in size since 1660 now sailed the seas of the world, bringing home tea from China, coffee from Arabia, spices, silks and cotton textiles from India, gold and ivory from Africa, sugar and dyestuffs from the West Indies, tobacco from Chesapeake Bay, raw silk and cotton from the Levant and wines and fruits from southern Europe and the islands of the Atlantic. Such goods were eagerly consumed in England, but much was also re-exported to other markets in Europe, a very profitable business which ensured that London would soon replace Amsterdam as the leading entrepôt of the world. England's 'commercial revolution' drew in merchants, brokers and sailors from all over Europe, and it was in the late seventeenth century that London first became a great cosmopolitan city which could be described justifiably as 'the chiefest Emporium, or Town of Trade in the World; the largest and most populous, the fairest and most opulent City at this day in all Europe, perhaps in the Whole World'.[5]

61 St Michael Royal	73 Dutch Church	85 St Hellens	97 St Katherine Coleman
62 St Stephen Walbrook	74 St Bennet Fink	86 St Bennet Gracechurch	98 St Botolph Aldgate
63 New Bethlehem	75 St Peter Poor	87 St Dionis Backchurch	99 St Olave Hart street
64 St Margaret Lothbury	76 St Edmund Lumbardstr	88 St Magnus	100 Alhallows Barking
65 St Swithin	77 St Michael Cornhill	89 St George Botolphlane	101 St Katherines Tower
66 Alhallows the Great	78 Alhallows Lumbardstr	90 St Andrew Undershaft	102 SSMary-Whitechappel
67 St Chrijstophers	79 St Peters Cornhill	91 St Margaret Pattons	103 Wappin Chapel
68 St Mary Abchurch	80 St Martins Outwich	92 St Mary Hill	104 St Paul Shadwell
69 St Mary Woolnoth	81 St Clement Eastchep	93 St Katherine Creechurch	105 Stepney Church
70 St Bartholmew	82 St Michael Crookedlane	94 St James Dukes place	
71 Royal Exchange	83 St Botolph Bijshopsgate	95 Alhallows Stainning	
72 Alhallows on the Wall	84 St Ethelborough	96 St Dunstans in the East	

REFERENCES for LONDON

LONDON

56. A view of London's churches after the Great Fire (anon., *c.* 1690).

Ten years later in 1700, neither England nor its empire would have seemed very different to the casual observer. And yet this last decade of the seventeenth century was fundamental in transforming many aspects of English life, so that the England of Queen Anne seems to the historian to be a very different place, in many ways a very modern place, compared to the England of the 1680s. Some of these changes, particularly those in the social and cultural lives of the English, are difficult to pin down to a single decade, although they certainly belong to this *fin de siècle*. Others are more obviously rooted in the 1690s, a period of warfare and taxation on an unprecedented scale, a period which so nearly coincides with the reign of King William III (1689–1702) that it is no surprise that the working out of the Revolution settlement which brought him to the throne should dominate the historiography of the decade.

Those who lived through it saw the 'miraculous deliverance from popery and arbitrary power' brought about by William in the Glorious Revolution of 1688 as the true *fin de siècle*, a major turning point whose date, like 1066 and 1588, became one of the few to be fixed firmly in the nation's collective memory. The end of the century itself attracted some millenarian attention as usual; the year 1699 was after all the sum of 1666, the Beast's Number, and

57. The Crown by Consent not by Divine Right. William III, arrived from Holland, and his wife
Mary, daughter of James II, have been crowned in London. They figure as Protestant liberators.

33, the years of Christ's life, and some predicted the rise of a great conqueror
who would 'give peace to the whole earth'. But such predictions were fairly
commonplace in the late seventeenth and early eighteenth centuries, a time
of general millenarian enthusiasm in which the earthquake of 1692 or the
conjunction of Saturn and Jupiter in 1702 might well have greater
apocalyptic significance than the mere end of a century.[6]

Archbishop Tillotson thought that the Revolution of 1688 was 'a thing
that cannot be paralleled in History, and which can only be resolv'd into the
over-ruling Providence of God',[7] but to those less obsessed with the dangers
of popery it seems so muted compared to other revolutions that it is easy to
forget just how important both the Revolution itself and the compromises of
the decade that followed it have been to English political life. After all, what
did it involve but the replacement of one man, the autocratic Catholic King

James II by his equally autocratic Protestant nephew and son-in-law King William of Orange, just another palace revolution with more than its fair share of farce? And yet the need to justify the ejection of a legitimate king and at the same time to check King William's desire to be an absolute monarch produced a classic compromise, a muddling through, which has stood the test of time and provided the nearest to a constitution that Britain possesses.

The details of this compromise need not detain us, since they belong more to a textbook than to an essay on a *fin de siècle*, but the results can hardly be ignored since they are the greatest legacy that the 1690s have bequeathed to later generations. This then was the decade that saw the resolution of nearly a century of quarrels between king and Parliament and made the memory of civil war seem little more than a bad dream. This was the decade which saw the triumph of parliamentary government and the rule of law which have ever since been taken for granted. Parliament has sat every year since the 1690s and sessions have been sufficiently long for legislation to have a fair chance of becoming law, a far cry from the previous situation where Parliament often did not meet for years at a time and when it did meet was quite likely to be dismissed after a few weeks or even a few days.

Parliament was still of course unreformed, an assembly of country gentlemen, merchants, lawyers and officers in the army and navy whose seats were usually obtained by careful attention to aristocratic patronage or by the expenditure of large sums of money on votes and rotten boroughs. Such a venal system of representation did not mean, however, that there were no loyalties, beyond those due to patriotism or 'revolution principles' or more specifically to a patron or oneself. For this same decade which invented parliamentary government also invented, or at least refined, that system of two-party politics, Whig and Tory, which in various forms has had such a long hold on English affections and affairs. Indeed, the decade went a little further than this since politics was complicated then as in other times by the emergence of a third party, the 'country party', whose interests and affiliations have bemused generations of historians. The psephologist may not have been born in the 1690s, but he had certainly been conceived.

The autocratic King William resented parliamentary restraints on his freedom to rule and he positively detested party politics. He soon discerned, however, that these were the price he would have to pay for the achievement of the main aim of his intervention in British royal affairs, the attachment of British wealth, manpower and especially naval power to his Grand Alliance against the all-conquering ambitions and love of *gloire* of Louis XIV. Parliament might control the purse-strings, but it had as yet made few inroads into the royal prerogative, and one of the most jealously guarded prerogatives of an English king was the right to determine foreign policy and declare war. King William was well aware of this and wasted no time in bringing his new kingdoms into the war against France, a decision which seems to have come as no surprise to his new subjects if one can judge from the reaction of the crew of the merchant ship *Expedition* trading in the Mediterranean. They refused to set sail without a naval convoy 'for that ye Prince of Orange as they said was come to England and they did not know but that they might have warrs with all the world'.[8]

This war was to drag these islands into the heart of European affairs for the first time since the fifteenth century and to lay the foundations for England's lengthy innings as a great power. There was to be no turning back. The country which had believed that a strong navy and a broad channel were sufficient to keep the unpleasant affairs of Europe at a distance was from now on to commit men and money on continental soil in war after war, down to the battle of Waterloo and of course long after that. The historian David Ogg remarked that William 'was the first English king who was a good European'.[9] The English themselves were reluctant Europeans in the 1690s, just as they are today, but King William's lead has ensured that being part of Europe is as much a legacy of the 1690s as that parliamentary price which the king had to pay to achieve his ambition.

King William's War (1689–97) was not itself a memorable war. It succeeded modestly in its aim to contain the expansionist ambitions of King Louis XIV and so ensured the survival of the revolutionary regime in England itself, but there was as yet no sign of that British military brilliance which was to shine forth under the Duke of Marlborough's command in the next decade. Marlborough himself (still plain Churchill) was in disgrace, suspected rightly of intrigues with King James's court in exile in France; and few but extreme military history buffs can find much to stir the blood in the battles of Steenkirk and Neerwinden or even in the capture of Namur, the king's solitary military success in this war that bears his name. The war was a bloody stalemate of marches and counter-marches and sieges, whose long-drawn-out tedium was enlivened for contemporary observers by gambling on the date on which such and such a town might fall to a besieging army. Such excitement is of course denied to the military historian, who can find little on which to comment except the substitution of firelock and bayonet for matchlock and pike, a small but murderous piece of technological change which was to ensure that the wars of the eighteenth century would be even more bloody than those of the seventeenth.

At sea also, where England expects some excitement from its sailors, the war fails to catch the imagination. There are probably few readers of history books today who can remember who won the battle of Beachy Head (1690) and who the battle of La Hogue (1692), yet the first resulted in a French victory which left the Channel free for an invasion that never came and the second was an Anglo-Dutch victory which destroyed the French navy as a serious threat, thus encouraging the French to devote nearly all their naval

58. Two islands, two faiths: the battle of the Boyne (1690), still echoing through the history of Ulster, was won by William III and the Protestants.

efforts to privateering – with devastating effects on English merchant shipping. Indeed, the only military event of the 1690s which is still well known today is the battle of the Boyne, which was fought on 12 July 1690. King James rode forward with resolution to meet his nephew William in battle, determined that 'he would not be walked out of Ireland without at least having one blow for it', but his resolution failed him on the day as he watched the collapse of his army and his hopes, a defeat which sealed the fate of Ireland for the next two centuries. The Boyne is still remembered with passion today and people still whistle 'Lilliburlero', the stirring Protestant marching song of the 1690s. Yet how many remember that the battle was fought as part of a general European war between France and King William's Grand Alliance, an alliance which was supported not just by some of the Catholic princes of Europe but for a time by the Pope himself?

The Boyne apart, the war of the 1690s is unusual in being remembered today not for its battles or for the men who fought in them but for the way it was financed. English rulers had long sought a solution to the perennial problem of paying for wars, hitherto without much success. This time the problem was even worse, for King William's War was on a scale greater than any previous military adventure, requiring as it did well over 100,000 men and an average expenditure of some £5.5 million a year. Raising men was not too difficult since poverty has always been an effective recruiting sergeant and there were more poor men than usual in the hard times of the 1690s. And if poverty should not prove sufficient to supply the men required, there were always the press gangs and the sweepings of the gaols. But raising money was quite a different matter and occupied the minds of the most ingenious men of the day.

New tax followed new tax. Some, like the land tax of 1692 or the many additions to the excise, were to prove long-lasting as sources of revenue; others like the strange tax on births, burials, bachelors and marriages or the poll tax (hated then as now) were to prove ephemeral. But increased taxation has never been sufficient to fund the demands of war, and the government was forced to turn increasingly to borrowing to pay its bills.

It was in this sphere of public borrowing that the men of the 1690s were to have their greatest successes, so great indeed that they have been graced by historians with the name of financial revolution. This is a complex subject, but three main aspects of this 'revolution' can be singled out, all with antecedents going back to the 1660s but all coming to full fruition in the 1690s. First, and very important, was the fact that borrowing in the 1690s and thereafter was raised not on the credit of the king but on that of Parliament, which, in turn was seen to represent the credit of the people. 'They who lend upon parliamentary funds', wrote Charles Davenant, 'have for their security the quick and dead stock of the kingdom; the land with its product; the arts, industry, labour and manufactures of this country.'[10] Such lending still represented a risk, since parliamentary credit itself required the survival of William's regime, but this was seen as preferable to the much more perilous risk of lending to a king, and loans were forthcoming.

Parliament soon found, however, that the demands of the war made it increasingly difficult to find sufficient money to pay its bills and interest payments and at the same time to repay the capital lent to it at the due date. Payments fell into arrears and claims on the government were sold by their disgusted holders at big discounts, a small hardship for financiers perhaps but a terrible one for the sailors of the Royal Navy whose 'tickets' (claims on the government for their meagre pay) were being bought for less than half their face value by speculators. Such financial crises were a regular feature of all wars, but this time a partial solution was to be found to one of the problems, the need to repay capital to the lenders. The answer here – the second aspect of the financial revolution – was to appeal to the English passion for gambling. Public lotteries were one successful innovation adapted from foreign examples. The Million Lottery of 1694, for instance, raised its million pounds in £10 tickets which earned their holders at least £1 a year for sixteen years while the biggest prize-winners got £1000 a year, a very substantial income for the period, large enough to support a life of idleness. Even more successful was the sale of annuities, a gamble on life expectancy.

These financial expedients, the product of a time of near panic, were to prove important precursors of future finance, for they were the first examples of deliberate long-term borrowing by the English government, as opposed to the unplanned long-term borrowing of the past when debts were simply not repaid for decades. As such, they mark the beginning of the famous national debt, which was to be organised in a slightly less frantic way in the eighteenth century and would enable England to raise money for her future wars with remarkable ease. In the 1690s, however, this happy outcome could hardly have been predicted since, regardless of lotteries and annuities, the government lurched from financial crisis to financial crisis until peace in 1697 brought a merciful, though only temporary, release.

The third pillar of the financial revolution was the Bank of England which was founded in 1694, again as a by-product of war finance. The idea of a national bank had been debated for decades, but had never met with much favour, partly because of the power that it would give to the 'moneyed men' who would inevitably control it, partly out of fear that such a huge accumulation of money would prove an irresistible target for a greedy or unscrupulous king. Fear of the king was diminished by the parliamentary control enshrined in the revolutionary settlement, but fear and hatred of big money were to remain strong well into the eighteenth century. Nevertheless,

59. The power of money. The Bank of England, incorporated by royal charter in 1694 was founded to fund war against France. It became a prop of the government and, by managing the national debt, became 'a part of the constitution'.

needs were to overcome caution in 1694 when a proposal to lend the government £1.2 million in return for a charter to establish a bank was accepted, and the Bank of England, whose capital was subscribed in just eleven days, came into existence. The Bank, like government finance in general, lurched from crisis to crisis in the 1690s, but like the government system it survived intact to become the respectable institution it is today.

One can also credit the establishment of a permanent civil service to the 1690s, though as with finance there were lengthy antecedents to this development. Here again, the war was instrumental in bringing about change since it necessitated a considerable increase in the personnel of government, both to administer the armed forces themselves and to manage and collect all the new taxes needed to pay for them. Once such posts had been established, they normally survived the intervals of peacetime, and the escalation of numbers employed in government service has been more or less continuous since the 1690s. Such bureaucrats joined an already large number of pen-pushers engaged in legal clerical work and a smaller but rapidly growing population of clerks and accountants employed in business, men like Thomas Leche of Covent Garden, who was 'a book-keeper to several master tailors in Burleigh Street', or Benjamin Hayne, who followed 'the buisnesse of writeing for any person who will employ him'.[11] Such men, and they were all men, were normally well educated and reasonably well paid. They formed a respectable and largely overlooked group in society whose behaviour and attitudes to their fellows prefigure those of the Pooters of Victorian London.

Many of these clerks were highly numerate by the standards of their day, the beneficiaries of a massive expansion in the teaching of mathematics and accountancy. Indeed, society as a whole had a passion for numbers, however spurious these might be, and by the 1690s such numbers had entered into the normal discourse of political argument. This was the decade which saw the triumph both of 'political arithmetic', what we might loosely call statistics, and of 'discourses of trade', the precursor of economics, both of which relied to a considerable degree on the ingenious manipulation of numbers. The first year of the decade saw the publication of the book which gave the new science its name, *Political Arithmetick* by Sir William Petty, who promised in his preface 'to express my self in terms of *number, weight,* or *measure*', a promise he fulfilled in some extraordinary calculations of the comparative strengths and prospects of England, France and Holland. 'To conclude, upon the whole it seems that though France be in people to Holland and Zealand as 13 to 1, and in quantity of good land, so 80 to 1, yet it is not 13 times richer and stronger, much less 80 times, nor much above thrice.'[12]

Even more ambitious were the calculations of the herald and number-cruncher Gregory King, who counted or pretended to count practically everything in England from people to rabbits and from houses to hats. Not to be outdone, the astronomer Edmond Halley (of the comet) calculated the area of each English county by cutting them out from a map and weighing the pieces of paper, while in 1692 the young Scottish physician John Arbuthnot introduced the theory of probability to Britain with a demonstration of how to calculate the odds in backgammon. He thought there were very few topics incapable of being reduced to mathematical reckoning: even politics was but 'a kind of analysis of the quantity of probability in casual events'.[13]

Numeracy, gambling, greed and an interest in probability also lay behind another remarkable phenomenon of the 1690s, the rise and rapid maturity of the London stock market. Speculation had been stimulated in the 1680s, suitably enough by dealings in the shares of treasure-hunting companies and more prosaically in those of the East India Company. But the early 1690s were to see the first great promotion boom in British history with dealings in well over a hundred English and Scottish joint-stock companies, ranging from the honest and useful to the totally fraudulent, as well as in the financial paper of the government. Almost immediately, all the paraphernalia of a modern stock market sprang into existence, brokers and jobbers, bulls and bears and a press providing listings of current prices for the benefit of the investors. Such activities naturally aroused the hostility of those who did not understand them and in any case disliked the moneyed man instinctively; but, despite restrictions on their activities, these 'yuppies' of the 1690s were here to stay.

All this might suggest that the decade of the 1690s was a very serious one, interested only in money and more money, with the occasional dash of politics. This is essentially true; it was indeed a serious decade, and many of the people who lived through it were types who worried about the war, politics, the Jacobite threat to the Revolution settlement, high prices, the state of the coinage, government finance and a host of other things of which money was the most important. There is however a lighter side to this somewhat intense *fin de siècle*, for the people of the 1690s were interested not only in getting money but also in spending it, and during that decade there were considerable changes in the way in which they did so.

It was, to start with, a period which saw a veritable revolution in dress, for both men and women. This is reflected in portraits and makes the people of the late seventeenth and early eighteenth centuries look very different from their predecessors. By the 1690s, men had abandoned the doublet and hose of earlier times and wore the three-piece suit of coat, waistcoat and knee-breeches which is so characteristic of the eighteenth century, the coats and waistcoats of the 1690s being so long that they almost concealed the breeches. The wearing of a wig on shaven heads, which started in the 1660s, had also now become general even in quite lowly strata of society. The

60. 'A veritable revolution in dress': male fashion
at the turn of the century. Fashions would
continue to change in the next century.

change in women's clothes saw the abandonment of the tailored costumes of
the mid-seventeenth century for more loosely fitting outer garments in the
form of the mantua and the gown. These normally trailed to the ground at
the back and were left open below the waist in front to reveal the petticoat
or petticoats, while, under all, their shape was determined by 'a pair of
bodies' (stays), normally quite tightly laced.

Details changed regularly as fashion took a firmer grip, such fashions
originating from Paris, war or no war. What was worn by the fashionable was
quickly imitated by the prosperous and expanding middle classes and even
by men and women in the lower strata of society who were able to buy cheap
ready-made clothing in the new fashions, this ready-made industry being yet
another innovation of the late seventeenth century. 'Many remember',
claimed a writer in 1681, 'when there were no new garments sold in London
as now there are, only old garments at second hand.'[14]

Furniture and the interior decoration of houses also changed significantly
in the late seventeenth century, especially in the 1690s; much that was
common in the reign of Queen Anne had not been present at all in the 1680s.

61. Female beauty: Lady Townshend, 1681–1711, painted by Sir Godfrey Kneller in the 1690s. Female fashion with a classical background.

One major feature of change was an increasing emphasis on light within the house. Small-paned windows were being replaced by the typical London sash-windows from the late 1680s, throwing more light into rooms whose ceilings were now more often plastered, which 'make by their whiteness the rooms so much lightsomer'.[15] Inside, there was a much greater provision of sconces and standing candlesticks, often backed by mirrors, and the general effect was enhanced by the use of vast mirror plates as chimney-glasses above fireplaces or as pier-glasses between the windows. The use of mirrors was indeed very much a feature of the age. They could be found in every room in middle-class homes, even in those occupied by the servants, suggesting an increasing interest in self-perusal as well as a desire to be able to see at all.

The rooms revealed by this more plentiful light were changing rapidly from the stark, bare and uncomfortable interiors of the recent past. Hedonism had entered into furniture design with the result that curves which fitted the human body now began to replace the upright, angular furniture of earlier days, while improvements in upholstery led to better padded seats and a more frequent use of cushions. Couches, sofas and

62. Light from without: Uppark, West Sussex, was built in *c.* 1690 for Lord Grey of Werke, first Earl of Tankerville.

settees became commonplace, while the 'easy chair', another innovation of the period, has been described by a furniture historian as 'a national symbol of comfort and ease'.[16] One finds also many oriental touches in these late seventeenth-century interiors, sometimes directly imported from the Levant, India or China, but often provided by English imitators. Eastern silks and cottons were increasingly used in upholstery, bed-hangings and window-curtains (themselves quite a recent innovation). Light and elegant canework was employed for upright chairs and other furniture, while japanning and other lacquerwork enhanced cabinets and chests of drawers.

A love of things oriental also manifested itself in the accumulation of objects within the home. Some of these were things which now suddenly seemed essential, such as clocks, or possibly useful, such as barometers or weather-glasses (which were the fashion of the 1690s). Others were mainly for fashionable or decorative display, the product of a collecting fever which is still with us. The most obvious example was china, which began to be common in domestic households in the 1690s and had become an absorbing craze by the following decade. But collecting went far beyond china. Bric-à-brac and ornaments of all sorts piled up in cabinets and on mantelpieces.

Walls became galleries, quite modest people often owning ten or twenty pictures. Oriental prints imported by the East India Company were very popular, but they shared space with locally produced art, landscapes, seascapes, portraits of the king and queen, and large numbers of 'family pictures', evidence of a growing self-awareness which produced a plentiful supply of work for portrait painters from the 1690s onwards.

It was also in this decade of innovation that hot drinks became common within the home. The coffee-house had first appeared in England around 1650, and it was in this public and very social new meeting-place that people first got a taste for all three of the exotic new drinks – coffee, chocolate and tea. But it was only in the 1690s that it became common to find the equipment for making and drinking coffee and tea in people's homes, and it is interesting that even at this early stage tea-kettles outnumbered coffee-pots by three to one. The English were just about to become a nation of tea-drinkers. Not that this should be taken as evidence of some new national passion for sobriety, for the 1690s saw the beginning of the biggest drinking spree in English history. It was then that port started to replace claret as the upper-class tipple, while spirits challenged beer as the consolation of the lower classes. Spirits consumption quadrupled between 1680 and 1710 and was to quadruple again by 1740, most of this being gin, which as Defoe

63. Polite society taking tea and coffee at home (a British School painting, *c.* 1690).

64. Taking coffee in public. Coffee houses flourished, places of pleasure and business (anon., *c.* 1700).

informs us was introduced to the English by their Dutch allies in King William's War.[17]

It would seem then that the people of the 1690s were not just interested in money, politics and war. They were also interested in drinking, comfort and possessions – and the analysis of these possessions may give some clues to what went on in their minds (though it must be admitted that making psychological inferences from the possessions of people in the past is a notorious quagmire for historians). The ubiquity of clocks presumes an interest in time and punctuality, in 'work-discipline and industrial capitalism', as E. P. Thompson once suggested. Collecting may have something to do with the accumulation of capital stressed by economists. Window-curtains suggest an interest in privacy, which can also be seen in other features of domestic interiors, such as the increasing use of corridors to provide each room with a private access. A taste for comfort may indicate a softening of the national psyche, a decline in stoicism which can also be observed in a leap in the demand for medical services of all kinds and in the consumption of such painkilling drugs as opium. Mirrors and family portraits may reflect self-awareness and vanity, or they may of course simply reflect fashion, which was itself becoming more pervasive.

Drinking and gambling may have been the most popular leisure occupations of late seventeenth-century English men and women, but more cultured entertainment provided considerable competition. Music and

65. A 1695 astronomical clock that tells more than the time. By Samuel Watson.

dancing were especially popular at all social levels, from the stately minuets of the court to music houses in taverns, public hops in spas and pleasure grounds and ballad singers in the streets. Musical interludes before, during and after plays became an important part of the entertainment offered in the theatres, while public concerts, which had made a tentative start in the 1670s, really began to flourish in the 1690s with the opening of the first purpose-built concert hall in York Buildings and of Thomas Hickford's famous Great Room off the Haymarket.

Such developments greatly increased the employment available for professional musicians, many of whom were foreigners attracted by English money, but they had the unfortunate side-effect of driving music out of the home so that the impromptu private concerts which were such a feature of the domestic life revealed by Samuel Pepys in his diary became rarer. This commercialisation of music was also accompanied by a decline in the native English genius, which was eclipsed by foreign competition after the death of Henry Purcell in 1695. The English were to hear and enjoy far more music in the years to come, but not so much of it was to be English music.

In drama and literature, the 1690s serve as a watershed between the Restoration and the Augustan age. Congreve was at the height of his powers and wrote all his plays between 1693 and 1700, the year of *The Way of the World*, but most of the other great writers who were alive in the 1690s produced their best work either earlier, like Dryden, Shadwell and Wycherley, or later, like Farquhar, Swift, Pope, Defoe, Addison and Steele. This does not mean that there was not much writing going on in the 1690s, because those years in fact produced more printed words than any previous decade in English history. This avalanche of print owed much to the collapse of censorship after the lapsing of the licensing laws in 1695, but it also reflected the social, economic and political problems of the decade. These provided the subject matter for thousands of pamphlets and other ephemeral literature and were also a major factor in vigorous expansion in the numbers of newspapers and periodicals, culminating in 1702 in the appearance of the first London daily. Such papers make dull reading today, though there is some light relief, such as the invention of the 'agony column' by John Dunton in the *Athenian Mercury*. They were read avidly, however, by contemporaries, who perused them and discussed them in coffee-houses and taverns or spelled them out to those of their fellow countrymen unable to make sense of the written word.

Concerts, newspapers, changes in dress and furniture were all examples of a commercialisation of society which was becoming more evident as the seventeenth century drew to a close, an important theme in English social history which has been described as the consumer revolution. The English were getting richer and they also seem to have been spending a higher proportion of their income – and spending it on a much wider variety of goods and services than had been available in the past. This change in what economists call the propensity to consume was quite apparent to the entrepreneurs of the age, who eagerly produced what the public demanded and on occasion anticipated that demand in imaginative ways. The growing importance of consumption, that often despised element in the economic equation, was also apparent to intellectuals, who were in two minds whether to praise or condemn the conspicuous spending of their fellows.

The traditional ideal was that one consumed what was necessary to sustain one's way of life and that to consume any more was a product of greed, vanity or some other sin which was subsumed under the general heading of 'luxury'. Luxury continued to be attacked as a vice throughout the eighteenth century, but more astute observers realised that it was a necessary vice if there was to be any economic growth. 'The main spur to Trade, or

66. Love without Honour.
William Congreve's frank comedy
The Way of the World, 1700.

rather to Industry and Ingenuity,' wrote the merchant Dudley North in 1691, 'is the exorbitant Appetites of Men, which they will take pains to gratifie, and so be disposed to work, when nothing else will incline them to it, for did Men content themselves with bare Necessaries, we should have a poor World.'[18] 'Prodigality is a vice that is prejudicial to the man, but not to trade,' wrote the speculative builder Nicolas Barbon, thus anticipating the 'Private Vices, Publick Benefits' paradox of Bernard de Mandeville, whose *Fable of the Bees* was published in 1714.[19]

Such ideas were still very much minority ideas in the 1690s, a decade in which praise of luxury and prodigality continued to be seen by most people as amoral, but this intellectual justification for materialism is just one more strand in the precocious modernity which illuminates this *fin de siècle*. People had always been greedy, of course, but they could now be greedy in the public interest. Accumulation remained a duty to one's family and to the state, but that conspicuous and wasteful consumption which underpins the

67. Up-to-date: a newsletter of 1699 designed to look as though it had been written by hand.

modern economy was now seen to be a necessity, if not a duty. 'Those who are guilty of Prodigality, Pride, Vanity, and Luxury, do cause more wealth to the Kingdom, than Loss to their own Estates,' wrote John Houghton, who epitomises the decade very nicely, being at once a pioneer of stock-market reporting and of advertising and an enthusiastic supporter of all types of mechanical ingenuity.[20]

The reinterpretation of luxury was just one theme in an intellectual revolution which was taking place in the late seventeenth century, a revolution which was to usher in the Age of Reason and undermine millennia of certainty based on revealed religion and an unwavering belief in Aristotelian physics. Nothing was safe, in the wake of Locke, Newton and Boyle, from determined sceptics who would not accept any belief which was not amenable to empirical proof. Miracles were examined and found wanting, contravening as they did the laws of God's own creation. Old Testament chronology was found to be inconsistent with the far longer history of man discovered by a study of Chinese or Egyptian historiography. Heaven and hell, angels and devils, were seen by many as merely metaphors suited to the simple-minded audience for whom the Bible had originally been written. Astrology was widely seen to be a false science, 'a ridiculous piece of foolery' according to John Harris in 1704, while witches were laughed out of court, except in old-fashioned puritanical Massachusetts, where the Salem witch-craze of 1692 marked one last triumph for the irrational in the Anglo-American world. Even God himself attracted the attention of the sceptic, though few denied Him completely, accepting the necessity of a first cause, a Supreme Being who had made this beautiful world whose secrets were daily becoming more accessible to intelligent and enquiring mankind.

Beautiful though the world might be, it had its social problems and these were more than usually apparent in the 1690s, for the high spending, comfort and ease noted earlier were mostly for the rich and middling people in society. For the poor, the 1690s were a time of great hardship caused by wartime disruptions to employment, very high food prices and manipulation of the coinage by the government. Unemployment soared, as did crime and disorder, and poor rates rose to unprecedented levels. Middle-class people's alarm at such threats to their pockets and security was compounded by a firm belief that they were in the midst of a wave of moral degeneration in the country as a whole. As usual, this was felt to be most serious among the poor, who were seen as idle, vicious and irreligious, a belief reinforced by an observed tendency among the poor to prefer their homes or the alehouse to church or chapel as a place to spend Sundays. Even the Toleration Act of 1689, which allowed Dissenters to worship in their own way, had little effect in this respect and indeed could well have been counter-productive since it made it far more difficult to monitor the religious practice of the poor. Such irreligion among the masses was disturbing since the pulpit was seen by the wealthy as the most effective instrument of social control, while it was clear to observers that 'no one could be both devout and lazy'.[21]

The moral regeneration of the poor and the problems of poverty itself were two more themes then in the complex history of the 1690s, the subjects of many of those pamphlets which we have earlier seen pouring off the presses. The solutions offered were very wide-ranging, but three approaches may be singled out as reflecting the social philosophy of the decade. First in time was the establishment of Societies for the Reformation of Manners, which were first set up in various places in the autumn of 1690 and were to proliferate throughout the country in the course of the decade. The Societies existed to bring prosecutions against those deemed guilty of such moral offences as blasphemy, drunkenness, breaking the sabbath or 'any other dissolute, immoral or disorderly practice', a conveniently vague catch-all which enabled virtually anyone and especially prostitutes to be rounded up. The Societies claimed for themselves very considerable success in the suppression of vice and they certainly punished 'a vast number of lewd and disorderly persons', but it seems doubtful if this hit-or-miss and often hypocritical campaign had any lasting effect on the morals of the poor.

A much more effective approach was introduced towards the end of the decade with the setting up of charity schools, a campaign which really got under way in 1699 with the foundation of the Society for the Propagation of Christian Knowledge, which operated as a co-ordinating body. These free schools were designed for the children of the poor, who were to be given 'a Christian and useful' education, 'useful' meaning fairly minimal, with an emphasis on humility, obedience, subordination and respect for their betters. Since charity-school children were thought to make very good servants, the campaign was strongly supported by the urban middle classes and it was in fact very successful, particularly in London, where there were some 5000 children attending the schools by 1729. Literacy levels had always been high in the metropolis; they now became even higher, for both men and women, ensuring a very large reading public for the ephemera produced by the city's printing presses.

Needless to say, not everyone approved of such schools. Bernard de Mandeville spoke for many when he claimed that knowledge itself was subversive. 'To make the society happy and people easy under the meanest circumstances, it is requisite that great numbers of them should be ignorant as well as poor. Knowledge both enlarges and multiplies our desires, and the fewer things a man wishes for, the more easily his necessities may be supply'd.' Such cynicism was not, however, the prevailing mood of the age, and most people thought that a little education for the poor was beneficial to society, as did Bishop White Kennett, who in 1706 addressed a charity sermon to a congregation of 'little children who are born of meaner parents'. 'You will come to say,' he predicted from the pulpit,

> Oh what had we been, if left unto our selves, and to our parents unable to help us! Left to play in the streets, and to linger and pilfer from door to door! What had we been, when come to age, but the lowest servants, and hardest labourers; or perhaps idle wanderers and beggars, or possibly strolling thieves and robbers.[22]

Many poor children did indeed linger and pilfer from door to door, and many grew up to be idle wanderers and beggars, a major problem of the age whose solution occupied the minds of many reformers in the 1690s. The problem here was to distinguish the treatment of the deserving poor – the old, the sick, abandoned mothers and orphans – from that of the undeserving or able-bodied poor, those whom the liberal late twentieth

68. Gratitude for charity; charity school children gather in the Strand to watch the world go by, 1713. Children, including foundlings, were among the main recipients of charitable giving.

century calls the unemployed. Few people objected to supporting the deserving with doles paid out of the parish poor rates, but the sight of someone both able-bodied and idle was anathema to ratepayers in a society which tended to believe that such unemployment was always voluntary, the result of individual moral failings and idleness.

Thus, the third solution to poverty, and the one most commonly adopted, was a harsh development which anticipated the social philosophy enshrined in the notorious New Poor Law of 1834. This was the workhouse movement, whose modern form began in Bristol in 1696 and was to be imitated in many other places in the early eighteenth century. The object of the workhouse was to confine the able-bodied poor and make them work for their keep under such a strict and unpleasant regime that most poor people would rather starve than endure it. Such workhouses certainly had the desired effect of reducing poor rates, since refusal to enter the house meant that 'such persons shall be put out of the parish books and not be entitled to relief', but one fears that, as reforming institutions they were less successful.[23]

The 1690s then was a decade of paradoxes, of good intentions and harsh solutions, religious enthusiasm, scepticism and indifference, increases in the consumption of both tea and gin, a passion for fashion and frivolity combined with a deadly seriousness. The 1690s may go down in the textbooks as the decade of King William, war and financial revolution, the triumph of parliamentary government and the rule of law. But, in the longer run of history, this *fin de siècle* can be seen as the birthplace of a host of other things, many of them inherently modern, such as newspapers, advertising, the three-piece suit and a belief in the possibility and desirability of social reform.

Those who lived through the late seventeenth century and into the eighteenth were well aware of these changes and welcomed most of them. They knew that they now lived in a new and much more 'modern' world. But for most of them the crucial turning point in England's social as well as political history would have seemed to be not the *fin de siècle* as such but the Revolution of 1688 by which it was inaugurated.

Notes

1. Bernard Capp, *Astrology and the Popular Press* (London, 1979), p. 162.
2. Peter Earle, *A City Full of People: Men and Women of London* (London, 1994), pp. 200–201.
3. E. Barlow, *Journal*, ed. Basil Lubbock (London, 1904), ii, pp. 433–4.
4. Daniel Defoe, *Reformation of Manners* (London, 1702), p. 17.
5. John Chamberlayne, *Angliae Notitia* (London, 1707), p. 347.
6. Capp, *Astrology*, pp. 176–9, 251–2.
7. Quoted in Gerald M. Straka (ed.), *The Revolution of 1688* (Lexington, Mass., 1963), p. 92.
8. PRO HCA 13/80, 21 October 1691, evidence of Peter Ciriach.
9. David Ogg, *England in the Reigns of James II and William III* (Oxford, 1969), p. 321.
10. Charles Davenant, 'Discourses on the Public Revenue' (London, 1698) in *Works* (1771), i, 153.
11. Earle, *City Full of People*, p. 89.
12. C. H. Hull, *The Economic Writings of Sir W. Petty* (New York, 1899), i, p. 244.
13. J. Arbuthnot, *Of the Laws of Chance* (London, 1692), preface.
14. Quoted in F. W. Galton, *Select Documents Illustrating the History of Trade Unions* (London, 1896), p. xvii.
15. Guy Miège, *The New State of England* (London, 1691), ii, pp. 31–2.
16. John Gloag, *The Englishman's Chair*, (London, 1964), p. 82.
17. Daniel Defoe, *A Brief Case of the Distillers* (London, 1726), p. 24.
18. Quoted by Joyce Appleby, *Economic Thought and Ideology in 17th Century England* (Princeton, 1978), pp. 169–70.
19. Nicolas Barbon, *Discourses of Trade* (London, 1690), p. 32.
20. Quoted by Appleby, *Economic Thought*, p. 171.

21. Tim Hitchcock, 'Paupers and Preachers', in L. Davison et al., *Stilling the Grumbling Hive* (Stroud, 1992), p. 152.
22. Bernard de Mandeville, *Essay on Charity-Schools* (London, 1723), p. 328; W. Kennett, *Charity of Schools for Poor Children* (London, 1706), p. 15.
23. *Account of Several Workhouses* (London, 1725), p. 108.

69. *Glad Day* (1795) by William Blake. The poet looks beyond his time to a new dawn.

The 1790s
'Visions of Unsullied Bliss'

Roy Porter

A new world was opening to the astonished sight. Scenes, lovely as hope can paint, dawned on the imagination; visions of unsullied bliss lulled the senses, and hid the darkness of surrounding objects, rising in bright succession and endless gradations, like the steps of that ladder which was once set up on the earth, and whose top reached to heaven. Nothing was too mighty for this new-begotten hope; and the path that led to human happiness seemed as plain as the pictures in the Pilgrim's Progress *leading to Paradise.*

(*William Hazlitt*)[1]

Of all the turns of the century, the years around 1800 were epochal indeed. They brought revolution in Paris, which the French exported across the continent, and overseas too, through military and ideological warfare, waged on a scale hitherto unimagined. They gave birth to the modern concept of revolution itself – the idea of a total transformation engineered by reason and the general will – designed to destroy the *ancien régime* and institute a new order, heralded in France by the promulgation of a new calendar commencing with *An* I, by the introduction of the metric system, and, not least, by the invention of a new religion, the Cult of Humanity.

There had naturally been much talk of 'revolutions' in the past, but the concept had always meant a wheeling back to an initial starting point, as with the orbits of the planets around the sun: the astronomer Copernicus had called his book *On the Revolutions of the Heavenly Spheres* (1543). Revolution had thus always been restoration, essentially conservative. But now reason was being applied to revolution, and insurrectionary activity was transformed into an instrument of human regeneration, a secular resurrection.

Hitherto, there had rarely been expectations of forging a fundamentally new *future*: previous utopias had all been in the past, or transcendental (like heaven itself), or nowhere at all (the literal meaning of Sir Thomas More's Greek term 'utopia'). Hence the decades around 1800 – or rather *An* IX - transformed the very concept of human destiny. Earlier eras had read the Book of Revelation and envisaged a Last Judgment; or fate had been conceived as endless natural cycles governing the rise and fall of empires and

70. A view of London from the top of Albion Mills, south of Blackfriars Bridge, 1792. Note that churches still dominate the skyline. There were to be many more panoramas of changing London in the next century

princes. Now progress itself was the watchword, and for optimists 1800 signalled the replacement of time's cycles by time's arrow. Whereas Christian theology had traditionally spoken of a vale of tears, now a new world was in the offing – embodied first in the new American republic (1783) and then in revolutionary France.[2]

> Bliss was it in that dawn to be alive
> But to be young was very heaven.[3]

Moreover, 1800 found Europe in the thick not of one but two revolutions: politically, the French, but no less the industrial. Britain was the prime mover of economic transformation, and this chapter will focus upon the British experience of these twin revolutions, their intersections and consequences.

Independently of such grand events, however, the face of England (and, to a lesser degree, the rest of the British Isles) had been in a state of more gradual yet substantial change during the eighteenth century. A child born around 1700, who had gone abroad and returned in extreme old age, say around 1785, would have been surprised to encounter myriad minor changes which, while individually slight, were cumulatively transforming the quality of life in Britain and giving the swelling throng of middling people, craftsmen and bourgeoisie, all sorts of new comforts and luxuries. Our octogenarian would have found in such people's houses a range of domestic goods that around 1700 had been the preserve of the rich: possessions like curtains and carpets, upholstered chairs, tablecloths, glass- and china-ware, tea-services, fancy pottery, looking-glasses, clocks, shelves of books other than just the Bible, prints or ornaments to put on the wall or the mantelshelf, and all manner of bric-à-brac and decorations. Shop-bought toys, games and jigsaw puzzles for children had become common. Diet was more varied, with a greater range of fruit and vegetables. People had more changes of clothes, particularly as cheaper cottons became available. Efficient oil-lamps put an end to the age-old gloom; gas lighting was just around the corner.[4]

Outside the home, urban space had been spruced up. In many towns, well-demarcated straight streets replaced the old warrens of alleys and yards. House numbering began, pavements and kerbs appeared, making sauntering agreeable and encouraging window-shopping – a new pleasure,

71. 'Fancy goods': a monthly magazine *The Repository* offers 'Novelty, Fashion and Elegance'. Here samples of fabric are pasted onto the page. Fancy goods shops offered a variety of new wares.

72. London by gaslight: spectators examine newly installed Pall Mall gas lamps outside the Prince Regent's residence, Carlton House, 1809. An etching by George Moutard Woodward and Thomas Rowlandson.

taking advantage of the much admired new-style retail shop, a far cry from the dingy workshops of old. Sophie von La Roche, a German visiting London in 1786, was impressed by the elegant bow-windows and the attention to display:

> Behind the great glass windows absolutely everything one can think of is neatly, attractively displayed, in such abundance of choice as almost to make one greedy. Now large slipper and shoe-shops for anything from adults down to dolls, can be seen; now fashion-articles or silver or brass shops, boots, guns, glasses, the confectioner's goodies, the pewterer's wares, fans, etc.[5]

During our octogenarian's lifetime many cities and market towns gained assembly rooms, a theatre, coffee-houses, parades and public gardens, to say nothing of a hospital, a gaol and a workhouse.[6] New turnpike roads and coaching services linked provincial centres such as York, Norwich and Exeter with the metropolis. Mental communications improved thanks to newspapers. George Crabbe's poem 'The Newspaper' (1785) dramatised the changes they made and the new excitement they caused:

> I sing of NEWS, and all those vapid sheets
> The rattling hawker vends through gaping streets;
> Whate'er their name, whate'er the time they fly;

73. New turnpike roads: entrance to Tottenham Court Road Turnpike in the middle of London with a view of St James's Chapel. An engraving by Heinrich Josef Schutz after Thomas Rowlandson, 1809.

> Damp from the press, to charm the reader's eye:
> For, soon as morning dawns with roseate hue,
> The Herald of the morn arises too;
> Post after post succeeds, and all day long,
> Gazettes and Ledgers swarm, a noisy throng.
> When evening comes, she comes with all her train
> Of Ledgers, Chronicles, and Posts again.[7]

Foreigners were struck by the sheer animation of English life. 'The road from Greenwich to London was actually busier than the most popular streets in Berlin,' judged the Prussian Pastor Moritz, 'so many people were to be encountered riding, driving or walking. Already we saw houses on all sides, and all along the road at suitable distances lamp-posts were provided.'[8] And with activity went speed – 'no country is so well arranged for comfort and rapid travelling as this', observed another traveller.[9] Most admired this bustle, though critics complained the English had no time for anything but making money. Ever pressed for time, the English even pioneered the fast-food take-away: 'I happened to go into a pastrycook's shop one morning,' observed Robert Southey,

> and inquired of the mistress why she kept her window open during this severe weather – which I observed most of the trade did. She told me, that were she to close it, her receipts would be lessened forty or fifty shillings a day – so

74. Fresh bread, announced by
a bell. An evocative engraving
by Richard Phillips, 1805.

many were the persons who took up buns or biscuits as they passed by and
threw their pence in, not allowing themselves time to enter. Was there ever so
indefatigable a people![10]

In short, independently of the industrial revolution as such, England was
being transformed during the eighteenth century into a commercial and
consumer society. Not all approved. 'Everything about this farm-house was
formerly the scene of *plain manners* and *plentiful living*,' remarked the
journalist William Cobbett, a traditionalist man of the people who deplored
the rise of the *nouveaux riches*. In his *Rural Rides* (1830), he observed of the
homes of rich and swanky farmers, 'there were the decanters, the glasses, the
"dinner-set" of crockery ware, and all just in the true stock-jobber style'.[11]
But the prosperity of the many, if not exactly the masses, made Britain the
envy of Europe and created the complacent feeling that it was good to be
John Bull.

Initially, John Bull rejoiced at the storming of the Bastille. 'How much the
greatest event that has ever happened in the world,' exclaimed the Whig

politician Charles James Fox; the midlands physician Erasmus Darwin thought it 'the dawn of universal liberty'.[12] And for a while the atmosphere was festive, with sober Englishmen going around saluting each other as *citoyen* – compare the destruction of the Berlin Wall and the events of 1989–90 in eastern Europe. The young William Wordsworth was thus not crying in the wilderness but leading the chorus when he celebrated the events of July 1789:

> I see, I see! glad Liberty succeed
> With every patriot virtue in her train!
> And mark yon peasant's raptured eyes;
> Secure he views the harvests rise;
> No fetter vile the mind shall know,
> And Eloquence shall fearless glow.
> Yes! Liberty the soul of life shall reign,
> Shall throb in every pulse, shall flow thro' every vein.[13]

To share in the exhilaration, the poet crossed the Channel in 1790 for a walking holiday, landing just before the celebrations of 'that great federal day', 14 July. Writing in the *Prelude* a decade later – by then the former radical had turned reactionary – he recalled:

> Europe at that time was thrilled with joy,
> France standing on the top of golden hours,
> And human nature seeming born again.[14]

And this rebirth, as he remembered, was not merely the product of a local insurrection, but the fulfilment of a revolutionary spirit:

> 'Twas in truth an hour
> Of universal ferment; mildest men
> Were agitated; and commotions, strife
> Of passions and opinions, filled the walls
> Of peaceful houses with unquiet sounds.
> The soil of common life, was, at that time,
> Too hot to tread upon.[15]

It was easy to rhapsodise over the overthrow of the *ancien régime*. But initial emotional fervour had to be consolidated by reason: the Revolution had to be understood within the grander scheme of history and politics. In 1789, the Dissenting minister Richard Price spoke at a dinner to toast the centenary of the Glorious Whig Revolution of 1688–9. That coup – the dethroning of James II – had gone down in British constitutional wisdom as a typically conservative revolution: the king, argued constitutional lawyers, had not been booted out, he had 'abdicated'; legality had never been threatened. Dr Price took it upon himself daringly to propose a link between those two revolutions separated by a century. The French Revolution, he argued in his address, was precisely like the Glorious Revolution. What Britons had begun, the French had thus continued: the tocsin had sounded for universal liberation. Hence his conclusions were radical. 'Tremble all ye oppressors of the world!' he thundered in the *Discourse on the Love of our Country,* the published version of his speech: 'Take warning all ye supporters of slavish governments, and slavish hierarchies! . . . You cannot now hold the world in darkness. Struggle no longer against increasing light and liberality.'[16] Price thus challenged his compatriots: if they truly supported the principles of 1688 and were honest believers in British liberties, they *must* embrace the French Revolution.

It was Edmund Burke who took up the gauntlet that Price had flung down and forged the ideology of counter-revolution. His *Reflections on the Revolution in France* (1790) was in no doubt about the magnitude of the *événements*: 'All circumstances taken together,' he maintained, 'the French Revolution is the most astonishing that has hitherto happened in the world.' But though a veteran Whig politician who had defended the American rebels back in the 1770s, Burke damned the Revolution: despite superficial appearances, it was not the erection of the new order but the wanton vandalising of an edifice of civilisation laboriously erected over the centuries:

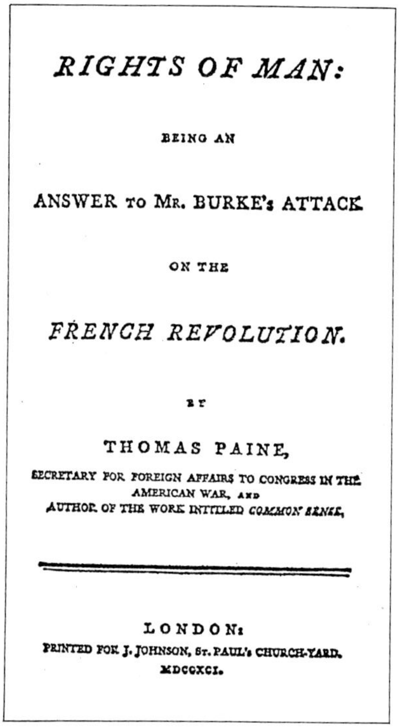

75. (*left*) *Rights of Man* (1791). Flyleaf of the first best-selling edition of Part One of Tom Paine's radical essay.

76. (*facing page*) Defending the Constitution: Edmund Burke (on the left) seeks to dispose of Tom Paine (cartoon by John Nixon, 16 January 1793).

RIGHTS OF MAN:

BEING AN

ANSWER TO MR. BURKE's ATTACK

ON THE

FRENCH REVOLUTION.

BY

THOMAS PAINE,

SECRETARY FOR FOREIGN AFFAIRS TO CONGRESS IN THE
AMERICAN WAR, AND
AUTHOR OF THE WORK INTITLED *COMMON SENSE,*

LONDON:
PRINTED FOR J. JOHNSON, ST. PAUL's CHURCH-YARD.
MDCCXCI.

The French have shown themselves the ablest architects of ruin that have ever existed in the world . . . They have completely pulled down to the ground their monarchy, their church, their nobility, their law, their revenue, their army, their navy, their commerce, their arts and their manufactures.

Burke countered with a conservatism that did not deny the need for reform – 'a state without the means of some change', he insisted, 'is without the means of its conservation'[17] – but insisted that reform must be gradual, lawful and consensual.

Even Burke's mesmerising rhetoric could not dampen the spirit of 1789, which was to fire native radicalism in the artisan workshops of London and the manufacturing areas of the midlands and north. Burke's *Reflections* sold 30,000 copies in two years; Tom Paine's *Rights of Man*, by contrast, sold seven times that number. From 1792, corresponding and constitutional societies sprang up in the provinces and in Scotland, comprising radical craftsmen and members of the petty bourgeoisie, often led by journalists, intellectuals or disaffected gentlemen. Clamour rose for cutting out corruption and securing constitutional reform. 'Frenchmen, you are already free,' declared the London Corresponding Society in 1792, 'but the Britons are preparing to be so.' Demanding parliamentary reform, the Society of Friends of the People observed in 1793 that Britain was not a temple of liberty but a prison of oligarchy. A majority of MPs were elected by just over 11,000 voters – only one Englishman in eight could vote, and no women at all.

Tom Paine provided the radical ammunition that returned Burke's fire. His *Rights of Man* argued the people's cause against a corrupt establishment and its toadies. Hereditary monarchy was absurd. Power came from the people and must ever reside in them:

> The vanity and presumption of governing beyond the grave, is the most ridiculous and insolent of all tyrannies. Man has no property in man; neither has any generation a property in the generations which are to follow ... Every generation is, and must be, competent to all the purposes which its occasions require. It is the living, and not the dead, that are to be accommodated.[18]

Paine derided the very names of monarchy and aristocracy, which, depending as they did on the accidents of hereditary succession, were insults to reason. The only means to check abuse of power by the privileged lay in universal manhood suffrage. Kings and courts wasted wealth on pensions, patronage and warfare. Taxation should instead be raised for poor relief, education, old-age pensions and other social benefits.

Attacking the tyrannical privilege of inherited wealth, Paine's *Rights of Man* spoke directly to the cobblers, printers, weavers, carpenters who were the soul of English urban radicalism. The pious bluestocking Hannah More – quite a progressive figure in her own way, supporting Sunday schools – was alarmed at the seepage of its message into the hamlets of the Mendips. Her response was a prayer: 'From liberty, equality and the rights of man, good Lord deliver *us*.'[19]

The government, led by William Pitt the Younger, was alarmed by Paine's extraordinary popularity. In May 1792 a Proclamation was issued against Seditious Writings. Paine prudently fled the country, but his influence remained. In 1793 his new book, *The Age of Reason*, carried the attack beyond politics to religion, popularising the assaults of Enlightenment *philosophes* upon established Churches. Christianity was an affront to reason, bishops were the tools of tyrants. The destruction of priestcraft would put an end to mind-forg'd manacles, and 'the present age', he insisted, 'will hereafter merit to be called the Age of Reason'. That term became a radical catchphrase. Asked if they were prepared to be no better than the 'footballs and shuttlecocks of tyrants', the Nore mutineers of 1797 rejoined: 'No. The age of reason has at last revolved.'[20]

It was reasonable to hope, or fear, that revolution itself would leap from Paris across the Channel. Jacobin doctrines were inflammatory, and the tinder of discontent was everywhere; rocketing inflation, agrarian disruption (notably over enclosures) and rapid industrialisation – all were creating dramatic social dislocation. For several years, insurrection was in the air. 'The late revolution in France', noted Thomas Somerville in his *Observations on the Constitution* (1793), 'has given rise to a spirit of political speculation, tending to depreciate our domestic privileges.'[21] The old paternalistic fabric seemed to be falling apart, deference was dwindling. An anonymous versifier warned the Quality:

> On Swill and Grains you wish the poor to be fed
> And underneath the Gullintine we could wish to see your heads.

A Somerset slogan urged 'half Starv'd Britons' to rise up:

> Then raise yr drooping spirits up
> Nor starve by Pitt's decree
> Fix up the sacred Guillotine
> Proclaim – French liberty!

Graffiti and chants called for an end to the war against France:

> Peace and Large Bread
> Or a King without a head

while a notice nailed to a Wiltshire church door capped anti-war views with a threat:

> Dear Brother Britons North and South Younite your selves in one Body and stand true Downe with your Luxzuaras Government both Spirital and temperal or you starve with Hunger they have stript you of bread Chees Meate etc etc etc etc etc Nay even your Lives have they taken thousands on their expeditions let the Bourbon Family defend their owne cause and let us true Britons loock to our selves let us Banish some to Hannover where they came from Downe with your Constitucion Arect a republick.[22]

The new political mood was assessed by Thomas Walker's *Review of Some of the Political Events which have Occurred in Manchester During the last Five Years* (1794). The people had grown aware, Walker noted,

> how the *few* have permanently contrived to live in affluence and luxurious indulgence, while the *many* drag on an existence laborious and miserable, in ignorance and vice, in pain and poverty! It is . . . a very instructive problem, to ascertain how it thus happened, that the great mass, not merely of a community, but of mankind, should have for ages submitted to this state of things.[23]

Yet the old order was not finally buried, either on the continent or in Britain. Jacobin attempts to force liberty, equality and fraternity on their European brethren excited ferocious anti-revolutionary nationalist backlashes in Spain, Russia and elsewhere, which eventually led to the defeat of Napoleon and the mastery of the reactionary powers at the Congress of

Vienna (1815). Meanwhile, the Jacobin Terror alienated many erstwhile supporters in Britain. Once France declared war, loyalties among British radicals were deeply divided; the properted closed ranks, and patriotic support – both spontaneous and staged – rose from the people in 'Church and king' demonstrations against foreign enemies and domestic 'traitors'. The Proclamation against Seditious Writings (1792) made quoting Tom Paine dangerous, and, although he remained widely read, he was also hanged in effigy in popular protests.

The Scottish Trials of 1793–4, in which radical leaders received sentences of transportation for attending a convention (an alternative parliament) at Edinburgh, served as a warning to militants elsewhere. Meanwhile in England Prime Minister Pitt set up spy networks to investigate the radical societies. Pitt believed, or professed to believe, that they threatened a 'whole system of insurrection . . . laid in the modern doctrine of the rights of man'.[24] In April 1794 Parliament suspended Habeas Corpus, and in the next month a prosecution was launched against leading London radicals. The jury found insufficient evidence for a treason conviction and, in the event, their acquittal proved a blessing in disguise for the government: conviction would have created martyrs and lent credence to the radical charge that Pitt was planning a police state.

77. Which is better, British or French justice? An etching by Thomas Rowlandson expresses rising anti-French sentiment among the public before the death of Louis XVI.

Radicalism dwindled, and after 1794 it was mainly economic misery that kept opposition alive. The year 1795 brought catastrophic harvest failures and soaring wheat prices. When stones were thrown in October at the king's coach on his way to open Parliament, Pitt seized the opportunity to batten down the hatches still further by means of the Two Acts. The Seditious Meetings Act prohibited assemblies of more than fifty people without a JP's permission, while the Treasonable Practices Act extended the sedition laws. Charles James Fox, one of the rump of Whigs who continued to oppose repression, retorted that all parliamentary reformers were, in theory at least, exposed under the Treason Act to transportation, while the poet and philosopher Coleridge, not yet turned Tory, predicted that 'the cadaverous tranquillity of despotism will succeed the generous order . . . of freedom'.[25] But theirs were rare voices.

Radicalism was thus muzzled by 1795, and public opinion fell into line behind the government, concluding that Britain's task was national salvation from Napoleon, and distrusting Frenchifying ideologies. If, however, the threat of revolution receded, perceptive commentators also grasped that the old stability was disappearing too. The very texture of society was in turmoil: England, never a static society, was ceasing to be essentially rural and agricultural. Many workers were leaving the land – or, to be more precise, were being thrown off it by enclosure and other innovations brought by agricultural capitalism. Former smallholders and cottagers were becoming urbanised as the labouring poor (or 'proletariat', as Marx was to call them). Economic change was recognised to be of the utmost political significance, heralding the advent of mass politics. 'Two causes, and only two, will rouse a peasantry to rebellion,' opined Robert Southey, radical turned Tory, 'intolerable oppression, or religious zeal either for the right faith or the wrong; no other motive is powerful enough.' But that moderately comforting scenario no longer applied:

> A manufacturing poor is more easily instigated to revolt. They have no local attachments; the persons to whom they look up for support they regard more with envy than respect, as men who grow rich by their labour; they know enough of what is passing in the political world to think themselves politicians; they feel the whole burthen of taxation . . . they are aware of their own numbers . . . A manufacturing populace is always ripe for rioting.[26]

Southey therefore felt obliged to warn England's ruling order: 'Do I then think that England is in danger of revolution?' he asked. 'If the manufacturing system continues to be extended, increasing as it necessarily does increase the number, the misery, and the depravity of the poor, I believe that revolution inevitably must come, and in its most fearful shape.'[27]

78. Enclosing the land: surveyors meticulously mapping Bedfordshire's open fields in 1798 (a watercolour drawing of a ward map by John Goodman Maxwell).

Hindsight suggests that Southey and practically all other nineteenth-century political analysts were wrong in their expectation that the rise of an industrial proletariat would spell revolution. Experience has shown that revolution succeeds in *peasant* nations – Russia, China, Mexico – whereas the urban working class rapidly becomes assimilated into the capitalist order, or at least is more easily controlled. What is relevant is that Southey had observed that the nation was undergoing momentous change, thanks to industrialisation. For if the French Revolution broadcast itself from the rooftops, the industrial revolution was relatively silent.

This is not to imply that nobody noticed the shooting up of textile factories and smoke-stack industries in the midlands and north of England, in South Wales and the midland valley of Scotland. Writers reflected ceaselessly on new mines, new ports, new canals, new factories, technological gadgetry and the new spirit of ingenuity and money-making. 'It is impossible', observed the economist Patrick Colquhoun, just after the turn of the century,

> to contemplate the progress of manufactures in Great Britain within the last thirty years without wonder and astonishment. Its rapidity, particularly since the commencement of the French revolutionary war, exceeds all credibility. The improvement of the steam engines, but above all the facilities afforded to the great branches of the woollen and cotton manufactories by ingenious machinery, invigorated by capital and skill, are beyond all calculation.[28]

79. A pit head. Coal and iron were the two master materials of early industrialisation cradled at 'Romantic' Colbrookdale on the River Severn (British School, 1790).

The point, rather, is that nobody dubbed these transformations a 'revolution'. That was perhaps because that term was still reserved for political events, and possibly contemporary commentators lacked the chronological perspective that would have confirmed not just the magnitude of socio-economic change but its continuance and cumulative nature – what was happening (we can see, but contemporaries could not be sure) was not just a random peak or a temporary boom. It may be significant that it was not until around 1870 that the term 'industrial revolution' passed into general use: by then, perhaps, its cataclysmic nature ('unbinding Prometheus') could be grasped.[29]

Even now debates still rage, and some scholars have discarded the term 'industrial revolution'. Change was gradual, revisionists argue; it affected only certain regions of the country. Before the railways, steam power was not all-important; hand-power, horse-power, wind-power and water-power remained predominant. 'Evolution', they argue, is a better term than 'revolution'. All this seems rather pedantic. There are strong reasons for re-establishing the older claim that Britain under George III was indeed undergoing the first industrial revolution, one of the great watersheds of human history.

A scattering of facts indicates the magnitude of change. Between 1750 and 1850, the British population increased threefold, from around six to around eighteen million (a matter of grave concern to some, as will be explored below). In 1801 some 20 per cent of workers were employed in manufacturing and linked occupations; that proportion had reached almost 66 per cent by 1871, while workers in agriculture and fisheries declined from 35 to 15 per cent of the workforce.

Industrial production grew rapidly. Averaging about £9 million a year in 1780, exports had shot up to £22 million by the end of the century. Annual iron and steel shipments, running at 16,770 tons in 1765–74, almost doubled by 1795–1804. Over the same period, export of cottons rose from £236,000 a year to a staggering £5,371,000. And output of many industrial commodities – yarn, iron, steel, coal and so forth – leaped, often by many thousand per cent, after 1800. Such figures speak for themselves. The changes they flag were creating an industrial order whose uniqueness provoked ceaseless comment from writers as different as Thomas Carlyle, Charles Dickens, George Eliot, John Ruskin and Benjamin Disraeli.

Britain did not sprint into industrialism from a standing start. The economy moved from a canter into a gallop. Britain had timeless advantages ready to be developed, above all abundant and accessible reserves of coal and iron in south Wales, the east midlands, south Yorkshire, the north-east and Scotland's central valley. By 1700 the nation was already heavily urbanised, with around 15 per cent of its population living in towns – a higher proportion than any country apart from the Dutch Republic. Manufactures, markets and exports all grew from the late seventeenth century. This general increase in prosperity, aided by low food prices, encouraged rising commodity consumption, leading to what has been termed the 'consumer revolution' of the eighteenth century (see above, p. 116), and inducing many economic historians to believe that robust *domestic* demand played a key role in fuelling the industrial revolution. The 'average family', it has been suggested, was buying £10 worth a year of British-made goods in 1688, £25 worth in 1750, and £40 worth in 1811. Capitalist farming permitted a rapidly growing population to be fed while releasing surplus labour for industry. Prosperity among landowners and farmers further enhanced demand.

Rising population spurred industrial development in many ways, creating a potential industrial workforce and also consumer demand. England was not alone in experiencing population growth, but other territories undergoing such a rise – notably Ireland – could not capitalise upon it for productive economic use, hamstrung as they were by the rigidities of subsistence farming and peasant proprietorship. In England agricultural change boosted the industrial revolution.

Transportation improvements also proved crucial. Canals expedited carriage of the bulk materials essential to industry, and, with turnpikes, laid the foundations for the mass market. Landowners and mine-owners were in the forefront of canal and turnpike investment. When in 1761 James Brindley's canal linked the Bridgewater mines at Worsley with nearby

Manchester, it halved the price of coal there. Canals soon linked the major rivers, Mersey and Severn, Trent and Mersey, Thames and Severn, so that by the 1820s some 4000 miles of navigable waterways were open to trade.

And if roads and canals facilitated internal trade, the growth of foreign trade provided vital opportunities. Imports, exports and re-exports (mainly of colonial goods sent via Britain to mainland Europe) increased by some 240 per cent between 1716–20 and 1784–8. The expanding American market stimulated production both of metal goods and of textiles – two-thirds of all cotton manufactures were exported, above all to America. The supremacy of the Royal Navy throughout the Napoleonic Wars gave British exporters an enormous advantage in winning markets overseas. As this suggests, the British government itself played a beneficial role in promoting industrialisation. Success in all eighteenth-century wars – the War of American Independence excepted – consolidated Britain's position vis-à-vis France and other potential economic rivals.

And while foreign and colonial strategies were helping to defeat rivals and open markets, new *laissez-faire* policies at home removed potential hindrances to investment and innovation. The absence of internal tariffs and tolls had long made Britain the largest 'common market' in Europe. Metalware towns like Birmingham and Sheffield operated in almost free-labour conditions. The repeal of labour laws facilitated recruitment of a mass workforce.

The British economy was thus uniquely poised for growth. Furthermore, Britain possessed the men and the skills to take advantage of such opportunities. While there was extensive aristocratic and gentry involvement in industry and economic improvement, Britain also enjoyed one of the most open societies in Europe, with opportunities for middle-class talent to rise. Moreover, religious Dissenters, denied access to government office, were well placed to play major roles in science, technology and industry. Iron manufacturers like the Darbys, Lloyds and Crowleys, bankers like the Barclays, Gurneys and Lloyds, and brewers like the Trumans, Bevans and Perkins were Quakers, while prominent cotton manufacturers like the McConnels and the Gregs were Unitarians.

Britain's industrial revolution depended on men of vision, ambition and greed. The captains of industry were self-made – raising capital for factories or other industrial enterprises, reinvesting profits, organising productive capacity, recruiting, training and deploying the workforce, calculating market trends and opportunities. The risks were awesome, but so were the opportunities for riches. Successful cotton-spinners began to rival traditional landowners, and their sons bought into the ruling class.

Notably in textiles, the new technology turned dreams into realities. Richard Arkwright was the model inventor and entrepreneur. In 1769 he patented a power-driven water-frame for roller spinning and a carding

80. (*right*) A King of
Cotton: Sir Richard
Arkwright grew rich and
powerful from the profits
of industrial expansion.
Engraving by John
Raphael Smith after
Joseph Wright, 1789–90.

81. (*below*) Arkwright's
mill at Cromford. The
mills sometimes never
closed. Shifts of women
and children provided the
main work force (painting
by Joseph Wright of
Derby, late eighteenth
century).

machine to prepare cloth for spinning in 1775. In 1771 he set up an early
water-powered factory at Cromford, Derbyshire, where more than 300
hands were employed. Knighted in 1786, on his death six years later he was
worth £500,000. The revolutionary expansion of the cotton industry spurred
by Arkwright was made possible by mechanised production first of spinning
and, some thirty years later, of weaving. Labour was saved, output soared
and products were cheapened. To process 100 lb of cotton, an Indian hand-
spinner would take 50,000 man-hours, a Crompton mule (1780) took 2000,
a power-assisted mule (1795) took 300, and by 1825 Roberts's automatic
mule took just 135 man-hours.

Entrepreneurs had to know not just how to produce but what to produce
and how to market it. In these respects, Josiah Wedgwood was the pioneer.
'Fashion', wrote the Staffordshire potter, 'is infinitely superior to merit in
many respects.' He appreciated the importance of tapping the aristocratic
market, knowing that his reputation as 'Queen's potter' or supplier to the
Empress of Russia carried maximum prestige. Wedgwood developed
numerous marketing strategies: travelling salesmen were engaged,
warehouses opened and advertising psychology pioneered. Like other
entrepreneurs, he thought big: 'I shall ASTONISH THE WORLD ALL AT ONCE,'
he declared to his partner, Thomas Bentley, 'for I hate piddling you know.'
Becoming, as he boasted, 'vase-maker general to the universe', he died (like
Arkwright) worth £500,000.

Of course, the development of new plant, mines, factories and technology
did not mean that everything had changed by, say, the end of the Georgian
era in 1820. Industrialisation probably did not have its most dramatic impact
until the coming of the railways in the 1830s. But momentous changes had
begun. Growing use of artificial power was opening prospects of unlimited
output. Thanks to domestic affluence and colonial expansion, markets were
being extended, rendering mass production worthwhile. An expanding
population could be sustained by more efficient agriculture and by industrial
profitability. A social order that for centuries had been relatively static,
because limited by the laws of climate, soil and harvest, was freed to engage
in unlimited growth by reason of its power to harness nature. Though the
industrial plant created by this first industrial revolution now lies largely
derelict, the pattern of transformation inaugurated around 1800 has never
been reversed.

Ceaseless change became society's law. Looking back in 1800 on the dying
century, the *Annual Register* reflected:

On a general recollection or review of the state of society or human nature
in the eighteenth century, the ideas that recur oftenest, and remain upper-
most in the mind, are the three following: the intercourses of man were more

82. The consumer society. Far from the potteries, where the Wedgwoods produced their wares, their London showroom attracts eager customers, 1809.

extensive than at any former period with which we are acquainted; the pro-
gression of knowledge was more rapid, and the discoveries of philosophy
were applied more than they had been before to practical purposes . . . This
present age, in respect of former times, may be called an age of humanity.
Whence this happy change? Not from the progressive effects of moral dis-
quisitions and lectures . . . but from the progressive intercourses of men with
men, minds with minds, of navigation, commerce, arts and sciences.[30]

Yet was it such a happy change? Debate raged about the virtues and vices
of market capitalism. Back in 1776, Adam Smith's *The Wealth of Nations*
had argued that capitalism must benefit the worker by encouraging 'the
liberal reward of labour':

The liberal reward of labour as it encourages the propagation, so it increases
the industry of the common people. The wages of labour are the encouragement of industry, which, like every other human quality, improves in
proportion to the encouragement it receives. A plentiful subsistence increases
the bodily strength of the labourer, and the comfortable hope of bettering his
condition, and of ending his days in ease and plenty, animates him to exert
that strength to the utmost. Where wages are high, accordingly, we shall
always find the workmen more active, diligent, and expeditious than where

they are low: in England, for example, than in Scotland; in the neighbourhood of great towns than in remote country places.[31]

That things were not so simple or favourable as Smith supposed was insisted
by the factory-owner and philosopher Robert Owen some forty years later.
Owen was a remarkable individual, one unthinkable except as a child of the
industrial revolution he helped create. Born in Newtown, Montgomeryshire,
he was first employed as an errand-boy. He gave this up at the age of ten for
a job in the drapery business, first in Stamford and then in London. He rose
to a partnership in a Manchester firm, and then, at the turn of the century,
became partner and manager of the New Lanark Mills on Clydeside, and for
eighteen years strove to combine entrepreneurship with social reform. His
most notable book, *A New View of Society* (1813), urged social rebuilding
on rational grounds. Manufacturing would provide the basis for universal
happiness if it could be divested of the arbitrariness of private ownership
and the market and organised according to socialist values. Steeped in the
Enlightenment, Owen was convinced that character could be moulded for
the better by experience and environmental influence.

Owen trumpeted the monumental changes being wrought by
manufacturing. 'Those who were engaged in the trade, manufactures, and
commerce of this country thirty or forty years ago formed but a very
insignificant portion of the knowledge, wealth, influence or population of
the Empire,' he contended in his *Observations on the Effect of the
Manufacturing System* (1815):

> Prior to that period, Britain was essentially agricultural. But, from that time
> to the present, the home and foreign trade have increased in a manner so
> rapid and extraordinary as to have raised commerce to an importance, which
> it never previously attained in any country possessing so much political power
> and influence.[32]

But, argued Owen, this narrow and shallow *laissez-faire* outlook was quite
inadequate for ensuring long-term prosperity and the welfare of the
workforce. Rather,

> the political and moral effects . . . well deserve to occupy the best faculties of
> the greatest and wisest statesmen. The general diffusion of manufactures
> throughout a country generates a new character in its inhabitants, and as this
> character is formed upon a principle quite unfavourable to individual or
> general happiness, it will produce the most lamentable and permanent evils,
> unless its tendency be legislative interference and direction.[33]

Owen was as convinced as Marx a generation later that industrialisation
promised untold human benefit. But the classical economists' faith in market
forces was misplaced: under competition, some grew fabulously rich but

others were pauperised. Hence, from factory floor to Whitehall, rational intervention and co-operation were needed to secure the potential social advantages of the manufacturing revolution.

Owen was an optimist, indeed a utopian. But the greatest prophet in England around 1800 was a giant of gloom: the Reverend Thomas Malthus, who, after a mathematical training in Cambridge, became an Anglican parson and an extraordinarily influential pundit on social and economic issues. His *Essay on the Principle of Population as it Affects the Future Improvement of Society, with Remarks on the Speculations of Mr Godwin, M. Condorcet, and Other Writers* (1798) forced readers to confront those two tremendous revolutions that have just been discussed: the French Revolution, with its faith in progress and perfectibility, and the economic transformation silently being produced by the individual desire to get on. For Malthus, they were incompatible and probably unrealisable.

Nobody grasped more clearly than Malthus the fact that change was the spirit of the age:

> The great and unlooked for discoveries that have taken place of late years in natural philosophy; the increasing diffusion of general knowledge from the extension of the art of printing; the ardent and unshackled spirit of inquiry that prevails throughout the lettered, and even unlettered world; the new and extraordinary lights that have been thrown on political subjects, which dazzle, and astonish the understanding; and particularly that tremendous phenomenon in the political horizon the French revolution, which, like a blazing comet, seems destined either to inspire with fresh life and vigour, or to scorch up and destroy the shrinking inhabitants of the earth, have all concurred to lead many able men into the opinion, that we were touching on a period big with the most important changes, changes that would in some measure be decisive of the future fate of mankind.[34]

The champagne fizz of revolution had naturally created great expectations – but were they rationally justified? The Enlightenment and the revolutionaries had promised the perfectibility of man, yet was mankind truly about to be emancipated from the limits imposed by nature? 'It has been said', Malthus noted,

> that the great question is now at issue, whether man shall henceforth start forwards with accelerated velocity towards illimitable, and hitherto unconceived improvement; or be condemned to a perpetual oscillation between happiness and misery, and after every effort remain still at an immeasurable distance from the wished-for goal.[35]

And that, in his view, was the dilemma facing mankind at the dawn of the nineteenth century.

Malthus never denied the allure of the 'new dawn' that radicals greeted in the Revolution.[36] His mood, though, was not sanguine but fearful. He believed faith in boundless progress was intrinsically flawed and self-defeating. For economic progress would create increasing wealth, wealth was bound to result in a population explosion – and that demanded attention to a few home truths:

> population must always be kept down to the level of the means of subsistence; but no writer . . . has inquired particularly into the means by which this level is effected: and it is a view of these means, which forms, to his mind, the strongest obstacle in the way to any very great future improvement of society.[37]

Malthus had thus identified the blind spot in the visionaries' dreams. In the opinion of Enlightenment thinkers, the higher the aggregate national population the better; all statesmen knew that underpopulated kingdoms lacked hands to till the soil, soldiers to defend frontiers, and taxpayers to fill the Exchequer. Traditional wisdom had been convinced that whatever boosted national population was desirable – population growth was the flag of a flourishing nation. But, countered Malthus, the implications of demographic increase had never been analysed – certainly not by prophets of progress like the Marquis de Condorcet, author of the *Esquisse d'un tableau historique des progrès de l'esprit humain* (1795), and William Godwin, author of *Enquiry into Political Justice and its Influence on General Virtue and Happiness* (1793), the man who had proposed the heady prospects of progress. Fantasising had thus outrun thinking: 'the cause of this neglect on the part of the advocates for the perfectibility of mankind, is not easily accounted for', teased Malthus, quietly but devastatingly scathing about the failure of visionaries to face facts:

> I have certainly no right to say that they purposely shut their eyes to such arguments . . . Yet . . . we are all of us too prone to err. If I saw a glass of wine repeatedly presented to a man, and he took no notice of it, I should be apt to think that he was blind or uncivil. A juster philosophy might teach me rather to think that my eyes deceived me, and that the offer was not really what I conceived it to be.[38]

Against the romantic dreamers, Malthus presented himself as a sober scientific realist, faithful to the facts and indifferent to 'mere conjectures'.[39] Debate had reached impasse because both progressive sides had descended to abuse. The radical branded his opponent as 'the slave of the most miserable, and narrow prejudices',[40] while in return conservatives dubbed radicals 'wild and mad-headed enthusiasts'.[41] Mankind's future, retorted Malthus, was not to be settled by rhetorical swordplay. The issue deserved cool reflection and a willingness to face 'unconquerable difficulties'.[42] He and he alone, Malthus insisted, had adopted the scientific approach to questions of production and reproduction 'explained in part by Hume, and more at large by Dr Adam Smith'.[43] The big issue lay in the relations between great expectations and demographic realities. 'Were the rising generation free from the "killing frost" of misery', he observed, 'population must rapidly increase', for affluence would permit earlier marriage and thus lead to larger families:

> Were every man sure of a comfortable provision for a family, almost every man would have one . . . Of this, Mr Condorcet seems to be fully aware him-self; and after having described further improvements, he says, 'But in this progress of industry and happiness, each generation will be called to more extended enjoyments, and in consequence, by the physical constitution of the human frame, to an increase in the number of individuals. Must not there arrive a period then, when these laws, equally necessary, shall counteract each other? . . . Will it not mark the limit when all further amelioration will become impossible?'[44]

But, having thus glimpsed the abyss of overpopulation, Condorcet had shrunk back without facing its implications – or rather had waved them aside as distant.[45] Malthus honoured Condorcet for recognising that rising population was not a solution, as traditionally represented, but an obstacle, yet blamed him for ducking the overpopulation issue.[46]

Where Condorcet was complacent Malthus saw cause for consternation.[47] For unchecked population increase would necessarily frustrate the political improvement imagined by the radicals. Their plans were doubtless ravishing:

> The system of equality which Mr Godwin proposes, is, without doubt, by far the most beautiful and engaging of any that has yet appeared. An ameliora-tion of society to be produced merely by reason and conviction, wears much more the promise of permanence, than any change effected and maintained by force . . . In short, it is impossible to contemplate the whole of this fair structure, without emotions of delight and admiration, accompanied with ardent longing for the period of its accomplishment. But, alas! that moment can never arrive. The whole is little better than a dream, a beautiful phantom of the imagination.[48]

From this, Malthus drew deeply pessimistic conclusions. Utopian bubbles were pricked by nature's realities. Zealots attributed all evils to the *ancien régime*; abolish the old order and, hey presto, everything was possible. But 'the great error under which Mr Godwin labours throughout his whole work, is, the attributing almost all the vices and misery that are seen in civil society to human institutions'.[49] For the real obstacle was nature. How then did nature operate in stabilising resources and population, how did it balance the capacity for work with the sexual drive, or the forces of production and reproduction? 'I think', Malthus proposed, 'I may fairly make two postulata':

> First, That food is necessary to the existence of man.
> Secondly, That the passion between the sexes is necessary, and will remain nearly in its present state.
> These two laws ever since we have had any knowledge of mankind, appear to have been fixed laws of our nature; and, as we have not hitherto seen any alteration in them, we have no right to conclude that they will ever cease to be what they now are, without an immediate act of power in that Being who first arranged the system of the universe; and for the advantage of his creatures, still executes, according to fixed laws, all its various operations.[50]

Population would thus inevitably outrun resources and precipitate crises – notably famine, epidemics and war. This was the great problem the radicals had never squarely faced – they had merely come up with frivolous suggestions, notably Godwin's conjecture 'that the passion between the sexes may in time be extinguished'. Poppycock! exclaimed Malthus:

> I will not dwell longer upon it at present, than to say, that the best arguments for the perfectibility of man, are drawn from a contemplation of the great progress that he has already made from the savage state, and the difficulty of saying where he is to stop. But towards the extinction of the passion between the sexes, no progress whatever has hitherto been made.[51]

The imbalance of production and reproduction presented a difficulty 'insurmountable in the way to the perfectibility of society'. Natural inequalities, in other words, frustrated dreams of social equality:

> All other arguments are of slight and subordinate consideration in comparison of this. I see no way by which man can escape from the weight of this law which pervades all animated nature. No fancied equality, no agrarian regulations in their utmost extent, could remove the pressure of it even for a single century. Consequently, if the premises are just, the argument is conclusive against the perfectibility of the mass of mankind.[52]

Grant these iron laws of the natural and economic order and pessimism about progress was the only realistic policy: 'that the superior power of population cannot be checked, without producing misery or vice, the ample portion of these too bitter ingredients in the cup of human life, and the continuance of the physical causes that seem to have produced them, bear too convincing a testimony'.[53] The first edition of Malthus' *Essay* spelt out a dismal future, with nature ever poised to avenge herself against the hubristic designs of man. Subsequent editions suggested that catastrophe could be avoided through what he termed 'moral restraint'. Population crises could be averted if those unable to support families at all, and certainly not large families, abstained from marriage entirely or, within marriage, desisted from irresponsibly gratifying their sexual impulses. (Parson Malthus, it should be emphasised, deeply disapproved of contraception: that was a sanction of vice little better than fornication.)

Malthus's *fin de siècle* gloom echoed the call of contemporary Evangelicals for moral rearmament as the basis of a safe and sound social order. In *A Practical View of the Prevailing Religious System of Professed Christians in the Higher and Middle Classes of this Country contrasted with Real Christianity* (1797), the Anglican MP William Wilberforce advocated 'back to basics' as the means to put new moral fibre into the ruling classes and thus ensure the obedience of the lower orders. Christianity's political message was not lost: it was 'to the decline of religion and morality', wrote Wilberforce,

> that our national difficulties must both directly and indirectly be chiefly ascribed . . . my only solid hopes for the well-being of my country depend not so much on her fleet and armies, not so much on the wisdom of her rulers, or on the spirit of her people, as on the persuasion that she still contains many who in a degenerate age love and obey the Gospel of Christ.[54]

Evangelicalism was nothing new; its novelty around 1800 lay in the willingness of the ruling classes to listen to its call for the reformation of manners. 'By the beginning of the nineteenth century,' commented that shrewd historian, G. M. Young, 'virtue was advancing on a broad, invincible front.'[55]

Confronted by the radicalism of the French Revolution and the disturbances of the industrial revolution, the British ruling elite sought to secure its title deeds by stressing the constraints of nature and the need for moral restraint. What we often dub 'Victorianism' was being born, not merely before the accession of the Queen (1837) but even before her birth (1819). The hypocrisy of such holier-than-thou-ism directed by the haves against the have-nots was not lost on fearless souls like William Blake:

> Is this a holy thing to see
> In a rich and fruitful land,
> Babes reduc'd to misery,
> Fed with cold and usurous hand?
>
> Is that trembling cry a song?
> Can it be a song of joy?
> And so many children poor?
> It is a land of poverty?[56]

The free spirit in the visionary poet was especially exasperated by Malthus' callously complacent defence of the status quo (anticipating Mrs Thatcher, he seemed to be insisting, 'There is no alternative'):

> When a man looks pale
> With labour & abstinence, say he looks healthy & happy;
> And when his children sicken, let them die; there are enough
> Born, even too many, & our Earth will be overrun
> Without these arts.
> Preach temperance: say he is overgorg'd & drowns his wit
> In strong drink, tho' you know that bread & water are all
> He can afford.[57]

The years around 1800 thus spawned unparalleled turmoil, high hopes, crushing disappointments. Radically opposed futures for mankind were held out, because, almost for the first time, the future itself had become the ground for debate. Many changed their minds, and others changed sides, erstwhile radicals like Coleridge and Southey becoming Church-and-king reactionaries – and being accused of turncoatism by one who never changed sides: the splenetic radical William Hazlitt.

Born in 1778, Hazlitt was the son of a Unitarian minister. At the age of twenty he met Coleridge and was captivated. Failing in his chosen career as an artist, he earned his living by his pen, becoming a prolific journalist. Turbulent, bitter and finally disillusioned, he remained a staunch Jacobin long after Wordsworth and Coleridge had abandoned their youthful enthusiasms. 'I am no politician,' he insisted in 1819 in the Preface to his *Political Essays*:

> and still less can I be said to be a partyman: but I have a hatred of tyranny, and a contempt for its tools; and this feeling I have expressed as often and as strongly as I could. I cannot sit quietly down under the claims of barefaced power, and I have tried to expose the little arts of sophistry by which they are defended. I have no mind to have my person made a property of, nor my understanding made a dupe of. I deny that liberty and slavery are convertible terms, that right and wrong, truth and falsehood, plenty and famine, the comforts or wretchedness of a people, are matters of perfect indifference. That is all I know of the matter; but on these points I am likely to remain incorrigible, in spite of any arguments that I have seen used to the contrary.[58]

Looking back, Victorians perceived the passing out of an old order around 1800. This point was never more evocatively made than in *Adam Bede*, published in 1859, the year of Darwin's *Origin of Species* – but set in 1806. In that novel George Eliot pictured a great watershed. On this side of 1800 lay modernity – the world of speed, size, turmoil, restlessness. And on the other? 'Leisure is gone,' she reflected,

– gone where the spinning wheels are gone, and the pack-horses, and the slow waggons, and the pedlars, who brought bargains to the door on sunny afternoons. Ingenious philosophers tell you that the great work of the steam-engine is to create leisure for mankind. Do not believe them; it only creates a vacuum for eager thoughts to rush in. Even idleness is eager now, eager for amusement; prone to excursion-trains, art-museums, periodical literature, and exciting novels: prone even to scientific theorizing, and cursory peeps through microscopes. Old Leisure was quite a different personage; he only read one newspaper, innocent of leaders, and was free from that periodicity of sensations which we call post-time. He was a contemplative, rather stout gentleman, of excellent digestion – of quiet perception, undiseased by hypothesis: happy in his inability to know the causes of things, preferring the things themselves. He lived chiefly in the country, among pleasant seats and homesteads, and was fond of sauntering by the fruit-tree wall, and scenting the apricots when they were warmed by the morning sunshine, or of sheltering himself under the orchard boughs at noon, when the summer pears were falling. He knew nothing of weekday service, and thought none the worse of the Sunday sermon if it allowed him to sleep from the text to the blessing – liking the afternoon service best because the prayers were the shortest, and not ashamed to say so; for he had an easy, jolly conscience, broadbacked like himself, and able to carry a great deal of beer and port-wine – not being made squeamish by doubts and qualms and lofty aspirations. Life was not a task to him, but a sinecure; he fingered the guineas in his pocket, and ate his dinners, and slept the sleep of the irresponsible; for had he not kept his charter by going to church on the Sunday afternoons! Fine old Leisure! Do not be severe on him, and judge him by our modern standard; he never went to Exeter Hall, or heard a popular preacher, or read *Tracts for the Times* or *Sartor Resartus*.[59]

Old Leisure had been superseded, according to Thomas Carlyle, author of *Sartor Resartus*, by the steam-engine age. 'Were we required', he wrote in 'Signs of the Times' (1829),

> to characterise this age of course by any single epithet, we should be tempted to call it, not an Heroical, Devotional, Philosophical, or Moral age, but above all others, the Mechanical Age . . . which, with its whole undivided might, forwards, teaches, and practises the great art of adapting means to ends.
>
> Only the material, the immediately practical not the divine and spiritual, is important to us . . . Our true Deity is Mechanism. It has subdued external Nature for us, and, we think it will do all other things.[60]

The Romantic, dyspeptic Carlyle damned the new steam age; Malthus believed that its aspirations, like Napoleon's, would meet their Waterloo, George Eliot had her misgivings. Whatever the response, nobody doubted that a new epoch in human history had dawned.

Notes

1. *Memoirs of the Late Thomas Holcroft, Written by Himself and Continued to the Time of his Death, from his Diary, Notes, and Other Papers*, edited by William Hazlitt, 3 vols (London, 1816), ii, p. 195, quoted in Philip Anthony Brown, *The French Revolution in English History* (London, 1965), p. 5.
2. Frank E. Manuel and Fritzie P. Manuel, *Utopian Thought in a Western World* (Cambridge, Mass., 1979). The new calendar attests the dawning, or creation, of a new age. The most radical calendar reform in modern history, it was adopted on 5 October, retroactive to 22 September 1792. Paradoxically for such a progressive change, the years were to be given Roman numerals. The year was divided into twelve equal months of thirty days, to be named in keeping with universal seasons or natural phenomena. To show the seasons, the months of autumn all ended in *-aire*, of winter in *-ôse*, of spring in *-al*, and of summer in *-or*. The months in order were Vendémiaire (vintage), Brumaire (fog) and Frimaire (frost); Nivôse (snow), Pluviôse (rain) and Ventôse (wind); Germinal (budding), Floréal (flowering) and Prairial (meadows); and Messidor (harvest), Thermidor (heat) and Fructidor (fruit).
3. William Wordsworth, *The Prelude*, xi, lines 108–9 in J. Wordsworth, M. H. Abrams and S. Gill (eds), *William Wordsworth, the Prelude 1799, 1805, 1850* (London, 1979), p. 397 (1805 version). See also p. 399:

    > Not in Utopia – subterranean fields, –
    > Or some secreted island, Heaven knows where!
    > But in the very world, which is the world
    > Of all of us –
    >
    > (*The Prelude*, xi, lines 140–43)

4. For the tide of goods, see Neil McKendrick, John Brewer and J. H. Plumb, *The Birth of a Consumer Society: The Commercialization of Eighteenth-Century England* (London, 1982); John Brewer and Roy Porter (eds), *Consumption and the World of Goods* (London, 1993); Carole Shammas, *The Pre-Industrial Consumer in England and America* (Oxford, 1990); Lorna Weatherill, *Consumer Behaviour and Material Culture, 1660–1760* (London, 1988).
5. Clare Williams (ed.), *Sophie in London* (London, 1933), p. 87.
6. Peter Borsay, *The English Urban Renaissance: Culture and Society in the Provincial Town 1660–1770* (Oxford, 1989).
7. George Crabbe, *The Complete Poetical Works*, ed. Norma Dalrymple-Champneys, 3 vols (Oxford, 1988), i, p. 182. The threat to traditional order posed by newspapers was well conveyed when the *Anti-Jacobin Review* declared in 1801 that 'the establishment of newspapers in this country' was 'a calamity most deeply to be deplored'. Quoted in Arthur Aspinall, *Politics and the Press, c. 1780–1850* (London, 1949), p. 9.
8. Carl Philip Moritz, *Journeys of a German in England: A Walking-tour of England in 1782*, trans. and introduced by Reginald Nettel (London, 1982), p. 25.
9. Friedrich von Kielmansegge, *Diary of a Journey to England in the Years 1761–1762* (London, 1902), p. 18.
10. Robert Southey, *Letters from England*, ed. with an Introduction by Jack Simmons (Gloucester, 1984), p. 58.
11. William Cobbett, *Rural Rides*, 2 vols (London, 1957), ii, p. 49.
12. Desmond King-Hele, *Doctor of Revolution: The Life and Genius of Erasmus Darwin* (London, 1977), p. 65.
13. Wordsworth, *Prelude* (1850 version, Book VI, line 339) in Wordsworth, Abrams and Gill (eds), *William Wordsworth*, p. 205.
14. Wordsworth, *Prelude* (1850 version, Book IX, line 161) in Wordsworth, Abrams and Gill (eds), *William Wordsworth*, p. 320.
15. Ibid.
16. Richard Price, *Discourse on the Love of our Country* (London, 1789), quoted in H. T.

Dickinson, *Politics and Literature in the Eighteenth Century* (London, 1974), p. 175.

17. Edmund Burke, *Reflections on the Revolution in France* (London, 1790). I have used L. G. Mitchell (ed.), *The Writings and Speeches of Edmund Burke*, viii (Oxford, 1989), pp. 60, 219, 207.

18. Tom Paine, *Rights of Man*, ed. Henry Collins (Harmondsworth, 1969), pp. 63–4.

19. W. Roberts (ed.), *Memoirs of the Life and Correspondence of Mrs Hannah More*, 4 vols (London, 1834), ii, p. 357. What next after the rights of man? Soon there would be heard, she forecast, 'grave descants on the rights of youth – the rights of children – the rights of babies!'

20. Paine, *Rights of Man*, p. 182. The mutineers are quoted in Brown, *The French Revolution in English History*, p. 157.

21. Thomas Somerville, *Observations on the Constitution and Present State of Britain* (Edinburgh, 1793), pp. 58–9.

22. For this and the preceding quotations, see Clive Emsley, *British Society and the French Wars 1793–1815* (London, 1979), pp. 86–7.

23. Thomas Walker, *Review of Some of the Political Events which have Occurred in Manchester During the last Five Years: being a Sequel to the Trial of Thomas Walker, and Others, for a Conspiracy to Overthrow the Constitution and Government of this Country, and to Aid and Assist the French, Being the King's Enemies* (London, 1794), pp. 1–2.

24. Quoted in Emsley, *British Society and the French Wars*, p. 161.

25. For this, including the quotations, see ibid., p. 56.

26. Southey, *Letters from England*, p. 375. For a contemporary assessment of Southey, see William Hazlitt, *The Spirit of the Age* (Menston, 1971), pp. 365–84.

27. Southey, *Letters from England*, p. 375.

28. Patrick Colquhoun, *A Treatise on the Wealth, Power and Resources of the British Empire* (London, 1814), p. 35.

29. For the industrial-revolution debate and the information in the following discussion, see P. Hudson, *The Industrial Revolution* (Dunton Green, 1992), P. Mathias, *The First Industrial Nation: An Economic History of Britain 1700–1914*, 2nd edn (London, 1983); P. Deane, *The First Industrial Revolution* (Cambridge, 1965); and D. Landes, *The Unbound Prometheus* (Cambridge, 1969).

30. *Annual Register* (1800), p. 1.

31. Adam Smith, *Inquiry into the Nature and Causes of the Wealth of Nations*, ed. R. H. Campbell and A. S. Skinner, 2 vols (Oxford, 1976), Book I, ch. VIII, p. 99.

32. Robert Owen, *Observations on the Effect of the Manufacturing System* (London, 1815), pp. 1–2.

33. Ibid., pp. 3, 9. Owen's most notable book was *A New View of Society* (London, 1813).

34. Thomas Robert Malthus, *An Essay on the Principle of Population as it Affects the Future Improvement of Society, with Remarks on the Speculations of Mr Godwin, M. Condorcet, and Other Writers* (London, 1798; I cite the facsimile reprint, London, 1966), pp. 1–2. For discussion of Malthus see also Catherine Gallagher, 'The Body Versus the Social Body in the Works of Thomas Malthus and Henry Mayhew', in Catherine Gallagher and Thomas Laqueur (eds), *The Making of the Modern Body: Sexuality and Society in the Nineteenth Century* (Berkeley, 1987), pp. 83–106; Patricia James, *Population Malthus: His Life and Times* (London, 1979); Kenneth Smith, *The Malthusian Controversy* (London, 1951). For Hazlitt's appraisal, see Hazlitt, *The Spirit of the Age*, pp. 251–76.

35. Malthus, *An Essay on the Principle of Population*, pp. 2–3.

36. Malthus came to be seen as the great conservative ideologue. But he presented himself as an honest enquirer, exploring the inherent tendencies of events more deeply and soberly than the intoxicated revolutionaries. Malthus may well have been a reactionary at heart, but his pose was that of a realist.

37. Malthus, *An Essay on the Principle of Population*, Preface, p. iii.

38. Ibid., pp. 8–9. Hazlitt commented thus on Godwin:

> The Spirit of the Age was never more fully shown than in its treatment of this writer
> – its love of paradox and change, its dastard submission to prejudice and to the

fashion of the day. Five-and-twenty years ago he was in the very zenith of a sultry and unwholesome popularity; he blazed as a sun in the firmament of reputation; no one was more talked of, more looked up to, more sought after, and wherever liberty, truth, justice was the theme, his name was not far off. Now he has sunk below the horizon, and enjoys the serene twilight of a doubtful immortality. Mr Godwin, during his lifetime, has secured to himself the triumphs and the mortifications of an extreme notoriety and of a sort of posthumous fame. His bark, after being tossed in the revolutionary tempest, now raised to heaven by all the fury of popular breath, now almost dashed in pieces, and buried in the quick-sands of ignorance, or scorched with the lightning of momentary indignation, at length floats on the calm wave that is to bear it down the streams of time.

(Hazlitt, *The Spirit of the Age*, pp. 31–2)

39. Malthus, *An Essay on the Principle of Population*, p. 10.
40. Ibid., pp. 4–5.
41. Ibid., pp. 3–4. Malthus was right: in the *Anti-Jacobin Review* George Canning memorably summed up the revolutionary case in a jingle:

> Reason, Philosophy, 'fiddledum, diddledum'
> Peace and Fraternity, higgledy, piggledy
> Higgledy piggledy, 'fiddledum, diddledum'.
> (G. Canning, 'The Soldier's Friend', in *Poetry of the Anti-Jacobin*, with explanatory notes by Charles Edmonds, 2nd edn (London, 1854), pp. 29–30)

42. Malthus, *An Essay on the Principle of Population*, p. 7.
43. Ibid., p. 8.
44. Ibid., pp. 150–52.
45. Ibid., p. 152.
46. Ibid., pp. 152–3.
47. Ibid., p. 174.
48. Ibid., pp. 174–5.
49. Ibid., p. 176.
50. Ibid., pp. 11–12.
51. Ibid., pp. 12–13.
52. Ibid., pp. 16–17.
53. Ibid., pp. 37–8.
54. William Wilberforce, *A Practical View of the Prevailing Religious System of Professed Christians in the Higher and Middle Classes of this Country Contrasted with Real Christianity* (London, 1797), p. 489.
55. Boyd Hilton, *The Age of Atonement: The Influence of Evangelicalism on Social and Economic Thought, 1750–1865* (Oxford, New York, 1988); F. K. Brown, *Fathers of the Victorians: The Age of Wilberforce* (Cambridge, 1961); G. M. Young, *Victorian England: Portrait of an Age*, 2nd edn (London, 1977), p. 24.
56. William Blake, *Blake's Complete Writings*, ed. G. Keynes (London, 1966), pp. 211–12, quoted in Ronald Walter Harris, *Romanticism and the Social Order, 1780–1830* (London, 1969), p. 160.
57. Blake, *Blake's Complete Writings*, p. 323, quoted in J. Bronowski, *A Man without a Mask* (London, 1943), p. 370.
58. William Hazlitt, *Political Essays* (London, 1819), p. vii.
59. George Eliot, *Adam Bede* (Edinburgh and London, 1859). I cite the Penguin edn (Harmondsworth, 1980), p. 557.
60. [T. Carlyle], 'Signs of the Times', *Edinburgh Review*, lix (1829), pp. 439–59, at p. 453.

83. The time span lengthens. Science opens up not only centuries but millennia. An evolutionary chart, 1880.

THE 1890s

Past, Present and Future in Headlines

Asa Briggs

The Coming Beast must certainly be reckoned in any anticipatory calculations regarding the Coming Man.

(*H. G. Wells,* Gentleman's Magazine*, 1891*)

'Speculations concerning the future', a book reviewer wrote somewhat tritely in the *Quarterly Review* in 1894, 'are probably confined to man alone. . . . Looking before and after, man seeks to peer beyond the narrow limits of the actual . . . . There are few thoughtful persons who do not now and then try to picture how "when the years have passed away" and we have passed away with them, it will fare with our children, our country, "the great globe itself".'[1]

The allusion to man's uniqueness – even when qualified by the adverb 'probably' – is explicable in terms of the fascination felt by many writers in the nineteenth century for the parallels between the dynamics of animal kingdoms and the dynamics of human societies. This was a century when the study of human history was transformed. So too was the study of the 'descent of man'. At least from Charles Darwin onwards the 'struggle for survival' seemed common to both studies: this was true also of 'evolution', as meaningful for anthropologists as for historians. In two or three generations the timespan of global history, geological and biological, had been lengthened from thousands to millions of years as efforts were made to trace back the wide range of species to their distant origins. The word 'prehistory' now entered the language.[2]

Meanwhile, newspaper headlines, when necessary printed in capital letters, proclaimed the news of the day for a greatly expanded reading public taught with public money how to read and write. 'The press is at once the eye and the ear and the tongue of the people,' wrote W. T. Stead, one of whose publications was the *Review of Reviews*, which drew on reviews from both sides of the Channel and of the Atlantic. The name *Globe* was at last an appropriate name for an evening newspaper. Another equally appropriate name, the *Daily Telegraph*, the first of London's daily newspapers, had been chosen as far back as 1855. Yet the name of the popular and highly successful *Daily Mail*, founded in 1896 by Alfred Harmsworth, the future Viscount Northcliffe, looked back to what was still the major form of

84. 'A wheat field in A.D. 1970': technology points to the future, offering new possibilities of material growth. *The Sphere*, 1907.

international private and business communication: the postage stamp, a nineteenth-century invention, had celebrated its half-century in 1890.[3]

The fact that the globe was already girdled with chains of communications that had been absent in 1800 intensified popular interest both in conflicts and in interdependencies on a global scale. Reuters news agency, 'following the cable', had established itself in London in 1851, and by the 1890s it had agents in most parts of the world. Not surprisingly, communications metaphors were by then popular. Thus, when the president of the newly founded Institution of Electrical Engineers replied in 1889 to an address by the Marquess of Salisbury, the last of Queen Victoria's prime ministers, he described how 'nowadays the whole earth resembles . . . one of our own bodies. The electrical wires represent the nerves, and messages are conveyed from the most distant regions to the central place of government, just as in our bodies, where sensations are conveyed to the sensorium.'[4] There was another place too to which the messages came – the City of London. This was a real sensorium, the financial capital of the world.

In the seventeenth century, when news travelled slowly and there were no newspapers or periodicals to disturb him, Bishop Usher, looking back confidently to Adam, had meticulously calculated the timing of 'creation'. Taking the sacred scriptures as his guide in working out 'astronomical reckonings', as Nostradamus had done in the sixteenth century, he had fixed it firmly at six o'clock on the evening of 22 October 4004 BC. Such a short but scriptural timespan – and there were many Christians who still believed in it in 1900 – left no place in the scheme of things either for the ends of human centuries or for the beginnings of new ones. It incorporated, however, the notion of a millennium – of a Last Judgment – the main theme of C. T. Russell's popular book *The Divine Plan of the Ages*, which had appeared in 1886.[5]

'Millennialism' had taken secular as well as religious forms in the nineteenth century, but its appeal was limited. As the century drew to a close and proposed millennial dates like 1881 had come and gone, far greater interest was taken, particularly in the press, in the length of Queen Victoria's reign. By then the Victorians had become used to celebrating centenaries, jubilees and anniversaries in words, events, buildings, medals and other objects fashioned out of metal or pottery or silk. The queen's life, however, registered in its last years in jubilees, had a distinctive interest of its own. On 23 September 1896 she had reigned longer by one day than any previous English sovereign, and when she died in 1901 almost every newspaper stated precisely that her reign had lasted for sixty-three years, seven months and two days. It was described as an 'era', and when the Privy Council was summoned to proclaim Edward VII there was no man alive who had ever taken part in the formal ceremonies associated with the death of a sovereign and the proclamation of a new one.

The sense of a century as well as of a reign had begun to take shape even before Queen Victoria came to the throne. Indeed, the nineteenth century, the first century to be thought of by most people as possessing a number, had been saluted at its beginning as a new dawn: A. W. Schlegel in his *Canonical Way of the Old and New Century*, a theatrical piece performed on 1 January 1801, had proclaimed that it was not the eighteenth century, a withered old hag, that was its parent. Instead, one parent was Genius, the other Freedom. There were some students of Nostradamus, hostile to such romantic utterances – and to the French Revolution – who considered the rule of Napoleon as the rule of the third Antichrist, but Schlegel had little time for such thoughts. Out of a turbulent present a new and better future would arise.[6]

A generation later, Thomas Carlyle wrote in 1831 that 'never since the beginning of time' had there been 'so self-conscious a society'. The 'spirit of the age' was frequently invoked, as it was to be sixty years later, and new *isms* multiplied, as they were to do into the age of 'imperialism', a term which acquired a new significance in Europe during the last decades of the century as vast areas of the non-European world were partitioned. In 1856, when it had not yet acquired that significance, the poet Tennyson had added '19th Century-ism' ('if you will admit such a word') to the already growing list of *isms*.[7]

Across the Channel *la dixneuvièmité* never needed apologies, and in time it came to suggest not a period, but a state of mind.[8] The novelist Stendhal, who died in 1842, used the adjective *triste* to describe the century: by contrast, Victor Hugo, who loved to deal in great effects, talked the language of triumph. By the 1860s, whatever the political regime in Paris, the time disease, *mal du siècle*, a phrase coined by the conservative Chateaubriand, was obsolete in France, although in England Matthew Arnold wrote self-consciously of 'sick-fatigue' and 'languid doubt'. *Fin de siècle*, coined in France, was to come later. The novelist Emile Zola, whose name often reached the headlines, used it in 1886, two years before two French playwrights, F. de Jouvenot and M. Micard, wrote a play with that name which was performed in Paris in April 1888. And, eleven years before that, what became an influential periodical, the *Nineteenth Century*, 'a modern

85. 'Janiform': looking backwards, looking forwards. The periodical the *Nineteenth Century* now adds the words 'And After' to its title.

THE

NINETEENTH CENTURY

AND AFTER

No. CCLXXXVII—January 1901

XX

XIX

This Janiform head, adapted from a Greek coin of Tenedos at the request of the Editor, by Sir Edward J. Poynter, P.R.A., tells, in a figure, all that need be said of the alteration made to-day in the title of the Review.

86. Poets and novelists survey past, present and future, with Victor Hugo prominent among them. The cover of an edition of Hugo's *La Légende des siècles* (1859, 1877 and 1883).

symposium', had first appeared in London on the initiative of and under the editorship of James Knowles, architect as well as writer: the title was to be changed in the early twentieth century to the *Nineteenth Century – and After*. Knowles's review found a place for science as well as the arts and for every kind of moral and religious issue, and in Janus fashion it looked both backwards and forwards.

During the first half of the century more comparisons were being made between the nineteenth century and its immediate predecessor, the eighteenth, than was to be the case when Knowles assembled his symposium. By then, indeed, comparisons with the thirteenth century had become common not only through the writings of John Ruskin or William Morris but in *Punch* cartoons and in Gilbert and Sullivan's comic opera *Patience*, first performed (with Oscar Wilde in the audience) in 1881. By the 1890s through shifts of fashion – and taste – it had become customary, as the term *fin de siècle* passed into general use on both sides of the Channel, to relate the nineteenth century to the whole of history that had gone before it. Thus, A. R. Wallace, the biologist, who had worked in parallel with Darwin before 1859, gave his own account in 1898 of the 'gains' and 'losses' of 'the wonderful century', the title of his book, in which after offering a centennial audit, he concluded that not 'only is our century superior to any that have gone before it, but . . . it may be compared with the whole preceding historical period. It must therefore be held to constitute the beginning of a new era of human progress.'[9]

Wallace deliberately chose the word 'wonder', which he incorporated in his title, to describe the reactions of his contemporaries to the many inventions of the century from safety matches to gas mantles and electric light bulbs and from postage stamps to telegrams: one of his chapters was called 'The conveyance of thought'. Likewise, the reviewer in the *Quarterly* in 1893, whose approach to past, present and future was quite different from that of Wallace, stated with awe that 'he yielded to none in the admiration of those stupendous conquests of the modern mind which have so marvellously increased man's dominion over matter and its forces, augmenting incalculably the world's wealth, amplifying indefinitely human comfort, and adumbrating an illimitable career of material progress for the generations to come'.

The book which the *Quarterly Review* was discussing in 1894 was as different from that of Wallace as was the review itself. Professor Charles H. Pearson's *National Life and Character: A Forecast*, which set out to identify the main tendencies or trends of the times, was one of a number of such books. H. G. Wells wrote several of them. His first success, *The Time Machine*, in which his time traveller looked ahead to the distant world of 802,701, appeared in 1895, and four years later he turned in his new novel *When the Sleeper Awakes* (1899) to a world 200 years ahead when disease had been conquered and everyone had a sufficiency of food and clothing.

For Wells the Victorian age at best had been 'a hasty trial experiment', and in a new century there would be necessary forms of redress through planned cities, better transport systems and, above all, educational advance. In 1902 he chose to include the word *anticipations* in the title of his meditations on the future 'reaction of mechanical and scientific progress on human life'. Wells, born in 1866, had been 'launched into life', he recalled later, 'with millennial expectations'. Now he was seeking with some humility to forecast, not to extol or to condemn, as he described a 'new republic' which would consist of 'all those people throughout the world whose minds were adapted to the demands of the big-scale conditions of the new time – a naturally and informally educated class, an unprecedented sort of people'.

Wells agreed with the social biologist Herbert Spencer, born in 1830, that the future would hold in store 'forms of social life higher than any we have imagined', but Pearson, born in the same year, was less sure. A former minister of education in the State of Victoria in Australia, who had travelled widely in the United States, he had written in his youth a *History of England in the Early and Middle Ages*, the period to which some of the most articulate Victorians had expressed a fervent desire to return. Now in 1894 he feared both a further increase in the power of the state in the twentieth century and a 'trivialisation of culture'. Already, he claimed, the state had superseded the Church 'in its hold upon popular imagination by the great benefits it assured to its members', and in the twentieth century it would gain further at the expense this time of the family. The marriage tie itself would be relaxed. 'We may imagine the State crèche and the State doctor and the State school, and the child, already drilled by the State, passing from the State school into the State workshop.'

Most people would live in cities and that in itself would inevitably narrow horizons and diminish the power of 'personality'. In the Britain of 1800 there had been no city, with the exception of London, with a population of more than 100,000; in 1891 there were twenty-three. For Pearson the consequences in terms of quality of life at work and in the home had already been disturbing, and in the future they would spread increasingly to leisure. 'Does any man dream that an excursion train, with its riotous mirth and luncheon baskets and a few hours freedom to stand on a pier or stroll through the streets of a country town, can compensate to millions of human beings for nature quite shut out?'

At this point the animals, so dear to the Victorians, came into the picture once again along with Nature, usually given a capital letter, which in its various manifestations could console, inspire or alarm them. 'What kind of children will those be who grow up when the best sanitary laws have restricted the intercourse with animals even more than is now customary in towns; who have never picked buttercups and daisies; who read in poems of the song of birds that they cannot hear, and of a beauty in the seasons which they only know by vicissitudes of hot and cold? Will not their eyes be dimmed for all the sights but those which a shop window can afford?'[10]

Pearson's perspectives in space were as extended as his perceptions in time. Much of his book was concerned with the United States and with Africa as well as Australia, and, not least, with China. He thought in terms of the globe. So, too, did the *Daily Mail*, which in a 'golden extra', replete with capital letters, which appeared on 31 December 1900, declared that 'the Passing of the Nineteenth Century and the Dawning of the Twentieth were celebrated all over the world by demonstrations of thankfulness and gratitude'. The longest article in the supplement was entitled 'The Golden Century: One Hundred Years of Glorious Empire', and it contemplated the

87. Slumland London, *c.* 1900, where Nature is shut out and there are few signs of human progress.

future more than dwelt on the past. 'The genius of a masterful race turns instinctively to forecast more readily than to retrospect; its leaders are ever more prone to prophesy than to search for precedent.'

If Pearson was far less sanguine than Herbert Spencer when he talked of 'forms of social life', he was even less sanguine than the editor of the *Daily Mail*. In the twentieth century, Pearson concluded, the day would come, 'and perhaps is not far distant, when the European observer will look round to see the globe girdled with a continuous zone of black and yellow races, no longer too weak for aggression or under tutelage, but independent, or practically so, in government, monopolizing the trade of their own regions, and circumscribing the industry of the European'.

Not everyone, looking around, took Pearson so seriously. Europe's population had more than doubled in a hundred years from 200 million to 430 million, and the population of North America had risen dramatically from 7 million to over 80 million. The number of Asians was still increasing, but whereas in 1800 they had constituted more than two-thirds of the world's population, in 1900 they accounted for only 51 per cent. Among them Indians were under the beneficent sway of an empress far away in London: they constituted 'the jewel in the British crown', while the Japanese were learners, not rivals. Africa too – after a process of partition – was largely under European control, and its population was growing relatively slowly. Darwin, summing up the recent past, had anticipated the *Daily Mail*. 'Looking to the world at no very distant date,' he had written, 'what an endless number of the lower races will have been eliminated by the higher civilized races throughout the world.' The leaders of those races included the makers of empires, some of them as controversial as Cecil Rhodes, but there were also new men who changed the map which, for the first time in 1900, included (federal) Australia.[11]

Thanks to men as adventurous as Rhodes the creed of empire was far stronger in the 1890s than it had been a generation before, and Queen Victoria's Diamond Jubilee in 1897 was a self-consciously imperial event. Messages of congratulation and loyalty had begun to arrive for her from distant parts of the empire in 1896, and they multiplied dramatically in 1897 itself. On 22 June 1897, a great day of public thanksgiving, a special Bank Holiday in a week of jubilee celebrations, the queen herself sent a message in return to her subjects everywhere. Pressing an electric button, she despatched a telegram to the empire: 'From my heart I thank my beloved people. God bless them.'

The London crowds were noisy on jubilee day, and there were many touches of colour as peddlars moved among them, selling flags and fireworks. Troops from different parts of an expanded British Empire proudly wore their national dress. The choice of the word 'diamond' to

88. Pomp and splendour: the Diamond Jubilee (1897) was an imperial as well as a national event. From the *Illustrated London News*.

identify the jubilee carried a cross-reference to Africa, for it was from South Africa that most diamonds came – along with gold that had been the symbol of the earlier jubilee in 1887. So also did ostrich feathers. Despite the complaints of the Society for the Protection of Birds, founded in 1889, women's hats in 1897 made lavish use of them. Queen Victoria in this connection was exceptional: she preferred bonnets.

By the end of the century display was muted. Long before any of Pearson's predictions had had time to register, Britain's imperial splendour was tarnished in South Africa; and in what was called at the time 'Black Week', from 10 to 17 December 1899, a week that contrasted totally with jubilee week in 1897, the British army suffered a series of military disasters at the hands of the Boers. It lost 3000 men and twelve guns. The war, which had controversial origins, was now to last far longer than had been contemplated, although a detachment of cavalry relieved Ladysmith after a siege of 118 days in February 1900. After the queen had sent telegrams of congratulation to general Sir Redvers Buller and to the garrison commander in Ladysmith, Sir George White, the commander, wrote happily that 'any hardships and privations are a hundred times compensated for by the sympathy and appreciation of our Queen'.[12]

Later in 1900, on 15 May, it was popular, not royal, reactions that amazed foreign visitors to London and stole the headlines. When news arrived of the liberation of besieged Mafeking, a wildly cheering crowd of 20,000 people gathered round London's Mansion House within five minutes. The comedian Dan Leno announced the news in the middle of his act at the London Pavilion, dancing a celebratory hornpipe, while at the Alhambra in Leicester Square it was a *Daily Mail* reporter who broke into the show with the cry 'Mafeking is relieved.' The audience there, like the audience at the even more famous nearby music hall, the Empire, rose to its feet and sang 'God Save the Queen'. All over the country railway engines blew their whistles and church bells rang out. At Rottingdean, near Brighton, Lady Burne-Jones, widow of the great pre-Raphaelite painter, friend of William Morris and aunt of the poet of empire, Rudyard Kipling, displayed a vast linen banner which she had prepared herself: it bore the words 'We Have Killed and Also Taken Possession'.

The killing in South Africa did not stop with the relief of Mafeking, a starving town. Instead, the struggle was transformed into stubborn guerrilla war, and the British had to maintain an army of 250,000 in South Africa. In all, around 22,000 British soldiers died, most of them from disease. The financial cost too was high, £250 million instead of the £10 million originally estimated.

During the Boer War, in which many black and coloured people assisted the British cause, Britain was politically isolated from almost every other country in Europe. Nonetheless, many of the foreigners who welcomed

Britain's reverses in South Africa in words and in cartoons would have shared Pearson's long-term forebodings in 1893. Indeed, in the same month as the relief of Mafeking, disturbances in China, whipped up by the anti-foreign 'Boxer movement', the 'Fists of Righteous Harmony', stirred the various legations in Peking, each following its own national policies, to appeal in unison for help. They were responding to what the German Kaiser, Wilhelm II, Queen Victoria's grandson, called 'a Yellow Peril'. Chinese forts were seized, but even after their seizure the German minister, Baron von Ketteler, was assassinated.

Relief was a word much in the news, and the legations were not relieved until the middle of August. An improvised international expedition had been hastily mobilised in which by far the biggest military contingent consisted not of Europeans but of Japanese. There were ill-prepared Americans also who wore winter uniforms, and the Russians, who were soon to be involved in war with the Japanese, had to travel without their cannon. Throughout the disturbances the Chinese Empire was presided over, as it had been for decades, by the formidable Empress Dowager, Tz'u-Hsi, whose attitude towards the Boxers was ambivalent. She liked to compare herself (favourably) with Queen Victoria, and like her subjects she followed a non-European calendar, based on the timing of each moon, which identified each hour: the hour of the monkey was at 3 p.m. Centuries played no part in such reckoning. Nor, indeed, did they in Queen Victoria's: in her diaries and in her letters she made no references to the end of one century and the beginning of a new.

Queen Victoria took a great personal interest in her subjects abroad, including soldiers from Canada, Australia and New Zealand who served in the Boer War. Yet 'high noon' imperialism, as expressed at the turn of the century, was not an exclusively British or 'Victorian' phenomenon. Japan, which borrowed from different western cultures in its ambitious industrialisation and modernisation programmes, developed its own distinctive version, became one of the 'Boxer Protocol' powers after the Chinese revolt was eventually crushed, and in 1902 entered into alliance with Britain, breaking decades of British 'splendid isolation'. American official preoccupations in 1900 were 'imperial' also, as newspaper headlines proclaimed, although 'imperialism' was as pejorative a word as ever in the United States. Moreover, just as there was bitter opposition in Britain to the Boer War, with David Lloyd George prominent among the 'pro-Boers', so in the United States there was well-organised opposition to President McKinley's policies of 'territorial expansion'. The Treaty of Paris with Spain, signed in December 1898, which removed Cuba, Puerto Rico and the Philippines from the Spanish orbit, had been ratified by only two votes in the Senate.

'I took Panama' was to be the terse comment of McKinley's successor, Theodore Roosevelt, when he summed up the great American 'adventure'

89. The White Man's Burden is taken up by Uncle Sam as well as by John Bull (1899). The cartoonist makes his 'Apologies to Rudyard Kipling' in the caption.

which made possible the building of the Panama Canal, started in 1904. McKinley, who had ordered the White House flag to be flown at half-mast when he heard of Queen Victoria's death in January 1901, had been shot eight months later by an anarchist at an exhibition in Buffalo. 'Anarchism' had been one of the bogey words of the 1890s. Violence was not associated solely with war. Roosevelt's heroes included gun-carrying frontier cowboys in the American West, a land where legends were born that were making their way throughout the world.

As in Britain, much American rhetoric of 'imperialism' was racial even when it was not racist. The Anglo-Saxon race itself was deemed superior. 'Manifest destiny' was held to be at work. The 'White Man', in the words of Kipling, who, it was claimed, whether he liked it or not, was 'in some sort American' – he was born in Bombay – bore a 'burden', and the best of his 'breed' on both sides of the Atlantic were called upon

> To wait in heavy harness,
> On fluttering folk and wild –
> Your new-caught sullen peoples
> Half devil and half child.

In the name of 'civilisation' the White Man had to be prepared to fight on tropical frontiers 'the savage wars of peace'. The first title of this well-known poem, 'The White Man's Burden', had been 'An Address to America', not to Britain.

Believers in the 'imperial idea' were as well aware of the fragility of imperial power as they were of its pomp. Nineveh and Tyre had left their lessons. And during the Boer War, in a poem which on this occasion was addressed initially to the British 'People', Kipling did not hesitate to criticise Britain's Islanders for putting sport before both wealth and power.

> Then ye returned to your trinkets; then ye contented your souls
> With the flannelled fools at the wicket or the muddied oafs at the goals.

This was a dangerous theme for Kipling to pursue, since sport had seemed during the middle years of the 1890s to be a necessary antidote to introversion and to decadence. There could also be an element of international idealism in it. The first Olympic Games, proposed by a Frenchman, had been held in 1896.

The 1890s was a decade of popular local and national sports, far removed from ancient Athens, aristocratic Badminton or even the playing fields of Eton. Yet while idealism coloured the 'amateur' cult in sport, it was professional clubs from the industrial north which began to dominate what became England's national game, soccer, as attendances of spectators rose. The Football Association Cup had first gone to the north (Blackburn Olympic) in 1883, and the first Football League was founded in 1888/9 (with a second division added in 1892). Until 1891 there were no linesmen and each side had its own umpire, but umpires were now abolished in favour of referees, and in 1893 a Referees' Association was founded.

The middle classes developed their own interest in sports in the 1890s, including golf and tennis (a game for women as well as for men); and in 1896 an anthology called *The Poetry of Sport* appeared in the widely read Badminton Library, volumes of which included all sports from archery to yachting. It was dedicated to the Prince of Wales, 'one of the best and keenest sportsmen of our time'. In the same year *Punch*, as always reflecting dominant middle-class moods, particularly in the metropolis, turned to popular sporting life to preach lessons after the trial of Oscar Wilde:

> Reaction's the reverse of retrograde,
> If we recede from decadent excesses,
> And beat retreat from novelists who trade
> On sex, from artists whose *chefs d'oeuvres* are messes
> 'Tis time indeed such minor plagues were stayed.
>
> Then here's for cricket in this year of Grace,
> Fair-play all round, straight hitting and straight dealing
> In letters, morals, art and commonplace
> Reversion into type in deed and feeling –
> A path of true Reaction to retrace.[13]

90. After the game between Sheffield United and Southampton at Crystal Palace: Cup Final spectators pose outside St Paul's Cathedral, 19 April 1906.

The Grace referred to, W. G., was the famous cricketer whose claims for a sporting knighthood were being energetically promoted in the highest circles.

The trial of Oscar Wilde has usually been treated, as it was at the time, as the turning point of the last decade of the century, characterised in its beginnings as much by melancholy as by wonder. '*Fin de siècle,*' Sir Henry had 'murmured' in Oscar Wilde's *Picture of Dorian Gray* (1890). '*Fin du globe,*' his hostess had answered. 'I wish it were *fin du globe,*' Dorian had said with a sigh, 'life is a great disappointment.' Passages from *Dorian Gray* were read out at Wilde's trial in 1895. Myth flourishes in such circumstances. So, too, in retrospect, does nostalgia, a far more lasting response than disgust. Before 1895, the myth-makers have implied, green carnations were growing: after 1895 Union Jacks were flying. Before 1895 readers were pouring over the *Yellow Book*: after 1895 readers were glued to the Yellow Press. Before 1895 there were still aesthetes in Piccadilly: after 1895 it was South African plutocrats in Park Lane who attracted public attention. 'Arrest of Oscar Wilde: Yellow Book under his Arm', the newspaper headlines of 1895 proclaimed. The fact that it was a yellow book and not the notorious *Yellow Book* was overlooked.

After Wilde had been led out of court to be sent to Reading gaol, it was the *News of the World* which announced on 26 May 1895 that 'the aesthetic cult, in the nasty form, is over'. When Wilde, 'the exponent of uncut hair', as the *Sporting Times* called him, had been present at the first performance of *Patience*, he had been described as 'Ajax-like, defying the Gods'. Now in 1895 he was cast into darkness, and the famous or infamous *Yellow Book*, the first number of which had appeared a year earlier, 'turned grey overnight'. Volume II, January 1897, bereft of Aubrey Beardsley's drawings and introduced by a poem by William Watson, is dull, the one quality that its editor would have regarded as unforgivable.[14]

The *Yellow Book*'s successor, the *Savoy*, had only a brief life, and there seemed to be a lesson in all this as there had been to Wilde's trial. 'They are not long, the days of wine and roses' was one of the most memorable lines of the poet Ernest Dowson, a member of a group of 1890s writers who frequented Soho cafés and public houses in the Strand; another was his call in feverish verses for 'madder music and for stronger wine'. He died in 1900, aged only thirty-three. Literary historians of the English 1890s have often gone on to note how some of the most characteristic figures of the period were dead by 1900.

They included not only Wilde, who died in exile in 1900 at the age of forty-four, but far younger writers and artists, among them Beardsley, who had appeared on the scene only in 1893 and who died in 1898, aged twenty-six. Through his image as much as through his drawings he had already given his name to a period. Others were Hubert Crackanthorpe, *Yellow Book* author, who had complained of this 'miserable, inadequate age of ours', and who had died even earlier in 1896, aged thirty-one; Lionel Johnson, who had written a prose satire called 'Incurable' for one of the many small periodicals of the period, the *Pageant*, and who died in 1902, aged thirty-five, and Henry Harland, literary editor of the *Yellow Book*, who died in 1905, aged forty-four. John Davidson, whose *Fleet Street Eclogues* (1893) had warned of the lies behind newspaper headlines, and who produced four *Testaments* early in the new century, died in 1909, aged fifty-two.

'Perhaps all that was mortal of them felt so essential to the Nineties that life beyond the decade might have been unbearable,' Holbrook Jackson suggested in his brilliant study *The Eighteen Nineties*, which appeared in 1913 just before the twentieth-century cataclysm, the 'Great War', the kind of protracted war that few people had forecast as the nineteenth century ended.[15] Nonetheless, as Jackson fully recognised, no account of the 'idea of the 1890s' would be complete unless the survivors are brought on to the stage also. Among them are Arthur Symons, the first English champion of the French symbolist poets, who was to stand out as the representative voice of the 1890s; W. B. Yeats, one of the most fascinating poets of any time; G. B. Shaw, who refused to treat drama simply as entertainment; Kipling, far more than a storyteller of empire, who was to receive the Nobel Prize for literature in 1907; Henry James, who contrasted the innocence – and

91. Oscar Wilde (1895),
'a strange being', as painted by
Toulouse-Lautrec.

vitality – of the United States with the corruption – and wisdom – of Europe; and, not least, Wells, whose belief in the power of education and of science was to falter in his last years.

Each of these writers had his own history, although their paths crossed and diverged and their reputations rose or fell more than once during the twentieth century. Shaw, who received the Nobel Prize for literature eighteen years after Kipling, lived to be a bearded Methuselah. Yeats, another winner – in 1923 – travelled up a 'winding stair', the title of one of his poems published in 1929. Wells quarrelled with James, who died thirty years before him in 1916, about the nature of the novel, of art, and of 'journalism'. James had described the year 1900 as 'dreadful', 'gruesome' and 'monstrously numbered'. It was Wells who had offered one of the most striking beginnings of a novel in the 1890s: the opening sentence of his *The War of the Worlds* (1898), which pitted Earthmen against Martians, reads:

> No one would have believed, in the last years of the nineteenth century, that human affairs were being watched keenly and closely by intelligence greater than man's and yet as mortal as his own; that as men busied themselves with their affairs they were scrutinized and studied, perhaps as narrowly as a man with a microscope might scrutinize the transient creatures that swarm and multiply in a drop of water.

From his own vantage point in 1913 Holbrook Jackson recognised, as all historians recognise now, that in order to 'place' the 1890s in time it is necessary to 'trespass' on the adjoining territories of the 1900s, after Queen Victoria had died, and of the 1880s before she reached her first jubilee. In a most perceptive study, *In the Nineties* (1989), John Stokes, seeking to observe the 1890s from within, has shown clearly how much that is associated with the late 1890s was already there before 1895 and has concluded rightly that it is not only the year of Wilde's trial that merits detailed investigation, but other neglected years, like 1893, when a revealing public debate raged about suicide, a topic that must be central in any decade to all talk of death and survival. The debate followed the publication of a posthumous letter sent to the *Daily Chronicle* by Ernest Clark, a carpet designer, announcing his forthcoming suicide, which he wished to be printed after his death. The editor's headline was 'Tired of Life', a description that passed into the language. The debate reveals just how important the crowded correspondence columns of newspapers were as well as their headlines.[16] So, too, of course, were the interviews they printed, another new feature, and the obituaries.

In the previous decade, before the 'new journalism' had developed its exciting but disturbing potential, J.-K. Huysmans's *A rebours* (*Against Nature*) depicted characters who had lost faith in themselves and their times, and Robert Louis Stevenson's *The Suicide Club* and Emil Durkheim's study *Le Suicide* had appeared. In such a setting Arthur Symons was doubtless right to use the phrase 'swift, disastrous and suicidal energy of genius' in referring to Dowson, whose poem in memory of Crackanthorpe, 'Vesperal', vividly evokes the death wish. The relationships between 'imagination' and 'action' and between 'fantasy' and 'reality' were becoming more complex in the 1890s as the religious props which had sustained traditional societies began to be knocked down and as the scale of economic enterprise was enhanced. The dead Sherlock Holmes, hero of the brilliant Conan Doyle stories, fell to his death in 1893 after mortal combat with Moriarty in 'The Final Problem', but he was restored again in deference to his readers, just as Tinkerbell in *Peter Pan* was to be restored to life at the will of J. M. Barrie.

Some of the most characteristic figures of the 1890s did not need to be restored to life. Then and in the related decades which preceded and followed it there were energetic tycoons whose zest for life was as prodigious as their zest for riches. One of them was William Lever, born in the year of the Great Exhibition of 1851, who created a huge international business, founded on soap, a commodity that was to figure more prominently in the twentieth century than in the nineteenth. His model village, Port Sunlight, was opened in 1888.[17] Within this context one of the most interesting fictional characters was the narrator George Ponderova's uncle in Wells's *Tono-Bungay*, which appeared in 1908: he created a highly successful 'mitigated water' patent medicine, Tono-Bungay, described as 'a mis-chievous trash, slightly stimulating, aromatic and attractive' by George, who benefited from its profits to follow his own life of science and technology (including 'aeronautics'). His uncle's last words, when transported by George (and by air) into exile were, 'it seems to me, George, always there must be something in me that won't die'. Unfortunately George could not reassure him that in 'some other world' (perhaps) there would not be 'the same scope for enterprise'.

It was part of the strength of Holbrook Jackson's survey of the 1890s, which inevitably left much out, that he did not ignore economic and social trends, including market trends, both in production and in publishing and advertising. His emphasis on the distinctive combination of curiosity and vitality during the 1890s remains valid. There was 'a quickening of the imagination' in many fields, an 'awakening' which represented 'not the realisation of a purpose but of a possibility'. The same point was made by one of the most discussed authors of the period, Max Nordau, the Jeremiah of the 1890s, whose widely read book, *Degeneration*, published in 1895, drew on evidence more from other European countries than from Britain. While suggesting that 'the disposition of the times is curiously confused, a compound of feverish restlessness and blunted discouragement, of fearful presage and hang dog renunciation', he also acknowledged the vigour of the age that he was holding up to judgment.

We have to set against his much quoted judgments that the prevalent theme of the decade, with Paris, not London, at its centre, was 'that of imminent perdition and extinction', and that 'mankind, with all its institutions and creations, is perishing in the midst of a dying world', a rarely quoted passage asserting that:

> the healthy – and the vast masses of the people still include unnumbered mil-lions of them – will rapidly and easily adapt themselves to the conditions which new inventions have created in humanity. The more vigorous, although they at first also have become bewildered and fatigued, recover themselves little by little, and their descendants accustom themselves to the rapid progress which humanity must make.

By the end of the twentieth century, therefore, it seemed likely to Nordau that 'a generation' would have come into existence:

> to whom it will not be injurious to read a dozen quire of newspapers daily, to be constantly called to the telephone, to be thinking simultaneously of the five continents of the world, to live half their time in a railway carriage or in a fly-ing machine, and to satisfy the demands of a circle of ten thousand acquaintances, associates, and friends. It will know how to find its ease in the

midst of a city inhabited by millions and will be able, with nerves of gigantic vigour, to respond without haste or agitation to the almost innumerable claims of existence.[18]

Nordau's argument which consisted largely of analysing the press, like so much of the 'analysis' of the 1990s, turned on the likely future relationship of the 'majority' – often dealt with sweepingly and condescendingly as 'the masses' – and 'minorities' – which included writers and artists whom Nordau described as 'degenerate'. So, too, did the early twentieth-century analysts of 'decadence', a word then much in fashion. Another much used adjective of the 1890s with layers of meaning was 'morbid'. Yet at the time the 'degeneration' and 'morbidity' of minorities had a deliberate and greatly prized element of contrivance ('artifice') about it. Whatever Pearson might say, for many writers and artists art was now more appreciated than nature.

Wilde dealt wittily with this theme, making imaginative use of paradoxes, designed to shock. Nonetheless, the case for 'artifice' always provoked resistance, as Max Beerbohm learned after he had written his notorious essay 'A Defence of Cosmetics' in the first edition of the *Yellow Book* in 1894: 'so far as anyone in literature can be lynched, I was', he wrote later. Beerbohm, writing as a young man in praise of 'times of jolliness and glad indulgence', himself used the favourite word of the period, 'new', which must always be set against *fin de siècle*, in the context of a key passage in his controversial essay: 'the Victorian era comes to an end and the day of *sancta simplicitas* is quite ended'.[19]

By 1894 the word 'new' was being applied, sometimes enthusiastically, sometimes pejoratively, to almost everything from gender to morality, from objects (not least advertised objects with their own branded names) to ideas, from fiction to art – the term *art nouveau* is the one application that has stuck – and, not least, to journalism, which had created the scenario. The Germans talked of the *Neuen Welt*. 'Not to be new in these days is to be nothing,' wrote the critic H. D. Traill in 1892.[20] Even when the sense of wonder expressed by A. R. Wallace was dimmed, there was often a mood of expectation. There were many references, indeed, during this last period of the nineteenth century to *new* inventions, a revealing adjective in itself given that the very word invention implied something that was new.

The names of the earlier inventors of the eighteenth century, which were being learned by heart in late-Victorian board schools (Kay, Crompton, Arkwright, Hargreaves, Watt *et al.*), were acknowledged through their inventions to have made possible an unprecedented increase in wealth. The term 'industrial revolution' was beginning to come into general use in the 1880s, and contemporaries were fully aware of how Britain's natural resources, particularly coal and iron, had been exploited, how the cotton industry, depending on imports and exports had developed, and through

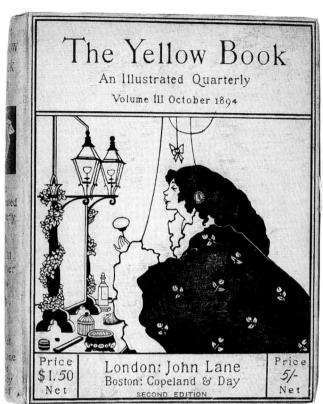

The Yellow Book
An Illustrated Quarterly
Volume III October 1894

London: John Lane
Boston: Copeland & Day
SECOND EDITION

Price $1.50 Net

Price 5/- Net

92. An edition of the *Yellow Book*, literary symbol of the 1890s. Cover by Aubrey Beardsley.

their own experience how the ways of work had been refashioned. Nevertheless, precisely because of such experience, there was ambivalence about the results.

The labour movement stressed human 'exploitation' and the continuing existence of 'poverty in the midst of wealth', and it won intellectual as well as working-class support. Even for those without industrial experience the social consequences of having 'unbound Prometheus' might be regarded as double-edged. Old values had been lost: Mammon had triumphed. Likewise, the social consequences of the invention of a new cluster of late nineteenth-century things were matters of debate also, although many of the inventions were associated with commerce more than with industry, with consumption more than with production, and with leisure as much as with work. Some contemporaries welcomed a push-button world with more gadgets ('novelties') and with more comfort. Others feared its advent, believing that twentieth-century people would be spoilt or manipulated.

There was, of course, considerable uncertainty about how new inventions would be employed once they had passed the 'toy stage'; and it proved difficult to separate out intelligent prediction from publicity, much of it promoted by moralising messages. Thus the telephone, demonstrated by Alexander Graham Bell at the Philadelphia Centennial Exhibition of 1876, was thought of in its early years as a possible instrument of entertainment or uplift as much as a personal facility of business communication.[21] You could listen to opera by telephone or hear a sermon. Bell once stated that his dream was that by means of the telephone all the people of the United States would sing 'The Star Spangled Banner' in unison.

The American Thomas Alva Edison, who more than any other individual was directly concerned with the future of many of the new things, from the electric light bulb to the phonograph, often had no more idea than his potential customers of how things would be used. While he recognised as early as 1878 that his phonograph, for example, would 'be liberally devoted to music', in his publicity he made just as much of its capacity to ensure 'the preservation of language by reproduction of our Washingtons, our Lincolns, our Gladstones'. Likewise, he thought at first of the kinetoscope, which pointed the way forward to the cinema, as a kind of peep-show. Edison was quick to learn, however, and concluded next that moving pictures would interest schoolchildren so much that they would cast aside their books and even before the bell would rush to school to learn their lessons from the screen.

The Frenchman Louis Lumière, born in 1864, seventeen years later than Edison, was more percipient, although he too described his first cine-matograph as 'a scientific curiosity with no commercial possibilities'. It was he and his brother Auguste who first introduced his device, which incorporated camera and projector, to London in 1896. Lumière, who for the price of a franc had already in 1895 shown to Parisians moving pictures of a train puffing into a railway station, a boy riding a bicycle and a baby eating, identified what activities would be most likely to entertain (as well as to instruct) his audiences. A comic interlude, *Teasing the Gardener*, was part of his first London show: it pictured a child stepping on a hose and the gardener (a key figure in Victorian England) getting drenched. In the same year, when Robert W. Paul tried to film the Derby, which was won by the Prince of Wales's horse, Persimmon, he got into a real-life fracas when a showman tried to overturn his wagonette and when the police, who later helped Paul, assumed they were both 'Punch and Judy men'. More seriously, when Queen Victoria saw Bert Bernard's film of the 1896 Lord Mayor's Show she found it 'very tiring to the eyes, but worth a headache to have seen such a marvel'.[22]

There remained more than a touch of magic in the cinematic process, even more than there was in early 'magic lantern' displays, some of which were used for instructional purposes. One of the first films in the *British Film Catalogue*, which goes back to 1895, shows a photographer trying in vain to take a picture of a ghost, while one of the first films of another pioneering Frenchman, the magician Georges Meliès, was called *The Vanishing Lady*: in it a skeleton by a dazzling time reversal becomes a living woman. Meliès also showed his audiences journeys to the bottom of the sea – and to the moon.

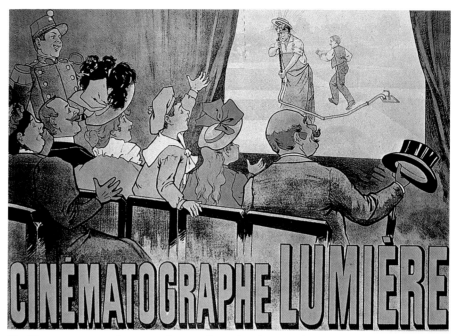

93. The screen was to become a feature of people's lives. In this cinema poster, *c.* 1895, the enthusiasm of the audience seems more convincing than what they are watching on the screen.

At the Paris Exhibition of 1900, where many new inventions were on display, twentieth-century 'talkies' were anticipated in a strange (but popular) combination of cinema and gramophone. Using discs, not cylinders, Emile Berliner – a German immigrant living in Washington – had patented his gramophone in 1894, and by 1900 the word 'record' was coming into use. At the same exhibition visitors could tour the site on moving belts, as they had been able to do at the Columbian Exhibition in Chicago seven years earlier, an exhibition which was said to have generated three-quarters of a mile of newspaper print before it even opened. There was excitement of this kind at most exhibitions which paraded novelties, as there was between exhibitions when readers perused the two 1880s volumes of the French writer and caricaturist Albert Robida – *Le Vingtième Siècle*, set in 1952, and *La Vie électrique*, set in 1955. These depicted revolutionary future forms of transport, along with juke-boxes and television (including visual telephones).

Some of Robida's drawings, like exhibits or displays at exhibition time or futuristic novels like *The Great War in Europe*, which appeared in 1894, focused not on peacetime progress but on military might. War was still associated less with an 'arms race', costly yet much publicised, than with dazzling uniforms and with dramatic 'spectacle'. There were many real-life spectacles also during the 1890s, most of them figuring in the *Illustrated*

London News, like the opening of the Kiel Canal in 1895, at which the sight of the 'gathering of the fleets' – and a great fleet was one of the dreams of Kaiser Wilhelm II – was said to be 'perhaps more notable than the mustering of manufactures of all nations at international exhibitions'. The print and the cartoon rather than the photograph were used as illustrations. Pictorial journalism long preceded journalistic employment of the camera. It was also well adapted to illustrating new things, sometimes satirically.

'As the nineteenth century draws to its close,' wrote the *Popular Science Magazine* in 1898,

> there is no slackening in that onward march of scientific discovery and invention which has been its chief characteristic. At the beginning of the century the telegraph was as yet undreamed of and the telephone and the dynamo utterly unimaginable developments. Had anyone dared to conceive that signals could be made to pass in a second of time between Europe and America he would have been considered a fit candidate for Bedlam.

Many of the new inventions of the late nineteenth century related to communications, as they had done since the rise of the railway and the telegraph two generations earlier. Indeed, the sense of a sequence of communications developments took shape long before there was any talk of a 'communications revolution'.[23]

When Guglielmo Marconi arrived in London in 1896 with a 'secret box' containing a bundle of radio devices, there seemed once again to be a touch of magic as well as of science in what he was offering, even though he conceived of wireless merely as a substitute for wire telegraphy and, like would-be investors in his company, deemed the broadcasting element that went with it to be an actual disadvantage. And, recognising its wartime value in defence and attack, he tried to interest the Royal Navy in it as diligently as he tried to interest the Post Office. Four years earlier, an English scientist, Sir William Crookes, had described as 'bewildering' the prospect that global communication could be carried on without wires. The 'ether' was considered 'mysterious'. Crookes himself was interested in 'spiritualism'. So also was Oliver Lodge, who patented his own wireless devices during the 1890s.

'Wireless is the nearest approach to telepathy that has been vouched to our intelligence,' wrote the *Popular Science Monthly*, which regularly crossed the frontiers between science and science fiction, discussing 'thought power' and 'thought control' as airily as electrically controlled clocks or Greenwich Mean Time. 'It [wireless] serves to stimulate our imagination', it went on, 'and to make us think that things generally hoped for can always be within reach.' 'A few years ago,' the *Electrical Engineer* observed in 1892, 'the public were content to send a message to London and get an answer within an hour; now they can get it in a minute or so; but still the cry is for quicker communication.' Wireless met a demand, and the fact that X-rays were discovered by W. K. Röntgen in 1895 in his laboratory at Würzburg did not seem coincidental. 'Illuminated tissue', the *New York Medical Journal* proclaimed; 'a new kind of light' was the comment of the *Journal d'Eclairage Electrique* in Paris. Meanwhile, cartoonists made the most of 'seeing through clothes'.

The first British radiographs were taken in Birmingham: they demonstrated the presence of a needle in a woman's hand. Röntgen was the winner of one of the first Nobel Prizes – that for physics – in 1901. There was irony as well as idealism behind the fact that these were to become the most prestigious international prizes of the twentieth century. The physics, chemistry and medicine prizes were offered to the men and women who had made the outstanding 'discoveries', 'inventions' or 'improvements' in science and medicine: the medicine prize was to be awarded in 1901 to Major Ronald Ross for his work on the causes of malaria. His research had taken him to the tropical areas of the British Empire. The prizes had been endowed by Alfred Nobel, the inventor of dynamite and the pioneer of nitro-glycerine, who owned among his many properties the giant armament works at Bofors in Sweden. Nobel had been deeply interested in many other inventions and discoveries, including celluloid and synthetic rubber, and in 1892 he had a yacht built at Zurich made almost entirely of aluminium.

One invention which was to receive no Nobel recognition – and was completely ignored by Wallace (it was also little noted by Wells) – was the internal-combustion engine, which was to change so many ways of life in the twentieth century, and incidentally to produce some of its most competitive and glamorous product advertising. It was the work of a number of individuals, outstanding among them Karl Benz, who produced the first workable engine using petrol in 1885, Gustav Daimler, who applied the engine first to a motor cycle and then to a motor car, and Rudolf Diesel, who perfected his heavy-oil engine in 1897.

Among the reasons why the full social implications of the automobile were only dimly discerned on either side of the Atlantic was the fact that at the end of the nineteenth century the automobile was still a luxury object, custom-built and cared for by servants. Driven in style by goggled owners or by uniformed chauffeurs, it generated more protests than enthusiasm. Yet in retrospect the first automobiles were to acquire a 'vintage' quality, and museums were to be devoted to them. One avid early collector of them was Kaiser Wilhelm II, who was to acquire twenty-five by 1912, keeping them in his stables and employing a staff of thirty-one to maintain them.

Only the fact that some of the first automobile inventors and dealers – like William Morris, later Viscount Nuffield, future benefactor of medicine, science and education – came from outside the privileged classes, and were

94. Transport and communications entangle in this vision of the financial future, from Albert Robida's *La Vie électrique*, 1892.

keen salesmen, suggested that in the new century automobiles would be owned by millions rather than by privileged elites. Costs of purchase were high. So too were running costs. There was usually laughter when it was suggested by enthusiasts that automobiles would spell the end of the centuries-old 'age of the horse'. There was, of course, no motoring infrastructure in 1900, and British roads themselves, while better than American roads, were not ready for automobile traffic. There were also legal limits to speed: the maximum in Britain was still twelve miles an hour.

The history of the bicycle had been quite different from that of the automobile, although some of the first bicycle enthusiasts – with journalists and salesmen among their numbers – became enthusiasts for the automobile also. It was the bicycle, not the automobile, that first offered travellers the 'freedom of the road'. Price was a major factor in customer choice and, after safety devices had been introduced in the bicycles of the 1890s and technical improvements had been achieved, bicycles described as the 'Working Man's Friend' cost as little as £4.50. There was a collective angle also. Bicycle clubs of many different kinds, including socialist clubs, extolled not only the freedom of the road but its 'fellowship'. In Britain the National Cyclists' Union, founded in 1883, preceded the Automobile Club, soon to become the Royal Automobile Club, by fourteen years.

Wells, who thought of himself as a socialist, was one of the early enthusiasts, who also included daring women, women who fully deserved the adjective 'new', an adjective that in this case was seldom used as a compliment. With the suffragettes around the corner it was foolish of one anti-feminist journalist of the mid-1890s to write that 'of the New Woman nothing is left but her bicycle'. There was another element of irony, however, in the fact that new women, who needed the publicity of the press to focus attention on their cause, were very soon its victims.

The newest of all the new communications inventions, still not perfected at the end of the century, was the 'heavier than air flying machine', an invention which was to transform peace and war. Before the secret of how to propel it was discovered, it was described in 1897 by Professor S. P. Langley, secretary of the Smithsonian Institution in Washington, as a machine which would emulate 'the effortless flight of the soaring bird'.[24] Again Wells was one of its prophets, outside as well as inside the pages of *Tono-Bungay*, but it was not until 1903 that the Wright brothers, who had first established their reputation as bicycle makers, succeeded at Kitty Hawk, North Carolina, in making the first powered flight, lasting only for a few seconds. It was during the first decade of the twentieth century that they and others on both sides of the Atlantic proved that flight over substantial distances could become a repeatable, regular and organised human activity. Langley perhaps foresaw this when he ended his account of his new flying machine with the stirring words: 'the great universal highway overhead is now soon to be opened'.

Like the highways on the land, which were to be transformed in the twentieth century, the aeroplane turned oil, a product known as long ago as

95. The newest of women, the Suffragettes, were to chain themselves, not their bicycles to the railings. A photograph of 1906

96. Reaching the skies. Professor Langley's model aeroplane flew on 8 August 1903 but the real thing would later crash, leaving the way open for the successful flight by the Wright brothers. Blériot crossed the Channel in 1909.

Herodotus and noted by Marco Polo, into one of the world's most valuable global commodities. But there was little sense in 1900 of how dependent upon it the twentieth-century world would be. The rise of oil had preceded the invention of the automobile, for it was in 1859 that the first oil well had been drilled at Titusville, later Oil City, in Pennsylvania. In 1870 J. D. Rockefeller had created the Standard Oil Company, a huge trust which by 1900 had assets listed at over $200 million. American production had then reached between five and six million tons, with the United States and Russia accounting for about 90 per cent of world output.

The structure of the oil industry, which in its origins and in its later development carried with it an obvious element of speculation, pointed to a new economic future for the world, based on enormous combines that would transform both production and distribution; and it was in 1901 that what was called 'the most gigantic deal ever known' was made across the Atlantic – the purchase of the giant steel company founded by the Scots-born tycoon Andrew Carnegie and six other companies by a trust or syndicate headed by the financier Pierpont Morgan. The world, it was said at the time, was being recreated not by God but by men, and there were to be unforeseen repercussions in this story, just as there had been in the history of Nobel or Nuffield: one was the Rockefeller Foundation, committed to the encouragement of research for the good of mankind; another was the charitable Carnegie Trust, which had a Scots dimension to it and which, among its other activities, endowed public libraries in both Scotland and England.

With its vast natural resources, the United States, drawing on human talent from overseas, was prepared (as in the McKinley tariff of 1891) to put its trust in protectionism. It was to play a dominating role in the twentieth-century world economy, and already by 1900 it was producing more steel than Britain. So, too, was Germany. Both the United States and Germany were ahead, too, in the use of electricity, such a fascinating source of power that it encouraged something like a cult: Henry Adams, an American visitor to the Paris Exhibition of 1900, could compare it with the thirteenth-century cult of the Virgin Mary.[25] Nonetheless, despite sometimes bitter, sometimes grudging British recognition of the fact that Britain was no longer the 'workshop of the world', as it had been at the time of the Great Exhibition in 1851, British industry was not in eclipse. Old industries were not wiped out. Birmingham, Manchester and Glasgow were among Europe's leading industrial centres.

During the 1890s the condition of the British economy was as complex and at times as controversial as the position of British 'culture', not least when it was assessed in terms of industrial productivity. The figures were open to debate. There was no doubt, however, that profit margins had fallen since the 1870s. There had been complaints too since the late 1870s of a great depression, affecting industry and agriculture, and while Queen Victoria's reign ended in an incontrovertible 'blaze of economic prosperity' the complaints were not stilled. In 1897 a book by the Duke of Bedford on the recent history of his 'ruined' estate, complete with statistics, served as a landowners' manifesto. There was a gloomy reaction too to the 1901 census figures showing a decline for the first time in the numbers of people working in textile factories. Nonetheless, the Duke of Bedford's selective figures ignored some of the more profitable sectors of his estate management, and the spinning capacity of the cotton industry was to increase by more than a quarter in the decade that was to follow. Even in the new electrical industry (power plant and traction) investment was substantial during the 1890s, and the tempo was to increase during the next decade. Part of the investment was American: Westinghouse and General Electric were among the huge American firms that were involved.

Meanwhile, Germany – and in this case France – played a bigger role in the early development of the automobile than Britain; and when F. W. Lanchester, inventor of the first British-made motor car in 1896, set up a company to exploit it in 1900, the business was not a success. The growth of the British motor car industry was to come later, and there was no early British counterpart to Henry Ford, the son of Irish immigrants to the United States, who after working as chief engineer of the Edison Company in Detroit formed along with others the Detroit Motor Company in 1899.

In Britain, there was worker as well as managerial resistance to the kind of standardisation of plant which Ford had pioneered and which had already developed in other branches of engineering. Frederick Winslow Taylor, 'father of scientific management', had been born in 1865, two years after

97. Automobile luxury was the theme of lavish advertising and scathing cartoons. Like other luxury, it depended on a plentiful supply of servants. An advertisement for a motor show in 1904.

Ford, and, although he did not publish his *Principles of Scientific Management* until 1911, he wrote his *Adjustment of Wages to Efficiency* in 1896. A year later there was a protracted strike in the British engineering industry which pitted the strong trade union, the Amalgamated Society of Engineers, against the newly founded and even stronger Engineering Employer's Federation. It ended in the defeat of the union without encouraging any significant shift in employers' attitudes to technological change.

Industry on both sides of the Atlantic clearly had two sides, and there were other bitter disputes in Britain, including a lock-out of the coal miners in 1893; and when in 1901 a legal verdict in the Taff Vale case overturned the assumption that trade-union funds were protected by law under the Trade Union Act of 1871, the trade unions were driven to using politics to demand remedial legislation. Unskilled workers had also been drawn into the struggles since the 1880s, which ended with the great dock strike of 1889, a strike that they won.

98. Down the mine. The start of a miners' shift, 1900. The dark world underground was a world of disasters as well as of work. From time to time there were bitter miners' strikes.

It was in a mood of resistance that the trade unions entered the twentieth century, having joined with socialist organisations to create the Labour Representative Committee at a meeting held in Farringdon Street, London, in February 1900. Seven years earlier, Keir Hardie, who had emerged from a coal-mining background, had become the leader of the new Independent Labour Party, brought into existence in industrial Bradford and one of a number of socialist organisations. However, the broader grouping of 1900 which was to lead to the creation of the Labour Party in 1906 included non-socialists as well as socialists. From its beginning the party was characterised by diversity, but its secretary, J. Ramsay MacDonald, was in 1924 to become Britain's first Labour prime minister, after the party had gained in strength and in organisation.

It had little immediate impact on what happened in the workplace, where the eminent French historian of Britain, Élie Halévy, who frequently visited the country and admired its institutions, concluded that there was frequent tacit collusion between both 'sides', employers and workers.[26] He also made much, as many far-sighted Englishmen did, of the inadequacies of the educational system. There were few ladders between the board schools and the higher reaches of education, and even near the base technical education, in particular, was rightly considered backward. Managerial education was unknown, except on the job. The benefits of scale were not fully appreciated.

It was in the oldest industries, textiles and coal, which had paid little attention to education and which had depended to only a limited extent on science, that Britain remained strongest. Early British industrialisation had depended on cheap coal: now, although the United States produced more coal, cheap British coal was fuelling other countries' industrialisation also, and coal exports, like coal output, were to rise to a peak in the four years before the cataclysm of 1914. (The only nightmare was that coal supplies would run out.) Coal miners were working in what were often difficult and dangerous conditions, and it was in some of the 'coal fields' that the antagonism of 'capital and labour' was most obvious. In other industries there could still be a deep sense of shared pride, strongest perhaps in the case of the shipping industry, which carried British exports around the world: Britain still ruled the waves, and throughout the 1890s controlled more registered shipping tonnage than the rest of the world put together. British shipping, too, seemed to offer an example: Japan was one of the 'new countries' which profited from it.

Closely associated with this British dominance of the oceans was control of the world's banking and insurance systems. The 'gentlemanly capitalism' of the City of London always depended on water – and paper – not on machines. The financial power of the City, with the Bank of England, a private institution, at the hub of the system, was so strong that the world, old and new, seemed to depend upon it. The golden sovereign was the supreme unit of currency, and the capital market flourished as net foreign investment rose from the equivalent of 67 per cent of gross domestic investment in the 1880s to 90 per cent in the years leading up to 1914. These were years when belief in the gospel of free trade and the authority of a self-adjusting gold

99. The power of Money. The Bank of England, a private institution nicknamed 'The Old Lady of Threadneedle Street', was at the centre of an expanding world economy. Its Governor, often criticised by other bankers was appointed on a rotating basis. The half-yearly General Court, consisting largely of non-bankers, met in the Bank Parlour, shown here in 1903.

standard remained the props of economic orthodoxy, even though there were provincial British industrialists, some of them never seeking to claim to be 'gentlemen', who were disturbed that their own interests seemed to be sacrificed in the process. Demands for protectionism were heard, for example, in Birmingham, although it was not until 1903 that Joseph Chamberlain, the most exciting politician of the period, who had crossed sides, came out to lead an unsuccessful, Edwardian crusade in favour of it.[27] Then and earlier, businessmen, like poets and novelists, usually spoke with more than one voice.

During the 1890s all kinds of orthodoxy were under attack – in manners and morals as much as in economics. Respectability was as much under scrutiny, therefore, as thrift. 'The more things a man is ashamed of, the more respectable he is,' Shaw was to write in *Man and Superman* (1903), directing attention, as he often did, to what he considered a core of guilt. 'To recommend thrift to the poor', Oscar Wilde wrote in his *Soul of Man under Socialism* (1891), 'is both grotesque and insulting. It is like advising a man who is starving to eat less. For a town or country labourer to practise thrift would be absolutely immoral.'

Wilde's epigrams should be set alongside the analysis of the effects of thrift in J. A. Hobson and A. F. Mummery's *Physiology of Industry* (1889), in which the argument was advanced – in flat contradiction of Samuel Smiles – that excessive saving was responsible for the under-employment of capital and labour in periods of bad trade at the troughs of the trade cycle. They should also be set alongside the statistics of the poor which Charles Booth, member of a prosperous Liverpool shipping family, had set out laboriously to collect and to classify during the late 1880s. Booth believed that cycles of booms and slumps were not only inevitable but useful, and he wanted to discover the facts of poverty, however it was produced.[28]

The first edition of what was to become a massive survey, *Labour and Life of the People,* volume I, *East London*, appeared in 1889. Volume VIII, which appeared in 1896, dealt with 'population classified by trades'. Booth began with public service and the professional classes, the numbers of which had increased significantly enough during the last years of the century, when they became sufficiently highly organised for the social historian Harold Perkin to be able to treat their rise as the major social trend of the period. Domestic service came next in Booth's categories: in the country as a whole out of four million women in employment in 1901 nearly half were in domestic service. On their drudgery or dedication – often both – the comfort of the large late-Victorian middle-class family depended, and no account of the period would be complete without registering their presence.

Their numbers varied, however: in Hampstead there were eighty female domestics to every hundred occupiers (in industrial Rochdale there were only seven, an index in itself of regional variation in Britain), and in Westminster there were no fewer than twelve manservants for every hundred occupiers. Booth's third category consisted of the '"unoccupied" classes', who included 'pensioners' (there was still no state-supported old-age pensions scheme, although Booth himself favoured one) and 'inmates of institutions', who lived carefully controlled lives out of sight.

The Victorians, impressive though they were in the creation and maintenance of 'charities', had created in parallel formidable public institutions which imposed tough disciplines on 'paupers' ('workhouses'), on 'lunatics' ('asylums') and on prisoners. They were so treated at the behest of better-off people, who thought of themselves as guardians of values and, equally important in an age dedicated to low taxation, custodians of the public purse. The workhouse, systematised in the pre-Victorian poor law of 1834, was still '*the* institution' for its inmates as much as for its guardians; and, although its disciplines had been relaxed during the last stages of Queen Victoria's reign, its role was still primarily as a deterrent. It was incapable of dealing adequately with the increasingly publicised problem of 'unemployment'. Nor was the prison capable of eliminating the activities of what was thought of as a 'criminal class'. There were still beggars in the streets, with charity, not the poor law, providing their only support, a charity that, however sharp the criticism, deliberately discriminated against the 'undeserving poor'.

The physical presence of the deprived was obvious in London and the great cities, as was the presence of the unemployed in small towns with vulnerable single industries, the fortunes of which registered the movements of the trade cycle. Some of the *Yellow Book* writers, fascinated by the sights of London, by night more than by day, left their own impressions. Thus Richard le Gallienne, an articulate if usually uninspired contributor, later self-exiled to the United States where he survived deep into the twentieth century, described in a prose-fancy of 1897 how the Sphinx, a favourite 1890s creature, 'telegraphed a smile' to a 'poor cab-opener' and dropped a large coin in his outstretched palm.[29]

'Among the many lessons' le Gallienne claimed to have learned from the Sphinx was 'the fair wage of the cab-opener'. 'When the red flags wave on the barricades, and the puddles of red blood beneath the great guillotine in Trafalgar Square luridly catch the setting sun, the Sphinx and I will have a friend in that poor cab-opener.' A more haunting set of images was offered by John Davidson in his *Fleet Street Eclogue* for St George's Day:

> I cannot hush! The poor,
> The maimed, the halt, the starving come
> Crying for help at every door.

There was as wide a gap between such deprived people and the 'working classes' as there was between the working classes, a heterogeneous group, and the equally heterogeneous middle classes, some of whom lived in straitened circumstances, described in a word now largely lost as 'penury'.

Class differences were firmly acknowledged. So, too, were social scandals. Jack London, delving into the depths, has described a place outside a hospital where:

> scraps were heaped high on a huge platter in an indescribable mess – pieces of bread, chunks of grease and fat pork . . . all the leavings from the fingers and mouths of the sick ones suffering from all manner of diseases. Into this mess the [poor] plunged their hands, digging, pawing, turning over, examining, rejecting and scrambling for. It wasn't pretty. Pigs could have done worse. But the poor devils were hungry.

By contrast, there was never any doubt that during the last years of the nineteenth century the working classes (when employed) were better fed than they had been in the earlier decades of the century. Real wages rose between 1861 and 1881 by 37 per cent and during the 1880s by a further 19 per cent; and from the 1870s onwards cheap American corn had begun to arrive in the country in large quantities, while refrigerated meat and fruit from Australia, New Zealand, Argentina and other parts of the world broadened daily diets. The annual consumption of sugar per household, 35 pounds in the first decades of Queen Victoria's reign, had reached 85 pounds by the end. It was already being claimed, although there were huge social contrasts (and continuing regional contrasts) in food consumption, as there were in housing and in health, that the luxuries of yesterday, thanks in considerable measure to 'imperialism', were becoming the necessities of today. The 'consumer age' so long long heralded, had now indubitably begun.

By the time that Booth's seventeenth volume, which included an index map of London, appeared in 1903, B. S. Rowntree had published his more politically influential *Poverty: A Study of Town Life* (1901), which gave carefully collected details of working-class family expenditure in York, an ancient city which had become a railway capital. Whatever social gains there had been, poverty there, Rowntree demonstrated, was as great as it was in the metropolis. A Quaker cocoa and chocolate manufacturer whose moral values were beyond doubt, Rowntree had started work on his survey in 1898, developing in the course of his enquiries what to him was a clear distinction between 'primary' and 'secondary' poverty, the latter characterised by family income that would have been adequate had not some of it been absorbed by other 'wasteful' expenditure. This included drink and gambling (a national pastime that united members of the working classes and the aristocracy), but also – for Rowntree was driven to draw hard lines in order to convince his readers – newspapers, books and entertainment.[30] He was dealing, as was Booth, not so much with individuals as with families, for it was the housewife who was forced to cope with the implications of her husband's 'wasteful' expenditure, and with how to bring up children.

The ways of life of working-class families – and they varied from one occupation and from one part of the country to another – were so different from those of middle-class families that it was difficult to communicate. Margaret Loane, a sensible district nurse who wrote several books, 'doubted if any real conversation between members of two classes is possible. All my conversations with my patients and their families have been of an exceedingly one-sided character.' And when Henrietta Barnett, wife of the founder of London's Toynbee Hall, the mission centre located in the East End in Whitechapel, exhorted the Metropolitan Association for Befriending Young Servants to counsel the girls to turn to the 'wholesale reading of monthly periodicals' she stressed how different they were from 'girls of our own class whose ignorance about sin we foster for fear of losing their innocence'. 'The girls, alas! many of them with naturally coarse minds . . . are conversant already with all the terrible facts of life.'[31]

Working-class families, larger than middle-class families, were all too aware of the facts of life, and while most were supremely 'respectable', there were others that they – and observers – knew to be genuine 'problem families'. The middle-class family itself, which was to be treated by John Galsworthy in terms of a saga, was still considered by most Victorians as 'the unit upon which a constitutional government has been raised which is the culmination and envy of mankind'. Yet it too had its problems, and during the last years of the nineteenth century it began to be regarded by rebels as authoritarian and despotic, cramping the life of mother and children alike. Moreover, the very conditions of happiness inside it began to be associated with 'illusions' and 'shams'. In his *Quintessence of Ibsenism* (1891), George Bernard Shaw, one of the most articulate rebels, concentrated on this theme. 'The family as a beautiful and holy national institution' was only 'a fancy picture'. Another rebel, Samuel Butler, whose *Way of All Flesh* was published posthumously in 1903, went further and claimed that families created more unhappiness than any other institution. 'The mischief among the lower classes is not so great, but among the middle classes it is killing a large number daily.'

The problems of the family – and of class relations – seldom reached the headlines during the late-Victorian years. Nor did those of the royal family. They were sometimes discussed, however, in correspondence columns. In most respects the role of the press at the centennial moment was crucial. It did much to herald it and even more to proclaim it. The Marquess of Salisbury might profess never to read daily newspapers and to have nothing

but contempt for the *Daily Mail* which he dismissed as 'a journal produced by office boys for office boys'. Yet when Frederic Harrison, a prolific writer and reviewer and the most famous of the Positivists, wrote his *Autobiographical Memoirs* in 1911, he described and interpreted 'the marvellous development of the Press' and with it 'the millennium of advertisement' which he had witnessed in his own lifetime. His choice of the adjective 'marvellous' did not imply that he approved of that aspect of nineteenth-century development, for he went on to assert that the press was 'a sort of monstrous megaphone which magnifies and multiplies the popular voice'. 'Politics, literature, art, manners' were now within 'the sphere of influence' of the daily press, which could make and mar 'governments, reputations, opinions and customs . . . Photography, wood pulp, and hungry journalists combine to make the world one great advertising bazaar.'[32]

It was the press, with the help of Kaiser Wilhelm II, that determined the perception of when the old century would end and a new century would begin. In correspondence in *The Times* some people demanded that the start of the new century should be 1 January 1900, a Monday, but others claimed that the world would have to wait until 1 January 1901, leading one of the former to suggest that 'a short Act of Parliament' should be introduced to

100 and 101. Unhappy families – deprived, in the East End of London, 1912 – and better off – in 1907 Bloomsbury. Both were patriarchal. In richer families, aristocratic and plutocratic, there was an upstairs/downstairs division (*A Bloomsbury Family* was painted by William Orpen).

make the first date stand. And although a correspondent to the *Illustrated London News* put his trust in 'the unreasoning habit of arithmetic, which will not allow a hundred to be ninety nine', Wilhelm II ostentatiously demonstrated that he did not choose to do so. He ordered the new century to be hailed on 1 January 1900 with a salute of thirty-three guns. Meanwhile, across the Atlantic, the *New York Times* devoted nearly four columns to a retrospective review of the nineteenth century on 21 December 1899, claiming optimistically that the world was now 'facing a still brighter dawn of civilization'; and at 12.01 a.m. on 1 January 1900 two young German Americans, hoping to be the first couple to be married in the twentieth century, went before the altar in New Jersey. Not surprisingly, there was talk of the new century clasping hands with the old.

Notes

1. For contributions to the *Quarterly Review* see W. Houghton, ed., *The Wellesley Index to Victorian Periodicals* (Toronto, 1966), pp. 692–782.
2. For the lengthening of the time span and history of the term 'prehistoric', first used in 1851 the year of the Great Exhibition, see P. Bowler, *The Invention of Progress, the Victorians and the Past* (London, 1989).

3. Chapter 8 of the detailed study by S. Koss, *The Rise and Fall of the Political Press in Britain: the Nineteenth Century* (London, 1981) is called 'Fin de Siècle'. For Northcliffe the huge biography by R. Pound and G. Harmsworth, *Northcliffe* (London, 1959) is indispensable. For a contemporary note on 'the new journalism' see E. M. Phillips, 'The New Journalism' in the *New Review*, August 1895. See also A. J. Lee, *The Origins of the Popular Press in England, 1855–1914* (London, 1976).

4. Address to the Institute of Electrical Engineers, October 1889.

5. Pentecostalism, far stronger in the United States than in Britain, developed the camp meeting, and American Evangelists could attract substantial audiences on the British side of the Atlantic. Dwight L. Moody and Ira D. Sankey campaigned in England for the first time in 1873. The Salvation Army, the most successful indigenous organisation, later active everywhere, was more interested in space than in time. William Booth, who published *In Darkest England and the Way Out* in 1890, with the cooperation of W.T. Stead, talked of carrying 'the Blood of Christ and the Fire of the Holy Ghost into every corner of the globe'.

6. Some people had given the eighteenth century a number, and the *London Chronicle*, 2 January 1801, noted how 'the good *Old Lady* known by the name of the EIGHTEENTH CENTURY, who resigned all sublunary cares on Wednesday night last, was quietly buried in the family vault of *Eternity*'.

7. See G. Tillotson, *A View of Victorian Literature* (London, 1978), p. 1.

8. See. P. Murray, *Le 19e Siècle à travers les âges* (Paris, 1984).

9. A. R. Wallace, *The Wonderful Century* (1898), p. 2.

10. See C. H. Pearson, *National Life and Character, a Forecast* (1894), esp. chs 4 and 5.

11. For Rhodes see J. G. Lockhart and C. M. Woodhouse, *Rhodes* (London, 1964), esp. pp. 24ff. W. T. Stead 'admitted' that 'the dread he inspired among those who disliked him was more widespread than the affection he commanded from those who came within the magic of his presence' (W. T. Stead, *The Last Will and Testament of Cecil John Rhodes* (London, 1902), p. 51.)

12. For the relief of Ladysmith and reactions to it see J. Montgomery, *1900, The End of an Era* (London, 1968), pp. 50ff.

13. *Punch*, CVII 1896.

14. See S. Weintraub, *The Yellow Book: Quintessence of the Nineties* (New York, 1964) and K. L. Mix, *A Study in Yellow* (Kansas and London, 1960).

15. H. Jackson, *The Eighteen Nineties* (Pelican edn, Harmondsworth, 1939), p. 117.

16. See J. Stokes, *In the Nineties* (New York and London, 1989), pp. 115ff.

17. See C. Wilson, *A History of Unilever*, Vol. 1 (London, 1954).

18. M.Nordau, *Degeneration* (London, 1895), p. 100. See also his 'A reply to my Critics' in *Century*, vol. 28 (1895), pp. 547–51.

19. In June 1894 Beerbohm, twenty-four years old, collected his early essays into *Works* (London, 1894) which also included a bibliography.

20. H. D. Traill, *The New Fiction and other Essays* (London, 1897), p. 1.

21. See A. Briggs, 'The Pleasure Telephone: A Chapter in the Pre-History of the Media' in *Collected Essays*, vol. 3 (New York and London, 1991), pp. 77–98.

22. See Montgomery, *op. cit.*, ch. 12, 'Animated Pictures'.

23. For contemporary prophecies see C. Marvin, *When Old Technologies Were New* (London and New York, 1988).

24. For Langley's failure to produce a satisfactory flying machine and the success of the Wright brothers, who started as fixers and sellers of bicycles, see R. M. Haynes, *The Wright Brothers* (Englewood Cliffs, New Jersey, 1991).

25. Adams went to the 1900 Exposition with Langley. For his record of his experiences see *The Education of Henry Adams* (New York, 1903).

26. Halévy's *History of the English People* covered the period from 1815 to 1850 and left a gap between then and 1895 (English translation, London, 1938). He noted that he felt that when he reached 1895 he was dealing with a different country.

27. See B. W. E. Alford, *Britain in the World Economy since 1880* (London, 1996); and D. Kynaston, *The City of London*, vol. 2, 'The Golden Years' (London, 1995).

28. H. Perkin, *The Rise of Professional Society: England since 1880* (London, 1989).
29. *The Savoy*, vol. 1 (1897). After the end of *The Savoy*, Le Gallienne wrote for a time for the *Daily Mail*.
30. B. S. Rowntree, *Poverty* (London, 1902), pp. 133–4.
31. See R. T. McKibbin in the *Transactions of the Royal Historical Society*, vol. 28 (1989).
32. F. Harrison, *Autobiographical Memoirs* (1911), Preface.

102. The Ferris Wheel: a British Airways project for a millennial wheel for London's South Bank that recalls the nineteenth century.

THE 1990s
The Final Chapter

Asa Briggs

'The sense of an ending is not a fact of nature,' wrote Frank Kermode in a study of the theory of fiction which appeared in 1968, an exciting year when the events of the present, *les événements*, dominated the headlines.[1] Everything everywhere seemed possible: all things were interconnected in what was proclaimed as a great 'global village'. It was during the turbulent but hopeful 1960s, still regarded by many as a decade 'on trial', that the experiences of the Second World War faded into the background. Yet the Cold War continued, and the nuclear bomb lay in the background, for a protesting minority the agent of apocalypse, for the majority the means of effective deterrence in a world divided by ideology as well as by interest.

There was talk now of a generation gap, and, although the century had many years still to run, Kenneth Boulding could write a book called *The Meaning of the Twentieth Century* in 1964 when the decade was little more than half-way through. At the end of the decade in 1969, the year when Britain's first Concorde 'roared into the skies', Neil Armstrong was the first man to step on to the moon, 'one small step for a man, one giant leap for mankind'. Space beckoned. A generation later, in 1994, the novelist Ian McEwan, a graduate of Sussex, the first of the new universities of the 1960s, which were designed to change the pattern and content of higher education, suggested, as the twentieth century was reaching its natural ending, that it should be treated as 'a gigantic sprawling novel' in which 'the plot thickens for the final chapter'. 'No one can put it down.'[2]

The century, he correctly insisted, had had many themes, not one, some connected, some disparate, but he did not go on to speculate on how the century might end nor point to possible alternative endings. Indeed, he did not mention the future once. He was wise in this, for since the late 1950s and 1960s, when speculation about the shape of the future began to quicken and predictive models were devised, there had been many largely unforeseen economic and political surprises – and these despite the fact that the study

of the future outside and inside science fiction had become more sophisticated than it had been before in history.

In the Soviet Union, which had inaugurated the space age with Sputnik in
1957, a book on *Life in the Twenty-First Century* had appeared with great
speed two years afterwards,[3] and eleven years later Denis Gabor in Britain,
who talked of 'inventing the future', published his book *Innovations:
Scientific, Technological and Social*. This was in the same year as Alvin
Toffler's best-seller *Future Shock* appeared. 'In the three short decades
between now and the turn of the millennium', Toffler warned, 'millions of
psychologically normal people will experience an abrupt collision with the
future.'[4] They would be 'strangers in a strange land'. Meanwhile, the Club of
Rome, founded in 1968, looked beyond the millennium, pointing to limits to
growth rather than growth itself.

References to the 'millennium' introduced what was to become a familiar
new element into what had already come to be called 'futurology', and as the
new millennium drew nigh the more frequent the references. Yet neither the
conclusions of the Club of Rome nor of Toffler went unchallenged. Critics
of the Club queried its methodology and its selectiveness. Early critics of
Toffler were not impressed by his preoccupation with technological change,
and in 1972 Krishan Kumar wrote in the magazine *Futures* of 'inventing the
future in spite of futurology'.[5] (The plural in the title of the magazine was
significant.) In 1969 Boulding had been right to tell his readers that 'the
testing of images of the future is unfortunately all too easy; all we have to do
is to wait and observe until the future becomes the past'.[6]

In looking ahead technology seemed easiest to envisage, and what subsequently happened to it was easiest to test. Yet few forecasters saw the
imminent dependence of business and individuals on 'fax', while the speed
of diffusion of more sophisticated technologies could never be predicted
with any certainty. The ramifications were open but vast. Throughout the
rest of the century the development of the computer, one of Gabor's main
themes and the key to much else in development, including space travel, was
to influence directly what happened in the skies, in the place of work and in
the home, and in thought and play, turning what had once been science
fiction into scientific fact. It affected manufacturing, distribution, banking
and, not least, communications, with the Americans inventing the ugly word
'compunication' to describe the first technological and social 'convergences'.
The latest of them was to be digitalisation, and by then computers had
diminished extraordinarily in size, against what had first been predicted,
now reaching the desk top. 'If the spirit of 1968 was counter culture,' *The
Times* wrote in 1988, 'the spirit of 1988 [not yet a whole generation on] is
surely the microchip. The sociologist has given way to the computer
programmer.' And much was to happen to microchips, storage capacity, lap-
top computers and computer programmers after that.[7]

103. Computer power is employed in games as well as in the laboratory, the factory and the office. It is a universal force, as is as shown in this cartoon from the *Philadelphia Inquirer*.

The human implications of technological change, including massive structural unemployment, created apprehension and a sense of uncertainty, particularly among those facing redundancy, some of them too old to find new jobs, some of them in hitherto secure occupations. There might also be robots around the corner.[8] There was concern, too, in some circles about new patterns of ownership and control not least of the 'media', a blanket word that included elements that were different in content, influence and impact, although almost all undergoing fundamental technological change. Technology, old or new, routine or run-away, must always be related to ownership – just as much in late twentieth-century conditions as in the early years of 'carboniferous capitalism'. The formation of huge global mergers during the last decades of the century strengthened the sense among some of the critics that in human organisation 'small is beautiful' and that cultural 'globalisation', which encompasses both information and entertainment, is not. Meanwhile, the roller-coaster advance of 'consumer culture', dependent on mass communications, mass credit and massive advertising, continued, though it was bound to disturb resistant minorities.

One cultural minority – that which was devoted to the study of 'culture' – increasingly large because of changes in education, was drawn into intense, intricate and incestuous debate about the meaning of 'the contemporary'. The much used, if awkward, word 'post-modern', one of a cluster of late twentieth-century adjectives beginning with 'post' (among them 'post-Christian', 'post-industrial', 'post-structural' and even 'post-cultural') deliberately blurred all boundaries.[9] Yet while most exponents of post-modernism rejected history, the adjective 'post-modern' was itself a historical label, a chronological indicator, however vague.[10] Moreover, while post-modernist writers claimed to be involved inextricably in the post-modern 'popular culture' that they were describing – and not to be separated from it by a 'critical distance' – they theorised about it in such self-absorbed fashion – and with so much cross reference to the opinions of others among their own spokesmen – that they separated themselves totally from the people whom they were describing.

The word 'inflation' has been applied to post-modernist language, which owed as much to anthropology as to sociology.[11] In its narrower sense, however, inflation was a preoccupation not of minorities but of the majority. As for technology, it generated a great increase in material wealth, but not everyone shared in it. Poor people and poor countries became relatively, if not absolutely, poorer during the 1980s and 1990s. Gaps widened both in Britain and in the United States. It needed not sociology but 'political economy', an old political framework revived, to explain what was happening. It was possible during the 1970s, the prelude to all that followed, for high inflation rates and large-scale unemployment ('stagflation') to coexist. It was inevitable, however, during the 1980s and 1990s that the play of market forces, accompanied by lower direct taxation and a shift to indirect taxation, would widen domestic inequalities. It was inevitable also that infrastructures of cities would be under-financed while expensive new private housing developments were on offer and while a new infrastructure would be created for carrying cable-information and entertainment, the staples of 'post-modern' analysis.[12] Meanwhile, economic questions concerning priorities, questions that had often been overlooked during the previous quarter-century of economic growth and social transformation, returned to perplex a generation that had experienced neither 'austerity' nor 'affluence'.

There were 'crises' too. The first of them, the 'oil crisis' of 1973, which seriously jolted the economic and social system, came before Boulding had explained to his readers how quickly the future turned into the past. It was an exceptional crisis, however, which ushered in a sequence of surprises. Its origins related less to 'oil' resources, which were the preoccupation of the Club of Rome, or to the statistics of energy use or automobile numbers (expressed in two-car garages and new 'motorways'), which were the preoccupation of critics of consumer culture, than to the politics of oil and the determination of oil prices. And after it was over its consequences were not widely understood. Arab surpluses deposited in banks that revelled in cross-boundary transactions made their way to Latin American countries that were already in debt. There would soon be a global bill to pay.

In the midst of this first international crisis there were two general elections in Britain in one year, 1974 (both of them lost by the Conservatives under Edward Heath), which avoided such issues and focused instead on coal, the oldest of Britain's resources. Coal was also to be at the centre of British politics ten years later after Heath's successor, Margaret Thatcher, Britain's first woman prime minister took office in 1979 following a grim 'winter of discontent' when trade-union power to disrupt reached its peak: Thatcher was to defeat the National Union of Miners in a protracted and bitter strike in 1984–5. The character, scale and reporting of the political upheaval of these years proved that in an age of computers Britain was still not a 'post-industrial society'. It was dogged by its past. And it proved, too, that consensus politics were over. At the same time, with the substitution of Thatcher for Heath the possibilities of Britain playing a major role in collective European advance diminished. That would have given it a stake in the future. Heath's continuing belief in Europe, a belief which had inspired Britain's entry into the European Community under his leadership, contrasted with the scepticism of many Conservatives and the hostility of many socialists.

Technology permitted a massive increase in miners' productivity during the 1970s. Coal, however – at least British coal – was doomed, and during the ten years that followed large numbers of mines were closed, including

104. Industrial conflict in 1984 centred on coal as it had done so often in the past. The police intervened in the Orgreave picket lines in a highly organised, costly and controversial operation.

the last deep coal mine in South Wales. There was symbolism in this, and nostalgia, for coal had been the basis of the industrial revolution and of the Victorian economy; mining communities were being destroyed, and the social costs were not adequately measured. As the twentieth century drew to its close the 'mining heritage' fascinated historians – and industrial archaeologists – far more than it did political economists. Trade-union resistance won sympathy. Trade-union leaders won less; their own tactics were questionable. Within ten years their voices would no longer thrill even the Trades Union Congress.

Ironically, oil, discovered in the North Sea in 1970, was a new source of economic wealth for Britain after it began to flow in 1975. The importance of 'energy policy' was recognised in Britain – and became an issue again in the early 1990s – yet there was a current of continuing complaint that after the first profits of oil had passed into private pockets the policy was muddled, leaving the public in the dark. Nor did the privatisation of gas, sold as an industry in one piece, and electricity, where two generating companies were set up, eliminate distortions in the domestic markets for fuel. The Thatcher governments and their immediate successor were committed to privatisation, however, and the climax of the policy, which also included the privatisation of water, was to be the privatisation of coal itself and of the railways.

During what came to be thought of as a 'Thatcher regime' or even a 'Thatcher era', which lasted in changing circumstances from 1979 to 1990, the prime minister, who gave her name to an adjective, Thatcherite, and to an *ism*, Thatcherism, totally un-post modern, demonstrated a remarkable ability to set the domestic political agenda for all the main political parties. She also exerted influence, sometimes through an understanding with President Reagan, sometimes through conversion, sometimes through aggravation, on international politics.[13] There were both 'crises' and surprises under Thatcher, beginning with the Falkland Islands crisis, when a nationalist Britain displayed independent political and military power in its dispute with authoritarian Argentina, and ending on the world stage with the most remarkable sequence of crises and surprises of all – the collapse in 1989 of Soviet power and, in the confident opinion of most observers at the time, Marxism with it.

The dramatic events of 1989, the bicentenary year of the French Revolution, included the fall of communist regimes in central and eastern Europe and the pulling down of the great wall separating the two Berlins. The events were largely unforecast except, it has been claimed unconvincingly, by Nostradamus, who was said to have prophesied the beginning of the Russian Revolution in 1917 and the European Community presidency of Jacques Delors in Brussels.[14] It was on west European issues, which were to change in character after the upheavals in the east, that Margaret Thatcher

105. Transformation scene:
Lenin gives way to a Marilyn
Monroe look-alike on May Day
in Moscow, 1990.

foundered, losing her office of prime minister in 1990 in what one back-
bench MP compared to an Elizabethan tragedy. It was a dangerous
comparison. The divisions of the party that were to loom large in the post-
Thatcher period, a party led by her own chosen successor, John Major, were
already there, and they were to last into the late 1990s. He won the general
election of 1992: she probably would not have.

As a result of internal strains in his party Major could not profit from
concessions that he won at a European Community conference at Maastricht
in 1991, and he found it increasingly difficult on his return, as criticism in the
press grew ever louder, to control Conservative politics. Meanwhile, the
Labour Party, which in the past had been renowned for its own inner
divisions on Europe, gained in strength in opposition, now supporting the
newly named European Union. Under its 'modernised' leadership, first
under John Smith, then under an untried but publicity-conscious Tony
Blair, 'new' became the essential adjective. Nonetheless, with a general
election pending and bound to take place in or by 1997, how Britain would
or could fare in Europe remained problematic. The decision about whether
to join a European currency at a future date, which Major wished to consider
pragmatically, seemed symbolic, and his decision to disrupt the Union's
political processes after 'Europe' had banned all British beef exports in the

wake of 'mad cow disease' imperilled what had hitherto been Britain's chief European concern – the establishment of an open European market. Throughout the story most sections of the press, not least in poster headlines, talked chauvinistically of confrontation between Britain and Europe, as if Britain were not itself a part of Europe, and 'blamed' Brussels for much for which it had no responsibility. The gap was huge between European federalists who put their faith in a twenty-first century 'new Europe' and those British politicians of all parties who clung tenaciously, as Thatcher had done, to an outdated concept of sovereignty. Meanwhile, many old links with the Commonwealth were scrapped. The Empire had faded into history, with Gibraltar and Hong Kong as awkward residues.

The European Community would doubtless have been more integrated had it not been for the political and ideological transformations in Eastern Europe, welcomed in Britain, which began (or seemed to begin) in Hungary in March 1989 and which followed on in domino-like fashion (to borrow an earlier Vietnam metaphor), changing European and world balances.[15] Yet nowhere were the transformations more welcome than in Germany, the dominant power in the European Community (though not without its own economic and social problems), where Helmut Kohl, who, like Thatcher, was to preside over a regime as well as a period of history, profited immediately. The collapse of the Berlin Wall, a symbol of liberation, and the unification of the two Germanies were more important events for the future of European politics than any event in recent British history. They seemed in a sense to mark the end of a period which has been described as 'the short twentieth century', a century which itself had begun not in 1900 but in 1914.[16]

What happened in 1989 further east had already had such wide-ranging consequences that they led one American writer, Francis Fukuyama, far from the scene of European action, to talk not of the end of a century – or of the end of an era – but of the end of history itself, *post-histoire*. The phrase, which had been used many times before in different contexts, carried what was taken to be 'good news' in that for many people it seemed that the victory of 'liberal democracy' constituted 'the end point of mankind's ideological evolution' and 'the final form of human government'. With it, Fukuyama himself claimed, the Hegelian and Marxist sense of history as a single and coherent process disappeared.

In an article of 1979, which had been as much publicised as the article in which Fukuyama first set out his findings, Jeane Kirkpatrick, briefly placed in political office in the United States and with her eyes fixed more on Latin America than on Europe, had written that 'the history of this century provides no grounds for expecting that radical authoritarian regimes will transform themselves'. That is why what happened a decade later in Europe's east seemed genuinely 'good news'. Yet Fukuyama declared himself unhappy about the outcome, believing that much would disappear from life in 'the old age of mankind', including 'the willingness to risk one's life for a purely abstract goal'. 'The world-wide ideological struggle that called forth daring, courage, imagination and idealism' would be replaced by 'economic calculation, the endless solving of technical problems, environmental concerns, and the satisfaction of sophisticated consumer demands'. In the post-historical period there would be neither art nor philosophy, only the perpetual caretaking of the museum of human history.[17] The Last Men would be bored.

Such conclusions were as melancholy as those of Charles Pearson at the end of the nineteenth century.[18] In both centuries, however, a great deal was left out of such analysis, including, in the twentieth century, the future role of Japan, which had difficulty in coming to terms with its own history, and of those parts of the Third World where little history had ever been recorded but where population was growing faster than ever before (the biggest increase being in Africa). There was an underplaying also of the future role of nationalism in Europe, a cause for which men would dare and die, as ambivalent a cause, constructive and destructive, as it had been in the nineteenth century, just as capable of inspiring aggression as of rallying resistance. In the Balkans, in particular, where old Communist Party leaders often remained in power in new guises in 1989, as they did in most of the old states of the Soviet Union, nationalism was to fire cruel civil war in Yugoslavia that ended in an uneasy peace arrived at in 1995, far from the scene of activity in the United States. Meanwhile, anti-semitism was not dead either in the east or in the west of Europe. Nor was xenophobia.

There was more than a trace of the latter, if not of the former, even in Britain, a multi-cultural society, whether it liked it or not, where Eurosceptics were willing to play on and incite populist national prejudice. Both were present in France, where a populist right-wing presidential candidate, Le Pen, could capture 15 per cent of the vote in 1995, a demonstration, as was the whole poll, that there was far more political uncertainty in Europe than there had been before 1989. Many of the people who voted for him were former members of the Communist Party. British politics remained less apparently bizarre, but in Britain even more than in France the media were steadfastly determined during the late 1980s and 1990s to investigate and spotlight the 'failures' (moral as well as political, some of them very strange) of people in 'authority', political, royal, professional, ecclesiastical. Some of the old distinctions between the 'quality' press and the 'tabloids' were narrowed during these years: there was common ownership of both, and both were attracted by the practices of 'investigative journalism' of a kind that seemed to large numbers of people to be an invasion of privacy. Indeed, privacy was as much of a theme of the 1990s as privatisation.

For these reasons neither Britain nor France after 1989 was conforming to a Fukuyama model, not least because there also remained in existence an unrepentant left, vocally represented in trade unions, including the National

Union of Teachers which had power to determine the atmosphere of schools. The biggest trade union in Britain, Unison, represented workers involved in local government and other public services, a very different constituency from coal miners or railway workers. In France transport trade unions were strong enough not only to paralyse Paris but to halt traffic through the Channel Tunnel, a gigantic, technically successful, financially hazardous operation linking two countries that had been separated by sea since prehistoric times. There was little sense of the long-term significance of this in England. Indeed, there seemed far more scope for rhetoric in the 'fish wars' when the Canadian maple-leaf flag flew in the harbour at Falmouth. 'Europe' was being defied.

Everywhere Fukuyama underrated prejudice and cynicism and overrated the attractive power of the word 'liberal', which figured in the title of one of his chapters, 'The Worldwide Liberal Revolution'. Already in 1989 the televised disturbances in June in Beijing's Tian-an-men Square were the prelude not to political liberalism but to a tightening of political authority in a vast country which seemed to many observers far from its borders to be the country of the future.[19] For the Chinese leadership subsequent events in the old Soviet Union (confusion, crime, above all fragmentation) were a warning, not an example. The Communist Party, however much it might embrace market economics, felt that it had to be tough, not soft. Meanwhile, 'liberalism' was never the prevailing philosophy in those countries, not far from China, along or near the 'Pacific rim' which enjoyed great economic growth often accompanied by corruption. There was talk there not of the 'Victorian values' dear to Thatcher but of 'Asian values'. They were proclaimed both in Japan and in South Korea and Malaysia and in Singapore. In the United States itself, with its own Pacific rim, successful Republican campaigns in 1994 and 1995 turned the word 'liberal' into a bogey-word. Even Democrats did not usually choose to employ it. President Clinton's own rhetoric became more conservative in his 1996 'State of the Nation' address when his political position was far stronger than it had been after the Republican victories in Congress.

At a deeper level than the workaday political, Fukuyama had little that was profound to say about a connected subject – religion in all its many versions, Buddhist, Christian, Islamic and Hindu. The versions of each of these religions that most appealed as the century was drawing to a close were often fundamentalist or irrationalist, not liberal. Some of the versions saw Armageddon, not 1989 or 2001, as the end of history. Others, like the richly endowed Asahara cult in Japan, prepared for a grim future – the end of the world – with perverted science. Meanwhile, a series of environmental 'disasters', some of them occurring before 1989, burst through history. Some of them were man-made, like the nuclear explosion in Chernobyl (1986), the chemical horror in Bhopal (1984) and the wreckage of an oil-tanker off

106 and 107. Chinese protest in Tian-an-men Square, Beijing hit the headlines and reached the television screens of the world in 1989; (*above*) laughter and (*below*) tears.

Alaska (1989): others were 'natural', among them droughts, floods, volcanic eruptions and earthquakes, devastating not only Third World countries but 'highly developed' societies like California (1989 and 1994) and Japan and Holland (1995).

Even when there were no disasters to shock people who were able to watch them or their immediate effects on the television screen – the medium which was still felt to have the biggest impact – there was an increasing public interest in the environment during the last decades of the century, making both for more concern and for more controversy, for struggles, indeed, which often called forth 'daring, courage, imagination and idealism'. Inventories of present and future world resources or scientific theories of possible environmental changes like 'global warming', the 'greenhouse effect', the evidence for which mounted, provided insufficiently satisfying fare for 'friends of the earth' who dismissed them as inadequate inter-governmental 'compromises'.

Environmental policy inevitably raised global as well as local, regional and national issues. At a time when grass-roots politics often focused on strictly local issues, the sense of the planet being one – 'Spaceship Earth' – was intensified. The future of the last rainforests, depending as it did on local pressures and resistances, logging and burning, became a global pre-occupation, as did the survival of endangered animal species. These now became topics for international conferences during the last decades of the century, the first of them at Stockholm in 1972, where the fifth principle set out in a Stockholm Declaration on Human Environment stated that 'the non-renewable resources of the earth were to be employed in such a way as to guard against the chances of their future exhaustion and to ensure that benefits from such employment were shared by all mankind'.

The frequent failure of short-term expedients, even when backed by international intervention, emphasised the need for 'sustainable growth' over long periods of time, and how best to achieve this now began to figure both in the manifestos of political parties, most of them committed by the political timetable to the short term, and in research programmes, some of which were financed (if precariously) from public funds. They had science at the core, but were increasingly interdisciplinary in character.

'Sustainable' was a new word to be attached to environmental control of 'Mother Earth', but to be effective 'sustaining' depended on governments taking the advice of 'experts' who did not always agree, resisting strong domestic interests, and finding adequate funds. The failure in effectiveness meant that the first word to be attached to 'environment' – 'crusade' – still did not lose its spell or its force even after the Rio conference on environ-mental issues in 1992. Yet there was a problem too in global crusading, generated in part by the uneven brokership of the media, in that during the 1970s, 1980s and 1990s, as in the 1960s, moral crusades, each with their own dedicated crusaders, also drew in militant fringe groups with a broader agenda and with a willingness, even an eagerness, to act outside the law.

The same groups were often also drawn to resist new pieces of legislation on other issues, like the restrictive British Criminal Justice Bill of 1994, which, as it made its way slowly and cumbrously through Parliament, aroused a wide range of angry protesters, including squatters, 'travellers', supporters of 'animal rights' and anti-hunt saboteurs. Such coalitions of minorities, however uneasy – as they were in protest against the export of live

108. Saving rainforests drew on an action network campaign which mobilised children as well as adults. This is the front cover of *Kids' Action Guide*.

calves – are likely to become a prominent feature in the politics of the next century. 'Conventional' public preoccupations and regular party loyalties may correspondingly be less strong, than they were in the middle years of the twentieth century. The relationship between the 'majority' and 'minorities' of all kinds, some of them 'infiltrated', is a crucial relationship for the future in that it raises the whole question of 'authority' at a deeper level than press publicity. It is not only fundamental in all consideration of 'culture' and the 'social fabric'; it also has serious implications for ballot-box democracy.

The 'majority' – as a concept debatable and open to rhetorical appeal and abuse outside the parliamentary process – is not always silent. Nor between elections does it necessarily abide by the verdicts of its elected representatives. In Britain people who speak in its name (among them the millionaire Sir James Goldsmith) can demand referenda, once thought of as thoroughly 'un-British'. The majority can meet anger with anger, yet it can easily dissolve, for the megaphoned sound of minority voices can induce not anger, fully reported by the media, but 'withdrawal symptoms', not so reported. Apathy is seldom news. In 1974 Michael Pawley, who left out reactions to pressure-group tactics in his chilling book *Private Futures*, concluded that twentieth-century 'withdrawal symptoms' can be prompted both by the commercially based 'consumer culture' and by 'counter cultures' designed to get out of it. For him 'music and drugs, like cars, houses and freezers', were all part of a 'wonderfully complex Western system of technotherapy which converts the pain of isolation into the onanistic pleasure of autonomy'.[20] There, indeed, would be the end of history.

After the collapse of the old Soviet system this 'wonderfully complex' western system can no longer be described simply as 'Western'. It has taken root also in large parts of the old 'Soviet empire' and in the Third World, and it draws some of its resources from Latin America and Asia. It is linked directly with corruption and crime. It may well be that awareness of its interdependences will make some minorities in the west more aggressive in their future tactics than they were in the past. Certainly conservative minorities, sometimes claiming to be the 'moral majority', will react, and as they react in the name of 'law and order', a key factor in the Russian general elections of 1996, they will themselves provoke reaction.

There are other issues too that challenge moral 'consensus', particularly those connected with human life and death, from abortion to euthanasia. Feelings about these are as strong as feelings about the threat to the environment or to wildlife, and they can grow in strength through uncertainty. There is even more uncertainty about the practical ramifications of changes in the life sciences, most of them based on controversial experiments, than there is about the human and social effects of digitalisation or environmental change or of 'black holes' and 'chaos theory'.[21] And 'experts' claiming professional authority show no signs of stopping on the way to further technological application of scientific theory – from various forms of 'gene engineering' to cloning. That 'the coming revolution in biology could overthrow many of our certainties about what it is to be human' was one of the themes in a *New Scientist* supplement on the future in 1994.[22]

There are, of course, other quite different elements in late twentieth-century experience that cast doubt on the notion of 'humanity', for example genocide in Cambodia and Rwanda, the former seen by millions on the television screen, the latter largely hidden, but devastating in its results. Those who flee genocide become despairing refugees, giving an alarming significance to the concluding image in Fukuyama's *End of History*, that of future 'mankind' appearing like 'a long wagon strung out along a road'. There was at least as much 'bad news' after 1989 as there had been before, as much evidence of evil (Satan was in fashion), with some of it focusing on crowds of refugees, most of them fleeing not from ideology but from their former neighbours with whom they had once lived, if uneasily, at peace.

In these circumstances, even leaving out pressing issues of economics, always relevant after 'yippies' had given way to 'yuppies' and the mid-century boom years to recession, it was not easy to stimulate a 'feel-good factor', a new term of the decade, in the Britain of the late 1990s. As the millennium approached, therefore, further separating Britain and the world from the landmark date of 1989, sophisticated versions of the future based either on the presentation through models of possible options or on extrapolation of existing 'megatrends' (the title of a highly successful book by John Naisbit and Patricia Aburdeen in 1982) were not now the versions to command most attention. The Club of Rome disintegrated: John Mortimer was not alone in finding no pleasure in *Megatrends 2000* with its glimpses of 'computerised and electronic joy to all mankind' in the year 2000.[23] Interest quickened instead in continuing argument about how (catastrophically?) the world was born and how it might end. There was also continuing speculation (in the wake of the dinosaurs) about the origins of man.* 'Boxgrove man', the remains of whom were found in a Sussex quarry in 1994, had a human shinbone said to be half a million years old. This was the oldest human bone ever found in Britain.[24]

Naisbit and Aburdeen themselves suggested that in the year 2000 there would be numbers of people clustering around 'a metaphysical bookstore, a spiritual teacher or an educational centre'. And already, before the millennium, bookshops were devoting large sections of their shelves to the 'occult', including, along with angels and demons, astrology, yoga and tarot

109. The New Age in New Zealand: miscellaneous wares on offer in Nelson, 1993.

---

* In 1996 an American university team in a laboratory administered by the Department of Energy claimed to have recreated by computer the call of the dinosaur sound organ (*New York Times*, 12 March 1996).

(an alternative to bridge), and 'alternative medicine', the best-known of alternatives, patronised in 'high', even royal circles. One sub-section was sometimes called 'spiritual and personal development' or, borrowing a Victorian term and using it quite differently, 'self help'. Outside bookshops there were large numbers of 'new age healers' of different kinds, some offering not messages but therapeutic and relaxing massages.

Critics of the intimidating volume of bookshelf material, which also included 'earth mysteries', folklore, and 'aura photography', have dismissed it as 'psychobabble', and critics of 'alternative practices' have described them as dangerous to the body as well as to the mind. Yet an active minority of 'pagan' devotees, proud of the adjective, have had their own sense of time and space in the late twentieth century, no longer content to stay submerged, as were the pagans of the 1890s. They look intently to the distant pasts of prehistory to connect with the distant future and link earth with space through 'extraterrestrial' messages or through the presence of real extra-terrestrials in our midst. They have nothing in common with the American and the Russian space-probers of the 1990s who, having once been space rivals, have joined, publicly at least, in a common endeavour.

The appeal of the esoteric has not been restricted to minorities. Astro-logical forecasts have figured prominently in popular newspapers, while astrologers with a publicity sense, some of whom described themselves as 'humanistic', offered private advice to clients, including political or business 'leaders', who sought 'insight and inspiration' into 'life paths and direction'. There can be odd collective implications also. It was reported in 1995 that one British true believer in astrology had warned that there were too many Taureans and Cancerians on Lundy Island, eleven miles off the North Devon coast, and that two couples born under those signs had already left.[25]

As the century grew old and the word 'progress', not for the first time in a hundred years, lost much of its power (despite or because of its current identification with the growth of material wealth), divination recovered some of its centuries-old spell and there was more fascination with the prophetic idea of a 'new age' than with the end of history. The 'Age of Aquarius', a new age of peace and love and harmony, had often been forecast before 1989, although there was never any agreement about its dating. Now the claim was made either that it had already begun or that it would begin soon: the 'seed beings' who would initiate it were already alive and active. There were different 'new age' sects, many with their origins in the 1960s, just as there were different charismatic, Pentecostal Christian sects seeking to transform humanity (men, women and children) both from within and from without. Names as well as visions seemed significant. Arnold Brown, writing for the World Future Society, proposed that the name 'Age of Aquarius' should be changed to the 'Age of Osiris', the Egyptian deity who was torn to pieces and reborn every year.[26]

'As we approach the year AD 2000 it is natural to wonder what will happen to us and our planet earth,' wrote A. T. Mann in his *Millennium Prophecies* (1992), drawing on pre-Christian, Christian and post-Christian religion, and showing how the range of possible answers had broadened since the prophet Isaiah proclaimed confidently 'then the moon shall be confounded and the sun ashamed, for the Lord of hosts shall reign'. Nonetheless, despite pseudo-science – or science itself – biblical prophecy had not lost its appeal, and Daniel's account of the 'destiny of the beast' was drawn upon (with the help of Nostradamus) to suggest that the European Economic Community was its embryo, though not yet the 'mature monster' that it would become.[27] In Britain there were various derivations from British Israelitism as the number of prophets multiplied. Yet some prophets had been outstanding men. The names of W. B. Yeats, Poet of the Golden Dawn, and T. S. Eliot, Poet of *The Waste Land*, could be invoked, and it was recalled that the great twentieth-century psychologist Carl Jung had written in his *VII Sermones ad Mortuos*, based on First World War visions, that 'when the greater world waxeth cold, burneth the star'.

Within such a kaleidoscopic spectrum, broader and more varied and more significant than most knowledgeable forecasters of the 1960s – or, indeed, of the 1890s – would have predicted, the world 'cult' acquired sinister undertones during the 1990s, and specially created bodies like Christian Rescue set out to arrange deliverance. Almost 2000 'cultish' organisations were noted in the database of INFORM, Information Network Focus on Religious Movements, ranging from the Central London Church of Christ and the Children of God to the Church of Scientology and flying-saucer worshippers. To computerise this data was evidence of the new force of computerisation in culture, expressed too in the computerisation of literary texts. 'Discover the incredible world of computers' was the invitation set out on the title-page of an advertising brochure. And there was an outstanding novel about it too, Umberto Eco's *Foucault's Pendulum*, translated from Italian to English in the *annus mirabilis*, 1989. 'Only for you, children of doctrine and learning, have we written this work', ran one of the two quotations that Eco used to introduce this book. 'Examine this book, ponder the meaning we have dispersed in various places and gathered again; what we have concealed in one place we have disclosed in another.' The quotation came from Heinrich von Nettesheim's *De occulta philosophia*.

The hermeneutic and the newsworthy were not compatible. At times, indeed, mysterious cults hit the world's headlines and television screens through disaster, for example, in April 1993 when eighty-seven people, twenty-five of them British and twenty-five of them children, died in an inferno in Waco, Texas, after a fifty-one-day siege of the heavily armed headquarters of the Branch Davidian cult; and in October 1994 Belgian-born Luc Jouret, founder of the Order of the Solar Temple, died in a chalet

214

Discover the incredible world of computers...

110. Exploration of inner spaces was accompanied by exploration of cyberspace. Outer space was left to the superpowers. An advertisement from Time-Life Books.

in Switzerland, where twenty-five bodies were found after what had apparently been a mass suicide. There was a further death toll in 1996. One of the earlier names of his cult had been the grand-sounding Académie de Recherche et Connaîssance des Hautes Sciences (ARCH). It had initiation rites, borrowed from the Rosicrucians as well as the Templars, and it proclaimed the imminence of the Age of Aquarius. There were no such resonances when members of American militia organisations were arrested in 1995 after a vengeance attack on a federal building in Oklahoma City where officers worked who had participated in the anti-Waco operations two years earlier. One immediate – and simpler – American reaction had been 'It's just like Beirut.'

It did not always take terrorism to hit the headlines during the last decades of the century. Established religions, including the Church of England, could hit them also. The Church was a different Church from that of a century earlier when statesmen, more knowledgeable about religion than their late twentieth-century successors, ascribed national and imperial greatness to the Providence of God. Many of the same hymns were still being sung, most of them to the same tunes, but a range of 'alternative services', significantly different in style and tone from the treasured Prayer Book, was now on offer. There had been liturgical changes also (including the use of vernacular languages in the mass) in the Roman Catholic Church following the Second Vatican Council of 1962.

The fortunes of the Church of England and the Roman Catholic Church, led since 1978 by a Polish-born pope, John Paul II, were increasingly interrelated after the controversial decision to ordain women in the Church of England was taken by its synod in 1992 and implemented in March 1994, when the first ordinations, low-key in character, were made in Bristol Cathedral.[28] One consequence of this was that a number of Anglican priests, including the recently retired Bishop of London, joined the Roman Catholic Church: with its rules of priestly practice, it provided, despite its changes in liturgy, a refuge for those who did not accept the validity of synodical change. The supporters of the measure had included determined and well-organised campaigners who spoke in the name of 'justice', some of them active and hopeful 'feminists', concerned more generally with women's rights in a predominantly secular society. Its opponents, active in both the Evangelical and the Anglo-Catholic wings of the Church, talked gloomily of the 'disintegration' of Anglicanism.

The Roman Catholic Church, which had been engaged for decades in an official 'unity dialogue' with the Church of England, first aspired to in the nineteenth century, did not completely escape the same pressures. Some women in the Roman Catholic Church themselves demanded ordination, while some laymen – and priests – were uneasy about the organised hierarchy. In Ireland sexual scandals disturbed the deeply entrenched Church, and in Germany and Holland there were theologians who questioned basic tenets of generally accepted orthodoxy. Moreover, if the Church of England had a controversial Bishop of Durham, across the Channel in Normandy the Roman Catholic Bishop of Evreux was dismissed from his post in 1995 for defending controversial causes, ranging from

111. The Bishop of Bristol solemnly ordains England's first thirty-two women priests, 1994.

advocacy of condoms to contain the spread of AIDS to a demand for the requisition of empty houses for the homeless.

From the central vantage point of the Vatican, Pope John Paul II, a redoubtable international traveller, firmly resisted all varieties of liberal pressure and appointed cardinals of conservative persuasion from all parts of the world. His travels forced him to concern himself – and the Church – with other established religions besides Christianity; and the Church of England likewise, itself at the centre of a worldwide Anglican communion, faced a similar challenge. Few had foreseen in 1900 (or in 1945) the appeal of Buddhism to English converts or (through immigration) the increasingly active role for Islam on British soil. In 1893, as the nineteenth century drew to its close, there had been a great conference of world religions in Chicago. Now most of them were represented in Britain itself.

Late twentieth-century papal encyclicals dwelt as much on questions of conduct as on questions of faith, and it was questions of conduct that could now produce strange alliances between Catholics and Protestant fundamentalists, some of them Pentecostalist, and even between the Church and Islam. Thus at the United Nations International Conference on Population and Development, held in Cairo in September 1994, the papacy in the name of 'family values' found itself in what critics called ironically a 'holy', if temporary, inter-faith alliance with sections of Islam against family planning, artificial birth control, abortion, confidential sexual advice to teenagers and the 'empowerment of women'.[29]

The Church of England was not bound by encyclicals or other authoritarian statements of position on such issues, and as a comprehensive national Church it was forced to acknowledge significant differences between its members not only on the ordination of women but on Christian attitudes to homosexual relationships, the latter a headline issue in the United States. It faced difficulties of a quite different kind, however, during the 1990s, including a financial crisis, caused in part by unwise, essentially speculative, investment by the Church Commissioners during the property boom of the mid-1980s. Even had the investment been sound there would still have been problems because of the growing pensions bill of the Church, which the Commissioners had to deal with from 1954 onwards: it accounted for half their expenditure.[30]

In this respect, as in others, the established Church was facing problems which reflected in microcosm the predicament of the nation's 'welfare state'. How would state pensions be paid in the twenty-first century? How would priorities be determined in a National Health Service that lacked adequate resources? In the United States, which was never a welfare state, President Clinton's ambitious health service plans were abandoned. In England many of the most vocal representatives of the Church were deeply attached to the welfare state, a term which had been popularised by William Temple, a mid-century Archbishop of Canterbury, and which politicians found it difficult to discard. Some of the most vocal Conservative Members of Parliament, however, believed that the welfare state should be thoroughly reformed, if not completely dismantled. Whatever else the late twentieth-century Church of England was it was not just the Conservative Party at prayer. In Scotland and Wales there were few Conservative Members of Parliament to take part in such discussion.

There was another parallel too between affairs in Church and state in Britain. The administrative implications of the Church's financial crisis added to the pressure for bishops, like university vice-chancellors and BBC departmental heads, to possess and, equally important, display 'managerial' qualities. One such quality was the ability to talk the fashionable jargon of management, as intricate as the culture jargon – the term 'corporate culture' provided a link – which evolved during the 1980s. By the 1990s it was required that this be spoken and written as a matter of course, not least on notice boards, in many private businesses and public organisations, particularly the National Health Service. Charismatic congregations might talk in tongues, but 'managers' had to talk of 'internal market mechanisms' and 'consumer [or producer] choice'. The word 'mission' acquired new significance.

Non-Christian cults might create prophets and martyrs, but in 'official circles' the required qualifications were grounded, above all else, in accounting skills. The 'secular order' had favoured accountants as managers when 'enterprise culture' was being extolled along with 'accountability' in the halcyon days of the mid-1980s. Accountants could do equally well, however, in bad times, figuring in the recession as 'saviours' brought in from outside or, with fewer haloes, as liquidators. Above all they figured as consultants, a freely used term. The University of Oxford had to resort to them in 1995.

Whatever the nature and scale of the problems facing the Churches and the Church of England in particular, they were no greater than the problems facing most traditional British institutions, including 'old' universities, the monarchy and 'the law'; and if haloes had been in short supply during the 1990s, crowns and wigs had not in themselves induced veneration. Within this context the Bishop of Oxford, Richard Harries, one of the more intelligent and articulate bishops – and one very familiar with the ways of the media – correctly observed in the early 1990s – from the vantage point of Robert Maxwell's Oxford – that there was nothing new in the cry of a Church in decline. He went on to point out that the figure of weekly attendance at Church of England services – one and a half million (out of five million attending services of all religious denominations) – was three times the number of spectators at football matches and larger than trade-union membership (which was still falling).[31]

112. Sport, national and international, was mediated through television which transformed the economics of football and the sociology of the Olympic Games. Here Mitsubishi advertises the far-away European Championships of 1996.

These were relevant comparisons, particularly the first, for sport, which figured prominently in the media, had come to serve as a religion for large numbers of people. With direct media intervention it had been almost unbelievably commercialised and internationalised during the 1970s and 1980s, with Rugby Union and Rugby League last in the line. Sport, now usually in the singular – the United States kept the plural – had also had its disasters, its scandals and its financial problems; and because of the behaviour of sections of the crowd at 'sporting events', particularly association football matches, it had raised both moral and political questions. There were, however, fewer critics of huge soccer salaries – and transfer fees – than there were of the disproportionately huge salaries of 'top businessmen', some of whom bought football clubs. 'Managers' in sport faced more risks than any other managers, even when they were not 'accountable'.

In one way sport was directly related to the Church. The Victorian sabbath lost its hold in the last decades of the twentieth century through the development of Sunday sport (including racing) as well as the extension of Sunday retailing. A majority of politicians, including Conservatives who knew little of the historic relationship between Church and state, legislated for the latter. Once again there were recalcitrant minorities – including in the case of Sunday trading, active trade unionists joining in chorus with traditionalist Evangelicals. Wales and Scotland had their own separate histories, though there were supermarkets common to both.

In his analysis Bishop Harries pointed to the fact that in England no fewer than 430 new churches had been built since 1969. (He did not discuss their architecture, a favourite topic elsewhere – not least with post-modernists and with the Prince of Wales). He noted also that by the beginning of the new decade in 1990 as many new churches had been opened as redundant churches (the subject of special architectural provision) were closed. Most of the latter, he added, had been built in the nineteenth century when more church buildings were provided than were necessary. This was to put that century in its place. Meanwhile, the Church itself had carried out careful and well-publicised enquiries into its strengths and weaknesses both in inner-city areas and in country parishes, many of them now amalgamated. There had been no nineteenth-century enquiries of such scope and depth. There had been no polls either, like the 1996 poll which registered serious ignorance of the meaning of Easter, which, like Christmas, had become a consumer festival.

Like the pope, the bishop moved on next to world issues and brought into his picture other faiths besides Christianity, suggesting that there was a 'cosmic optimism' which united Christianity, Judaism and Islam (as well as some other faiths) and claiming rightly that in Britain Islam ('as varied a phenomenon as Christianity') was looking to the Church rather than to secular liberalism as a sympathetic ally.[32] Bishop Harries did not refer, however, to the case of Salman Rushdie, whose assassination had been demanded in 1989 (back yet again to the *annus mirabilis*) by the Iranian Ayatollah Khomeini, leader of Islamic fundamentalism, although it was in Bradford in Yorkshire – a city with a large Asian immigrant population –

113. Condemning Salman Rushdie's *Satanic Verses*: prayers outside the House of Commons, 1989.

that Rushdie's *Satanic Verses* had been burned in the streets. The terrifying *fatwa* was to apply throughout the world. Television was to carry it, although in 1995 a different ayatollah was to secure a ban of satellite television dishes in Iran itself. Iran, along with Iraq (enemies before the Gulf War) and Libya, were treated as pariah states, responsible not just for threatening talk but for acts of 'international terrorism', including the PAN AM air disaster at Lockerbie, Scotland in 1993.

Through different media of communication political news of what was happening in Iran or Iraq or Libya, offered in patches rather than day by day, spread rapidly throughout the world in the late twentieth century, particularly at moments of 'crisis', raising every kind of issue as it did so. Religious news was patchy too, while business news was always regular and always up to date. Whatever appeared on the screen, the public was expected to understand ups and downs on the currency exchanges and new and awkward words like 'junk money', 'junk bonds' and 'derivatives'. It was also expected to follow (partially informed) the details of the many 'peace processes', including that in Ireland, which were usually in jeopardy through what was always labelled 'terrorism'. It is impossible, therefore, to understand late twentieth-century perceptions and preoccupations, economic, political, cultural or religious without turning to the so-called 'communications revolution', a term first used in the 1950s.

In what was regarded as its first phase during the 1950s and 1960s the revolution had pivoted largely on the role of the newest medium, television. Later during the 1990s it focused on the devising of 'interactive' systems that, through digitalisation, provided text, statistics, graphics, sound and moving video, including 'video on demand', on a home computer screen, with games added to the mix. In its first phase the public service monopoly of the British Broadcasting Corporation, entrenched since its foundation in 1922, had been broken, in 1955, although competition, dependent on advertising, was regulated by an Authority and the system became, in effect, a duopoly until a lively new Channel 4 came into existence in 1983. In the 1990s the emphasis was not on standards but on choice, and B-Sky-B attracted a huge paying audience.

The metaphors changed, too, as television itself was 'put into place', from 'window on the world' to electronic 'superhighway', for a time a 'buzzword'. 'Hitchhikers' Guides' to travelling on it appeared. Yet this metaphor too, like 'buzzword' itself (we currently talk more of 'sound bites') is beginning to sound archaic in an age of 'networks' and 'webs'.[33] When the Internet was created in the 1960s in the United States its purposes were limited and it had no central authority having been designed to serve academic and military needs. With the incentive still coming from below, its range spread quickly, far beyond any initial forecasts, so that by the mid-1990s it had become an 'electronic post office', operating worldwide, and incorporating a far wider range of activities, among them marketing and pornography, than any post office. The key word now was 'cyberspace', along with all the cyber words, not yet figuring in most dictionaries, that go with it – from 'cybernauts' to 'cyborgs'.[34]

With the Internet some observers welcomed a switch of power from suppliers to users and from providers to participants. Communication was developing from below not from above. Others, however, feared individual retreats into 'cyberspace' and, at a different level, the consequences of a new 'cyberstate' reducing the nation state to a large property management company. The implications for 'culture', starting with 'cyberpunk', have been the subject of serious study particularly in the United States. In consequence, the word 'terminal' has acquired a further significance.[35]

Present difficulties between the United States and Europe may well narrow. In 1990 Europe as a whole was far behind the United States in computer development, and France, the country with the most advanced plans for *télématique*, a new information society, preferred television-related technology, videotex, to computer-based technology on the American model. In Britain governments took a market-oriented approach to the issues of a 'global information society' which, in this as in other matters, differed from that of its European partners: in the words of a British White Paper of 1988 change was both inevitable and desirable. (The subtitle of the paper was 'Competition, Choice and Quality'.) A British White Paper on broadcasting, now developing within a new communicative context, also described changes as both inevitable and a good thing.[36]

114. The persistence of history on the screen where fact and fiction are often confused. Sky Television advertises a new history-only channel, operating on both sides of the Atlantic.

be there when it happens again

Announcing a landmark event in British television: the arrival of **The History Channel**. Experience the definitive moments in world history, captured in groundbreaking original programming, fascinating documentaries and spellbinding dramas. From epic battles to notorious scandals; from revolutions to legendary sporting achievements; the history of the world comes alive every evening.

115. The world as available on the Internet. 'Addicted to the net? Then you'll love what we deal in.' An advertisement for one of the many Internet service providers, Planet Internet.

Meanwhile, issues of transportation rather than of 'compunication' (except for mobile telephones and cable) preoccupied both governments and the public in Britain during the early 1990s – the widening of the over-worked M25 orbital road round London; the technical and financial problems of the London Underground that affected the daily routines of millions of people; and railway privatisation, which divided the political parties more sharply than any other issues. The correspondence columns of newspapers were full of letters on these subjects, and even after the revision of Clause 4 in its constitution 'new Labour' continued to put its trust in public service railways.

In fact, while Britain, 'a car-dominated society', with multi-storey car parks and armies of traffic wardens, had solved none of its traffic problems, a *Times* headline of 1995 could read 'Drive into history at 850 mph. This car will try to smash the sound barrier. Is this pilot [Andy Green] crazy or Britain's bravest man?'[37] Was Britain crazy? Circuit racing was a popular middle-class sport to which 'quality newspapers' devoted far more photographs and even more intricate paragraphs than they did to cricket, an historic game in trouble. There were other important background facts about automobiles. Britain's last British-owned firm to produce them had been sold to a German firm in 1994, but by courtesy of Germany, Japan and France more automobiles (most of them for export) were being produced in Britain in 1994/5 than in any year since 1973. And, given the oil crisis of 1973, that was a perfect reference point.[38]

Many of the reference points in the last decade of the twentieth century are further back in time, though usually not too far back. For all the talk of the millennium and of how best to reach it (by 'superhighway' or by fast car), most reference points related to the end of the nineteenth century or the middle of the twentieth: 1945. This was partly because of what historians had to say in 'post-modern conditions'. Still active, if less listened to at the end of the twentieth century than they had been a hundred years before, they concentrated increasingly on recent English history, and when it came to the millennium they poured scorn on suggestions that there had been a particularly strong sense of expectation or foreboding when the first millennium ended. They had authority for this. Although there was no shortage of apocalyptic prophecy earlier or later – and there were waves of millenarianism that attracted Christians of very different dispositions – it was not until the fourteenth century that myths concerning popular attitudes in the darkness of the tenth century began to circulate. The great French medieval historian, Georges Duby, described their content as a *mirage historique*.[39]

There were, however, modern French historians – and historians everywhere – who claimed that in the twentieth century we were returning to the middle ages, ages that did not know their name, *Demain le moyen age*, and as early as 1949 Étienne Gilson, theologian as well as historian, warned his readers that 'if the terrors of the year One Thousand are not a certainty for today's historians, those of the year Two Thousand will surely be so for future historians'. The American historian Barbara Tuchman's *The Distant Mirror* (1978), looking back at the fourteenth century, had found parallels there which were missing in the nineteenth century. Violence, holocaust, corruption and complicity were at the heart of the 'gigantic sprawling novel called the Twentieth Century' as they were at the heart of many of the novels which were published as the century closed.

Whatever other mirrors were there, there was a revival of late twentieth-century interest in the 1890s, strengthened by the incidence of much publicised centenaries – for example, those of X-rays, the cinema and of radio – even of an earlier Barings crisis – and by a re-evaluation of old attitudes designed belatedly to redress what seemed to be past injustices. Thus, on the day of the centenary of Oscar Wilde's *The Importance of Being Earnest*, 14 February 1994, a stained-glass window to Wilde was unveiled in Poets' Corner, Westminster Abbey, Sir John Gielgud read from *De Profundis*, the Irish poet Seamus Heaney, soon to be a Nobel Prize winner, gave an address, choirboys sang a traditional Irish melody, and Dame Judi Dench and Michael Denison performed the famous 'handbag scene'. *The Importance of Being Earnest*, staged in each new generation, had triumphantly survived both the trial and the century. This was not quite an act of rehabilitation, Wilde's grandson insisted, but, in Heaney's words, a 'reconciliation'.[40] In the same month as the ceremony in Westminster Abbey press publicity was given to re-evaluation of the play which suggested that Lady Bracknell, its most memorable character, was based on Lady Salisbury, the wife of Victoria's last prime minister.

There was a similar note of reconciliation – and re-evaluation – at a deeper level later in the same year, when the holocaust, one of the most terrifying experiences of the twentieth century, was recalled fifty years on before the victory of the Allies was celebrated. Centuries had been celebrated before with jubilees, the first of them Pope Boniface VIII's Jubilee in 1300. Now, like holidays, jubilees had lost almost all their religious significance. Time had been rescheduled.

The year 1995 saw the centenary of H. G. Wells's short novel *The Time Machine* which encouraged speculation on changes in attitudes towards time since 1885. 'There is no difference between Time and any of the three dimensions of space except that our consciousness moves with it', Wells had posited in 1895 as he contemplated 'Three-Dimensional represen-tations' of a 'Four-Dimensioned being'. A decade later, Albert Einstein, who with others revolutionised the subject of physics, questioned Newton's account of time and space, then an orthodoxy, suggesting that time was relative, varying with the relative speed and position of observer and observed. Einstein fascinated the general public who had not read anything that he had written but had been told of his work in newspapers and in books.[41]

Late in the century Stephen Hawking's *A Brief History of Time* (1988) was to be a much discussed, if too little read, best-seller. Time at the end of the twentieth century seemed terminal and space orbital, with common issues being raised in science and in literature.[42] The views of theoretical physicists were widely reported, as were biologists' views on the very different science of genetics, which interested the late twentieth century as much as it had interested the late nineteenth century – and Wells. Genetic codes provided evidence concerning transmission, and the word 'code' came to be used increasingly outside the natural sciences. Much remained uncertain in science as in history within the context of post-modernism, with one author, Jean Baudrillard, a guru *malgré lui*, suggesting that society and culture no longer existed in layered time – his own 'philosophy' does – but instead in what can only be described – and is being described – as 'virtual reality'. 'Meaning' has gone, and already the twentieth century is being wiped from memory. 'The Gulf War did not take place.' Not surprisingly, on the superhighway Baudrillard (mixing metaphors as he does deliberately) is one of 'the most referred-to people in the intellectual firmament'.[43]

Britain, a country with long memories, no more conforms to a Baudrillard model or to a 'post-industrial' or 'end of history' model. An articulate section of its middle classes still stands fast by St George, 'a decent sort of saint', and the prime minister can happily quote the socialist George Orwell, author of *1984*, a year which has come and gone, to soothe dog-loving conservatives who still prefer the pub, the green and 'the long shadows on the county grounds' to the market, even the much transformed stock market. Major might well have quoted T. S. Eliot too on the essential qualities of 'Englishness', though few of these mean much in Scotland or Wales.[44] Memories and myths are strong in Sunday colour supplements, figuring not only in articles but in the advertisements that serve as their main *rationale*. Taken together they express the unique balance in English history between continuity and change.

The content of the colour supplements also revolves around social stratification, which even under the disguise of income-group classification cannot leave out English perceptions of 'class' (according to a Gallup poll 85 per cent of the population believed in the existence of an 'underclass'); the 'home' and every gadget that sustains it and (for balance) the spectre of 'homelessness'; the sense of an island, coexisting with invitations to travel to the most exotic places; love of the countryside and the desire to escape there, along with a passion for gardens (beautifully photographed); delight in gossip about the great, particularly, but by no means exclusively, about the royal family. There are other stars of television (and cinema) with whom privileged members of the royal family like to be identified as 'celebrities'.

The most apposite metaphor to cover this cluster of phenomena is not superhighway but roundabout. Images recur, ideas recur, dreams recur, problems recur. 'Buzzwords' and 'sound bites' change. The problems can seldom be completely evaded. They take the form of 'issues', the word used in the title of *Big Issue*, a lively magazine produced and distributed by London's homeless people. The prime minister pleads for a 'classless

116. Homelessness: an all-too-familiar London 1990s scene registering its consequences.

society', but the difference between relative and absolute poverty continues to shape all discussion on social stratification.[45] London expresses this visually. Buskers, beggars, sleepers-out and squatters generate conflicting reactions that would have been familiar at the end of the pre-industrial sixteenth century. The home is idealised as the centre of the family – and over two-thirds of the population live in owner-occupied houses – yet when the last decade of the century began one in five of all British families was headed by a single parent, with nine out of ten of those parents mothers.[46] The sense of one island confronts the fact that in both Scotland and Wales there are pressures to live in the island not separately but independently. (As for the other island, there is a bigger cultural divide between England and Protestant north than there is between England and Catholic south.) Garden centres thrive, but the countryside is threatened by suburban developments in many villages: urban sprawl has swallowed up almost two million acres of countryside since 1945.[47]

Gossip about the royal family has been so extensive (and so expensive to collect) that it has become as much of an irritant to considerable numbers of readers as it has become to the beleaguered royal family itself. Because it is a family that is under scrutiny, the gossip raises general issues about divorce, now treated very differently from the way in which it would have been in the late nineteenth century. Should it be 'no fault'? A Lord Chancellor is in the thick of the fray. He is a Scot, and his own religion is old-style 'free' Presbyterian. His critics include people who have themselves been divorced.

There are, of course, new elements in the late twentieth-century mix, like the striking increase in women's work between 1973 and 1993 (much of it part-time), which has been described as a 'genderquake'; the opening up of higher education to a far larger section of the population than ever before and the conversion of all polytechnics into universities (even if the funding was squeezed calamitously in the process); and the spread of AIDS, unanticipated even in the 1970s, which has prompted some changes in sexual habits, as earlier sexually transmitted diseases had done.[48] There were limits, however, to the parallels. Few people drew the same lessons out of AIDS as were drawn out of the Black Death at the end of the fourteenth century, syphilis at the end of the fifteenth century, or cholera in the nineteenth, possibly because the numbers affected seemed small, but some people demanded tackling it not with condoms but with 'Victorian' moral guidance.

Drugs, not a new twentieth-century problem, were in part responsible for the 9,865 AIDS-related deaths before 1994, and how best to deal with drugs raised a broader set of issues than AIDS, some of them new, some of them old, most of them raised in other contexts too – like the role of the police, the motives behind crime, the length and bindingness of court sentences, and the state of the overcrowded prisons. The government's vigilant Chief

117. Fighting AIDS. A Health Education Authority poster, part of a campaign, 1994.

Inspector of Prisons, Judge Stephen Tumim, who was not reappointed to his post in 1995, would not have been an unfamiliar figure a century or even two centuries ago. Although juvenile crime has revealed new twentieth-century horrors unknown to Charles Dickens, the scandals would have been familiar to him as would the conflicts between Home Secretary and judges. He would have been shocked but not surprised by the resistance to change of the Prison Officers' Association.

Dickens would have understood too the significance of one of the colourful symbols of the roundabout – the 'traditional' pomp and ceremony of the Corporation of the City of London, 'medieval flummery', that remained appealing after the abolition of the Greater London Council, the 'big bang' in the City, and the spectacular East End funeral of one of the Kray brothers who had been in prison for appalling crimes. Some observers believed that City livery companies, like local accents, now 'Estuary' if not pearly Cockney, would survive the House of Lords, even the monarchy: the 667th lord mayor waved to crowds estimated at 200,000 in the Lord Mayor's Show in 1994. There were twenty marching bands, sixty floats and eighteen carriages, drawn by 200 horses. The lord mayor's theme was 'The City – heart of the nation', and his designated charity was the British Heart Foundation.[49]

It was appropriate that this should be a charity concerned with health, for health and the National Health Service, the latter a great achievement of the century, have been major preoccupations, private and public, at the century's close, raising issues of risk in a highly complex society where the aged, 'senior citizens', are living longer than ever before in history. It was less appropriate, given City pomp, that London should be the place where two of the leading ancient hospitals of the nation, St Bartholomew's and Guy's, should be in jeopardy. But it was the Victorians who had abruptly ended St Bartholomew's Fair. And it was they who had devised the great Ferris Wheel which was being considered a century later as a feature of the skyline for the beginning of the new millennium. Round and round.

There is one final reason for taking the word 'roundabout' as a metaphor. It carries with it a sense of fun, including all the fun of the fair – and all the fun of a gamble, risk in a different context, in old or new games where the dice is thrown. If 'meaning' is in danger in the 1990s, fun has become an obsessional theme, not only in Britain but in the world's proliferating theme parks, Disneyesque or 'traditional', with heritage itself becoming a 'fun industry'. In the film *Back to the Future 2*, released in 1989, the actor Michael J. Fox touches down in his home town in 2015 to see the town square converted into a futuristic fun park complete with flying cars and aerial skateboards, with nostalgia being catered for in a 'Café 80s', complete with computer images of Ronald Reagan and Ayatollah Khomeini. *Jaws 19* is playing at the cinema.[50]

In the distant days of August 1989 two articles appeared on the same page of the *International Herald Tribune*, one supremely serious, one self consciously light-hearted: they were entitled 'Gorbachev's Risky Journey towards Historical Truths' and 'Mr. Millennium's Advice: Get Ready for the Oh-Ohs'. In between there was a picture of a Warsaw Pact tank in the 'rough neighbourhood' of the Berlin Wall. The serious article, written by Anthony Lewis, who had long served the *New York Times* in London through all its changes in the 1960s and 1970s, raised questions about the risk of facing up to the truth about a people and a society, with particular reference to the question of whether or not Gorbachev himself would survive. The other

118. Assembling contemporary history: a revealing page from the *International Herald Tribune*, 30 August 1989.

Gorbachev's Risky Journey Toward Historical Truths
By Anthony Lewis

Rough Neighborhood.

Mr. Millennium's Advice: Get Ready for the Oh-Ohs
By Lewis Grossberger

article, by Lewis Grossberger, which focused on the 'Big Two Triple O', claimed that the United States needed 'a catchy name for the next thousand years'. How about 'the World Peace, Human Brotherhood and Doo-Wop Nostalgia Millennium'? It also raised the same trivial question – trivial at first sight at least – that had been raised by the Kaiser and others during the 1890s. 'When does this century end and the new millennium begin?' 'Most people', Grossberger responded, 'would say 1 January 2000, but mathematicians and other know-alls insist on 1 January 2001. Imagine how many irritable letters to the editor this dispute will produce! To have any hope of settling it in time for [a millennial] party we must start squabbling now.'[51]

In Britain Peter Brooke, then national heritage secretary, a revealing title, provoked a *Times* leader, 'Brooke's Millennium', after he had declared in the autumn of 1993 that the twentieth century would end not on the stroke of midnight on New Year's Eve 1999, but twelve months later after the year 2000, which for good or ill would still be part of the old century. 'The Millennium inspires feelings, not the need for facts', the leader ran, and Brooke should concern himself with feelings. 'Tell that to the pedants' was Philip Howard's vernacular reply to Brooke in an article only slightly less trivial than Grossberger's called 'Getting Ready for the Fun de Siècle'. If Peter Brooke insisted on going to bed early with a good book on 31 December 1999 he would be alone in his devotion to accurate chronology. Brooke himself acknowledged that many people would ignore his ruling. Meanwhile, a spokesman for the United Nations stated unhelpfully that he did not believe that 'we have thought that far ahead'.[52]

The national heritage secretary had been responsible among his other achievements for launching a National Lottery, suggested as long ago as 1967 by television pundit Robin Day (not then Sir Robin), and supported by the Rothschild Royal Commission on Gambling in 1978.[53] The contract was won by a consortium called Camelot, a name now more reminiscent of President Kennedy than of King Arthur. It was awarded the licence despite the fact that Richard Branson, a new man of the late century who straddled many fields, including entertainment and transport, had promised to give all the profits to charity. 'Technical clout' in the management of the lottery business triumphed. There was more 'fun', most of it contrived – BBC television at its worst – on the day of its launching in November 1994 (and in successive lottery programmes) than there was of talk of the enrichment of life that lottery proceeds would make possible. One of its beneficiaries, however, was to be a Millennium Fund, entrusted to commissioners chosen by and chaired by the heritage secretary and given the task of identifying national projects of long-term value that otherwise would not have been affordable. There would also be Millennium Bursaries and a Millennium Festival in the year 2000. The scheme had the support of both government and opposition. Indeed, it was the shadow heritage secretary who described the Fund as 'an opportunity to change the face of our country for good'.[54]

Millennial projects, a test of imagination but an inevitable source of controversy, were already on the table. They included an opera house in Cardiff Bay, turned down under a new national heritage secretary (while Covent Garden benefited enormously); a network of bicycle tracks; the clearing of a continuous waterway between the Forth and the Clyde to make use of existing Scottish canals and of new locks; 'Albertopolis', an arts and science centre, looking back to the dreams of the past, linking the Albert Hall, the great national museums and Hyde Park, where the 1851 International Exhibition had been held in the Crystal Palace; and a Millennium Centre in the vicinity of Heathrow Airport, which would incorporate 'a giant re-cycling unit' and 'a museum of computing and communications. Another proposal was for a History House, 'a museum for our collective memory', drawing (without commercialisation) on more than a millennium of national experience. By 'collective memory' its sponsors insisted that they meant not simply a one-island or a one-part-of-an-island memory, but the memory of a 'constellation of islands', including Ireland, 'of which this island is a part and not leaving out the links with Europe, old as well as new, and with the rest of the world'.[55]

The stream of projects continued to flow after the first successes and failures were announced. One, mooted in April 1996 (with a comet visible in the sky, named Hyakatake after the Japanese amateur astronomer who discovered it), was to add to the chalk-hill figures on the hills of Britain a pattern of a microchip. Among the potential sites was Pillmore Hill, ten miles south of Lanark in Scotland – in full view of the main railway line and the M174 motorway. Its sponsor, Tom Newton (the right surname), claimed that in a thousand years 'man will be able to look at the chalk design [he is himself a designer] and identify it as symbolising the very beginnings of microchip technology . . . Everything that man might create in the next millennium will be attributable to one thing – the chip.'[56]

Notes

1. F. Kermode, *The Sense of an Ending: Studies in the Theory of Fiction* (1968).
2. *Financial Times*, 24/25 December 1994.
3. Edited by M. Vassiliev and S. Gousebev. The Russian study was published in an English translation by Penguin Books (Harmondsworth, 1961). See also V. V. Ivasheva, *On the Threshold of the Twenty-First Century* (translated by D. Bradbury and N. Ward, New York, 1978).
4. See A. Toffler, *Future Shock* (New York, 1971), esp. ch. 17.
5. *Futures*, December 1972.
6. K. Boulding, *Values and the Future* (London, 1969).
7. *The Times*, 1 March 1988. Cf. *The Economist*, 23 March 1996, 'That Astonishing Microchip'. See also *Time*, 'The Strange New World of Internet', 25 July 1994. On 24 August 1994 *The Times* was issued free by courtesy of Bill Gates's Microsoft which

inserted a twenty-eight-page supplement, 'Windows'. See also 'Technology Titans Sound off on the Digital Future' in *US News and World Report*, May 1993.

8. See C. Norman, *The God that Limps, Science and Technology in the Eighties* (New York and London, 1981), pp. 113ff. Two early articles by Peter Marsh in the *New Scientist*, 12 June 1980 and 31 July 1980, dealt with early robotry in Britain. The first was called 'Robots See the Light'. *Hemispheres*, February 1996, describes 'serbots', service robots working alongside humans as among the first 'walking, talking and thinking androids'.

9. See the collected essays in I. Hassan, *The Postmodern Turn, Essays in Postmodern Theory and Culture* (Columbus, Ohio, 1987).

10. Historically 'the post-modern moment' can be conceived of as 'a break initiated by modernism . . . the transitional period between nineteenth-century romanticism and the current cultural scene' (E. A. Kaplan (ed.), *Postmodernism and its Discontents* (London, New York, 1988)). Yet some post-modernists refuse to equate 'post' and 'after' when relating 'modernism' to 'post-modernism', the second 'ism' incorporating a sense of the first. For an a-historical approach to the definition of post-modernism, treating it as a constant cultural state, see the influential book by J. F. Lyotard, *The Post-Modern Condition: a Report on Knowledge* (first translation published in French; English translation 1984). For 'post-modernism' as 'a reformation of temporality' see E. D. Manches Ermath, *Sequel to History: Post modernism and the Crisis of Representational Time* (Princeton, 1992). The post-modernist case against objective history and the claim that there is a 'real knowable past' is well summarised by P. M. Rosenau, *Post-Modernism and the Social Sciences* (Princeton, 1992), p. 63.

11. For literary post-modernism viewed as 'the act of fiction in an age of inflation' see C. Newman, *The Post-Modern Aura* (Evanston, 1985). For a Marxist view of the relationship between economics and aesthetics in a consumer culture see F. Jameson, 'Postmodernism and Consumer Society' in H. Foster (ed.), *The Anti-Aesthetic: Essays on Postmodern Culture* (Port Townsend, Washington, 1983). There is an essay in the same volume by J. Habermas, 'Modernity – an Unfinished Project'.

12. See A. Briggs, *A Social History of England* (London, 1994 edn), pp. 230ff. For the coal crisis viewed comparatively see M. Parker, *The Politics of Coal's Decline: The Industry in Western Europe* (London, 1996).

13. For Thatcher and Thatcherism see H. Young, *One of Us* (London, 1992, rev. edn); M. Thatcher, *The Revival of Britain* (London, 1989); P. Riddell, *The Thatcher Decade* (Oxford, 1989); and R. Skidelsky (ed.), *Thatcherism* (London, 1991). See also M. Loney, *The Politics of Greed* (London, 1986).

14. See E. Leoni, *Nostradamus: Life and Literature* (New York, 1961).

15. For an interesting immediate reaction by a French historian see E. Le Roy Ladurie, '1989 Annus Mirabilis' (*Contribution au Forum Européen*, 1990).

16. E. Hobsbawm, *The Age of Extremes* (London, 1994), p. 5.

17. Fukuyama's article 'The End of History', printed in the *National Interest* in Summer 1989, was written before the Berlin Wall fell. His book *The End of History and the Last Man* followed. It appeared in a Penguin edition in Britain in 1992. For earlier discussion of 'the end of history' thesis see L. Niethammer, *Post histoire: Has History Come to an End?* (Zurich, 1993).

18. See above, pp. 162–4.

19. See, for example, 'The 21st Century Starts Here: China Booms. The World Holds its Breath', the *New York Times Magazine*, 18 February 1996. Compare W. Gungwu, *The Chineseness of China* (Oxford, 1991) and S. Lipset, *American Exceptionalism* (New York, 1996).

20. M. Pawley, *Private Futures* (1974), ch. 8, 'The Private Future: Battle of the Two Realities'.

21. See B. Mandelbrot, *The Fractal Geometry of Nature* (New York, 1982); J. Gleick, *Chaos: Making a New Science* (New York, 1987).

22. See also, for example, a headline in *The Times*, 18 March 1996, 'Cloning breakthrough sounds ethical alarm'.

23. 'Here Comes the 21st Century', *Sunday Times*, 11 February 1990.

24. *Time*, 14 March 1994.

25. *The Times*, 14 February 1995. See also 'The Magic of the Millennium', a series of horoscopes by Jonathan Caines, *Daily Mail*, 25 April 1996 in the 'Femail' section.
26. *Dialogue* (1981), a print of a paper published in 1980 by the World Future Society.
27. NATION, *Intimations of Empire: The Great Powers in Prophecy* (London, 1993), p. 43.
28. *The Times*, 12 March 1994. The news report, which noted that the Bishop of Bristol altered the gospel reading to remove exclusive references to 'he', had an accompanying article 'Fractured Church Reflects an Angry State' by Mary Loudon, author of *Revelations: The Clergy Questioned* (London, 1994), a survey of the attitudes of the clergy.
29. M. Sheridan, 'A Holy but frail alliance', the *Independent*, 3 September 1994. See also the *Financial Times*, 8 September 1994, and for the Cairo Conference in retrospect *The Earth Times* (Geneva, New York), 15 March 1996.
30. M. Adonis, 'Church with its future in the balance', *Financial Times*, 17/18 December 1994. See also ibid., 11/12 July 1992, 'Unholy Saga, the Church's missing millions' by John Plender.
31. R. Harries, 'Has Religion a Future?' in W. H. Smith, *Contemporary Papers* (London, n.d.), p. 2.
32. Ibid., p. 12.
33. See L. McGill and A. Szanto, *Headlines and Sound Bites: Is That the Way?* (Freedom Forum Report, New York, August 1995). The *Wall Street Journal*, 15 November 1993, described the superhighway as beset by 'potholes, accidents and traffic jams'. See also *Media Studies Journal*, Winter 1994, 'Highway to the Stars or Road to Nowhere'.
34. For the history of cyber words, beginning with cybernetics, a word coined by Norbert Wiener in 1947, and including 'cyberbabble', see W. Clements, 'Cyberplenty' in the *Toronto Globe and Mail*, 16 March 1996. The most successful word in the cyber cluster has been 'cyberspace', coined by William Gibson in his novel *Necromancer* (1984). The sub-title of the *Time* number on Internet, 25 July 1994, was 'Battles on the Frontiers of Cyberspace'. For a radical critique see F. Owen 'Brain Lords and Cyberserfs: Class and Caste in the Age of New Media' in *The Village Voice*, 8 February 1996.
35. See S. Bukatman, *Terminal Identity* (Durham, North Carolina, 1993).
36. See also the later report of OECD, 'Global Information Infrastructure and Society (Paris, 1996) and the BBC Report, 'Extending Choice in the Digital Age' (London, 1996).
37. *The Times*, 'Car 95', 4 February 1995.
38. *Daily Telegraph*, 21 April 1995; *Sunday Telegraph*, 23 April 1995, 'Motown Britain'.
39. G. Duby, *L'An Mil* (Paris, 1967). See also D. Milo, 'L'An Mil, un problème d'historiographie moderne', *History and Theory*, vol. 27 (1988).
40. *Daily Telegraph*, 15 February 1995. See also D. Pannick, 'When Justice went Wilde', *The Times*, 14 February 1995.
41. For Wells see N. and J. MacKenzie, *The Time Traveller* (London, 1973) which discusses Wells's attitudes to century's end. For Einstein see D. E. Mook and T. Vargish, *Inside Relativity* (Princeton, 1987). A 1912 Einstein paper in German, bridging special and general relativity, which was auctioned in 1996, was described by Rubin Pogrebin in the *New York Times*, 15 March 1996, as showing how 'science can be art'.
42. See N. K. Hayles, *The Cosmic Web: Scientific Field Models and Literary Strategies in the Twentieth Century* (Ithaca, 1984) and *Chaos Bound: Orderly Disorder in Contemporary Literature and Science* (Ithaca, 1990). For other common issues see H. R. Pagels, *The Dreams of Reason: The Computer and the Rise of the Sciences of Complexity* (New York, 1989). See also P. Coveney and R. Highfield, *Frontiers of Complexity: The Search for Order in a Chaotic World* (London, 1996).
43. See M. Poster (ed.), *Jean Baudrillard: Selected Writings* (Stanford, 1988).
44. See T. S. Eliot, *Notes Towards the Definition of Culture* (London, 1947).
45. See, for example, 'Class You've either got it or you ain't', a supplement to the *Independent*, 18 April 1996.
46. The annual reports and other publications of SHiL, Single Homelessness in London will be essential reading for social historians. The object of SHiL, an all-party group set up by the London boroughs, is 'to bring together statutory, voluntary and private sector

organisations involved in providing services for people who are homeless and single in London' and 'to contribute policy and action on issues concerning single homelessness'.

47. 'Rural England Lost in Concrete', *Guardian*, 29 July 1993. For the blending of fact and fiction see 'Ambridge's Verdict on Gummer's England', *The Times*, 18 October 1995.

48. *The Times*, 1 January 1987, reporting a commissioned MORI poll. Almost half the adult population believed that the AIDS problem would not have arisen but for 'the permissive society' (a convenient portmanteau phrase). The first government education plan relating to AIDS was launched in 1986 and cost £20 million. See S. Garfidd, *The End of Innocence: Britain in the Time of AIDS* (London, 1994). For drugs see K. Leech, *A Practical Guide to the Drug Scene* (London, 1974, rev. edn).

49. For the heart metaphor see also 'The BBC at the heart of your home', a brochure guide of 1996.

50. For an illuminating review of the film by Nigel Andrews see the *Financial Times*, 23 November 1989. Headed 'Spaced out time shuttles', it included a letter to Einstein. 'I am writing to you on my interdimensional fax machine to see if you can help. Many of us here on earth can no longer work out the time-space complexities of Hollywood movies.' For Hollywood movies, history and the historian see V. Sobchack (ed.), *The Persistence of History: Cinema, Television and the Modern Event* (London, 1996). For a Glasgow museum described as fun see J. Russell Taylor 'In the house of fun', *The Times*, 30 March 1996. See also the Jersey Museum Service brochure, 'We Say History is Fun'.

51. *International Herald Tribune*, 30 August 1989.

52. *The Times*, 3 November 1994.

53. Ibid., 25 November 1967; 4 November 1994. On the eve of the change a Lottery Promotion Company was formed with Lord Birkett as chairman and the Earl of Harewood and Lord Montagu of Beaulieu among the members.

54. Ibid., 29 November 1994. *Lottery Update*, an occasional paper, lists awards and provides guidance to applicants.

55. The letter setting out details of the proposal was in *The Times*, 17 April 1995. The signatories were Professors John Elliott, Patrick Collinson, Peter Hennessy and Roy Porter, Neil Cossons, Elizabeth Goodall, Patrick Green, Allan MacInnes, Lord Montagu of Beaulieu and myself. Backers included Kenneth Hudson, administrator of the European Museum of the Year Award, Peter Catterall, the director of the Institute for Contemporary British History, Gordon Marsden, editor of *History Today*, and the co-editor of this volume, Daniel Snowman.

56. Ibid., 4 April 1996.

119. Our ending: how the world may end as seen by Hogarth in 1764.

Further Reading

THE 1390s: *The Empty Throne*

A reliable historical survey of the late fourteenth and early fifteenth centuries may be found in May McKisack, *The Fourteenth Century, 1307– 1399* (Oxford, 1959) and E. F. Jacob, *The Fifteenth Century, 1399–1485* (Oxford, 1961).

Different aspects of social history are treated in more specialised studies. On aristocracy and chivalric ethos, see Maurice Keen, *Chivalry* (New Haven, 1984). The later-fourteenth-century peasantry and its discontents is treated in R. H. Hilton, *Bond Men Made Free: Medieval Peasant Movements and the English Rising of 1381* (London, 1973). Documents bearing on the Rising of 1381 and its interpretation may be found in R. B. Dobson, *The Peasants' Revolt of 1381* (London, 1970) and Steven Justice, *Writing and Rebellion: England in 1381* (Berkeley, 1994). The situation of women in late medieval society has been discussed by, among others, Mary Erler and Maryanne Kowaleski, *Women and Power in the Middle Ages* (Athens, Georgia, 1988) and P. J. P. Goldberg, *Women, Work, and Life Cycle in a Medieval Economy: Women in York and Yorkshire c. 1300–1520* (Oxford, 1992). For an overview of social structure and the problem of its representation in documents of the time see Jill Mann, *Chaucer and Medieval Estates Satire* (Cambridge, 1973).

Conditions of material life have been authoritatively portrayed by Christopher Dyer, *Standards of Living in the Later Middle Ages* (Cambridge, 1989). A lively picture of the general economic situation may be found in R. H. Britnell, *The Commercialisation of English Society, 1000–1500* (Cambridge, 1993). The terms of a continuing debate on the city vs the country as the premier site of later medieval economic development are captured in T. H. Aston and C. H. E. Philpin (eds), *The Brenner Debate: Agrarian Class Structure and Economic Development in Pre-Industrial Europe* (Cambridge, 1985).

Useful collections on cultural life at the end of the century include V. J. Scattergood and J. W. Sherborne (eds), *English Court Culture in the Later Middle Ages* (New York, 1983) and David Aers, *Culture and History, 1350–1600: Essays on English Communities, Identities and Writing* (Manchester, 1992) – the former concentrating on elite art and education, and the latter more broadly couched. The intersection of literature and history is explored in Barbara Hanawalt (ed.), *Chaucer's England* (Minneapolis, 1992). Exceptional books on major writers of the period include: J. A. Burrow, *Ricardian Poetry* (London, 1971); Derek Pearsall, *The Life of Geoffrey Chaucer* (Oxford, 1992); Lee Patterson, *Chaucer and the Subject of History* (Madison, 1991); Morton W. Bloomfield, *Piers Plowman as a Fourteenth-Century Apocalypse* (New Brunswick, 1962); John H. Fisher, *John Gower: Moral Philosopher and Friend of Chaucer* (New York, 1964).

Persistent elements of late medieval Catholicism are described in the opening chapters of Eamon Duffy, *The Stripping of the Altars: Traditional Religion in England, c. 1400–1580* (New Haven, 1992). A view of the sacramental centre of the late medieval Church, suggesting a great deal more inner diversity, is Miri Rubin, *Corpus Christi: The Eucharist in Late Medieval Culture* (Cambridge, 1991). The principal English alternative to orthodoxy is surveyed by Anne Hudson, *The Premature Reformation: Wycliffite Texts and Lollard History* (Oxford, 1988). The prophetic strain in medieval Christianity is discussed in Marjorie Reeves, *The Influence of Prophecy in the Later Middle Ages* (Oxford, 1969). Relevant studies by the leading continental historian of the period – especially 'Merchant's Time and Church's Time in the Middle Ages' – are found in Jacques Le Goff, *Time, Work, and Culture in the Middle Ages*, trans. Arthur Goldhammer (Chicago, 1980).

THE 1490S: *Continuities and Contrasts*

Historical writing on this period has tended to concentrate upon the nature of Henry VII's monarchy (including his court and its culture) and its success. Recent work – on fifteenth-century England in general – has also focused on relations between centre and localities, and on the role of both gentry and noble families in local and national politics. Some of these themes (and much else) are discussed in S. B. Chrimes, *Henry VII* (London, 1972), R. L. Storey, *The Reign of Henry VII* (London, 1968), J. A. F. Thomson, *The Transformation of Medieval England, 1370–1529* (Oxford, 1983) and J. Guy, *Tudor England* (Oxford, 1990). Other important studies include G. R. Elton's essay on 'Renaissance Monarchy' in his *Studies in Tudor and Stuart Government and Society*, i (Cambridge, 1975) and J. R. Lander, *Crown and Nobility, 1450–1509* (London, 1976). The shift away from constitutional and parliamentary history towards the study of the court as a power-centre is reflected in D. M. Loades, *The Tudor Court* (London, 1986, repr. 1992) and D. Starkey (ed.), *The English Court, 1470–1640* (London, 1987). Culture and propaganda are dealt with in S. Anglo, *Spectacle, Pageantry and Early Tudor Policy* (Oxford, 1969) and G. Kipling, *The Triumph of Honour* (Leiden, 1977). There is much useful information about the impact of printing in N. F. Blake, *Caxton: England's First Publisher* (London, 1976). For religious life and devotional practices M. Aston's volume of essays entitled *Lollards and Reformers* (London, 1984), K. V. Thomas's *Religion and the Decline of Magic* (Harmondsworth, 1971) and, most recently, E. Duffy's *The Stripping of the Altars* (London and New Haven, 1993) approach a multi-faceted subject from differing points of view. A useful and accessible selection from the Paston letters (in modern spelling) can be found in *The*

Paston Letters, ed. N. Davis (Oxford World Classics, Oxford, 1963, repr. 1983). For the 'new world' see P. M. Watts, 'Prophecy and Discovery: on the spiritual origins of Christopher Columbus's "Enterprise of the Indies"', *American Historical Review*, vol. 90 (1985).

THE 1590s: *Apotheosis or Nemesis of the Elizabethan Regime?*

The most readable biography of Elizabeth remains J. E. Neale, *Elizabeth I* (London, 1934), and the most up-to-date is that of W. MacCaffrey, *Elizabeth I* (London, 1993); more iconoclastic is C. Haigh, *Elizabeth I* (London, 1988). Haigh has also edited a valuable collection of essays, *The Reign of Elizabeth I* (London, 1985). For a recent political narrative of the 1590s see W. MacCaffrey, *Elizabeth I: War and Politics, 1588–1603* (Princeton, 1992). There is an enormous literature on Elizabethan religion. For divergent perspectives, see P. Collinson, *The Elizabethan Puritan Movement* (London, 1967), C. Haigh, *English Reformations: Religion, Politics, and Society under the Tudors* (Oxford, 1993), and D. MacCulloch, *The Later Reformation in England, 1547–1603* (London, 1990). The best introductions to the social and economic history of the period are K. Wrightson, *English Society, 1580–1680* (London, 1982) and D. M. Palliser, *The Age of Elizabeth: England under the Later Tudors, 1547–1603* (London, 1983). P. Slack, *Poverty and Policy in Tudor and Stuart England* (London, 1988) and J. A. Sharpe, *Crime in Early Modern England, 1550–1750* (London, 1984) provide excellent surveys of their respective themes. The demographic impact of the crisis can be surveyed in A. B. Appleby, *Famine in Tudor and Stuart England* (Liverpool, 1978), and Peter Clark provides a good account of urban responses in his essay, 'A Crisis Contained? The Condition of English Towns in the 1590s', in his *The European Crisis of the 1590s* (London, 1985). Local studies provide sidelights on aspects of the crisis: see I. W. Archer, *The Pursuit of Stability: Social Relations in Elizabethan London* (Cambridge, 1991); A. Hassell Smith, *County and Court: Government and Politics in Norfolk, 1558–1603* (Oxford, 1974); and D. MacCulloch, *Suffolk and the Tudors: Politics and Religion in an English County* (Oxford, 1986).

THE 1690s: *Finance, Fashion and Frivolity*

An overview of the decade can be found in David Ogg, *England in the Reigns of James II and William III* (Oxford, 1955). For politics see, among many other works, Henry Horwitz, *Parliament, Policy and Politics in the Reign of William III* (Manchester, 1977); J. H. Plumb, *The Growth of Political Stability in England, 1675–1725* (London, 1967); J. P. Kenyon, *Revolution Principles: The Politics of Party, 1689–1720* (Cambridge, 1977); Geoffrey Holmes, *Britain after the Glorious Revolution, 1689–1714* (London, 1969) and for an insight into the actual working of Parliament see Henry Horwitz (ed.), *The Parliamentary Diary of Narcissus Luttrell, 1691–93* (Oxford, 1972). For the European background to the Revolution of 1688 see John Carswell, *The Descent on England* (London, 1969).

For a recent succinct study see Henry Roseveare, *The Financial Revolution, 1660–1760* (London, 1991) and for war finance and much else D. W. Jones, *War and Economy in the Age of William III and Marlborough* (Oxford, 1988). For the rise of the professions and the civil service see the masterly work of Geoffrey Holmes, *Augustan England: Professions, State and Society, 1680–1730* (London, 1982) and for the excellent study of the rise of the state John Brewer, *Sinews of Power: War, Money and the English State, 1688–1783* (London, 1988).

Valuable studies covering other subjects considered in this essay include Joyce Appleby, *Economic Thought and Ideology in 17th Century England* (Princeton, 1978); Paul Hazard, *The European Mind, 1680–1715* (London, 1953); J. Harley, *Music in Purcell's London* (London, 1968); Dudley W. R. Bahlman, *The Moral Revolution of 1688* (New Haven, 1957); M. G. Jones, *The Charity School Movement* (London, 1938); Lee Davison et al., *Stilling the Grumbling Hive: The Response to Social and Economic Problems in England, 1689–1750* (Stroud, 1992); Neil McKendrick et al., *The Birth of a Consumer Society* (London, 1982); Walter Minchinton (ed.), *The Growth of English Overseas Trade* (London, 1969). The present author's two recent books are about London in the late seventeenth and early eighteenth centuries and both include extensive bibliographies. Peter Earle, *The Making of the English Middle Class: Business, Society and Family Life in London, 1660–1730* (London, 1989) and *A City Full of People: Men and Women of London, 1650–1750* (London, 1994).

The quickest way to get a feel for the period is to read in the contemporary literature. The following short list is designed to be both varied and entertaining. Daniel Defoe, *Moll Flanders* and *Colonel Jack*; E. Ward, *The London Spy* (ed. Ralph Straus, London, 1924); Christopher Morris (ed.), *The Illustrated Journeys of Celia Fiennes, 1685–c. 1712* (London, 1982); Richard Gough, *The History of Myddle*, ed. D.Hey (London, 1981); Gregory King, *Two Tracts*, ed. George E. Barnett (Baltimore, 1936); Jonathan Swift, *A Journal to Stella*, ed. Harold Williams (Oxford, 1948); Dudley Ryder, *Diary*, ed. W. Matthews (London, 1939) and of course the incomparable Pepys, even if his diary was written in the 1660s.

THE 1790s: *Visions of Unsullied Bliss*

Many of the books providing background, information and interpretation on particular aspects of this essay have already been listed at the appropriate point in the Notes. There are some superb overviews of British history in this period; Asa Briggs, *The Age of Improvement 1783–1867* (London, 1979) and Eric Evans, *The Forging of the Modern State: Early Industrial Britain, 1783–1870* (London, 1983) take the long view; more focused around 1800 are Clive Emsley's *British Society and the French Wars 1793–1815* (London, 1979) and Philip Anthony Brown, *The French Revolution in English History* (London, 1965). Continental and international dimensions are prominent in Paul Johnson's exhilarating *The Birth of the Modern* (London, 1991) and Robert R. Palmer's classic, *The Age of the Democratic Revolution: A Political History of Europe and America 1760–1800*, 2 vols (Princeton, NJ, 1959–64). Specifically for events across the Channel, Simon Schama's *Citizens:*

A Chronicle of the French Revolution (London, 1989) conveys the confused drama. E. P. Thompson's *The Making of the English Working Class* (London, 1963) examines the dawn of class politics in Britain and in the process shows how social and political values based upon the notion of tradition gave way to an idealisation of the new. The intellectual background to the new sense of newness is explored in David Spadafora's *The Idea of Progress in Eighteenth-Century Britain* (New Haven and London, 1990); while in *Representations of Revolution 1789–1820* (New Haven, Conn., 1983) the art historian Ronald Paulson analyses the often horrified responses of artists and cartoonists to the new world of 1800.

THE 1890s: *Past, Present and Future in Headlines*

There are two collections of essays to complement Holbrook Jackson's memorable survey *The Eighteen Nineties* (London, 1913; reprinted Harmondsworth, 1976) – J. Stokes (ed.), *Fin de Siècle/Fin du Globe: Fears and Fantasies at the Late-Nineteenth Century* (Basingstoke, 1992) and M. Teich and R. Porter (eds), *Fin de Siècle and its Legacy* (London, 1990). See also J. Stokes, *In the Nineties* (New York and London, 1989) and G. A. Cevasco (ed.), *The 1890s: An Encyclopedia of British Literature, Art and Culture* (New York and London, 1993).

For the details of late nineteenth-century British history see R. Shannon, *The Crisis of Imperialism, 1863–1915* (London, 1974); R. C. K. Ensor, *England, 1870–1914* (Oxford, 1936); and the latest study, J. Harris, *Private Lives: Public Spirit: A Social History of Britain, 1870–1914* (Oxford, 1993). For contemporary accounts see T. H. S. Escott, *England: its People, Polity and Pursuits* (1879, new edn 1890) and *Social Transformations of the Victorian Age* (London, 1897). The anthology edited by C. Harvie, G.Martin and A. Scharff, *Industrialization and Culture, 1830–1914* (Milton Keynes, 1970) is useful.

See also for controversial but illuminating monographs M. J. Wiener, *English Culture and the Decline of the Industrial Spirit, 1850–1950* (Cambridge, 1981) and A. L. Friedberg, *The Weary Titan: Britain and the Experience of Relative Decline, 1895–1905* (Guildford, 1988). Compare C. E. Schorske's brilliant *Fin de Siècle Vienna: Politics and Culture* (Princeton, 1981). See also B. Denvir, *The Late Victorians; Art, Design and Society, 1852–1910* (London, 1984); J. K. Walvin, *Leisure and Society, 1830–1950* (London, 1978) and E. Royle, *Modern Britain: A Social History, 1750–1985* (London, 1987). G. M. Young, *Victorian England: Portrait of An Age* (Oxford, 1936) is shot through with insights.

Within the context of R. Williams, *Culture and Society, 1760–1950* (Cambridge, 1958) and *The Long Revolution* (London, 1961) read J. H. Burrow, *Evolution and Society* (Cambridge, 1966); F. MacCarthy, *William Morris* (London, 1994); G. Beer, *Meredith: a Change of Masks* (Cambridge, 1970); M. Holroyd (ed.), *The Genius of Shaw* (London, 1989); B. Bergonzi (ed.), *H. G. Wells, A Collection of Critical Essays* (London, 1976); N. and J. Mackenzie,*The Time Traveller* (London, 1973) and *The First Fabians* (London, 1978); and R. Ellmann, *Oscar Wilde* (London, 1987). See also B. Ford (ed.), *The Cambridge Guide to the Arts in Britain*, vol. 7, *The Later Victorian Age* (Cambridge, 1989) which includes valuable bibliographies.

For 'generation' and 'decadence' see Max Nordau, *Entartung*, translated as *Degeneration* (London, 1892); R. Gilman, *Decadence: The Strange Life of an Epithet* (London, 1979); and J. E. Chamberlain and S. L. Gilman (eds), *Degeneration: the Dark Side of Progress* (New York and Guildford, 1985).

For material culture see A. Briggs, *Victorian Things* (London, 1988); A. Forty, *Objects of Desire* (London, 1986); A. Adburgham, *Shops and Shopping, 1800–1914* (London, 1964); H. Fraser, *The Coming of the Mass Market, 1850–1914* (London, 1981); J. Burnett, *Plenty and Want: A Social History of Diet in England from 1815 to the Present* (London, 1966); R. W. Fox and T. J. Jackson Lears (eds), *The Culture of Consumption* (New York, 1989); and I. F. Clarke, *The Pattern of Expectation, 1644–2001* (London, 1979).

See also C. Marvin, *When Old Technologies Were New* (New York and London, 1988); J. Beniger, *The Control Revolution: Technological and Economic Origins of the Information Society* (New York, 1986); T. P. Hughes, *Networks of Power, Electrification in Western Society* (Baltimore, 1983); H. Perkin, *The Age of the Automobile* (London, 1976); D. Edgerton, *England and the Aeroplane* (London, 1991); W. H. G. Armytage, *A Social History of Engineering* (London, 1961); and S. Kern, *The Culture of Time and Space, 1880–1918* (Cambridge, Mass., 1983).

For science see C. G. Bernhard, E. Crawford and P. Sorborn (eds), *Science, Technology and Society in the Time of Alfred Nobel* (Oxford, 1982).

For statistics see D. C. Marsh, *The Changing Social Structure of England and Wales, 1871–1951* (Oxford, 1958); Charles Booth's multi-volume *Life and Labour of the People of London* (London, 1891–1916); B. S. Rowntree, *Poverty* (London, 1901); and T. M. Porter, *The Rise of Statistical Thinking, 1820–1900* (Princeton, 1986). For the press see S. Koss, *The Rise and Fall of the Political Press in Britain: The Nineteenth Century* (Chapel Hill, 1981); A. J. Lee, *The Origins of the Popular Press in England, 1855–1914* (London, 1976); and D. Read, *The Power of News: the History of Reuters* (Oxford, 1992). See also R. N. Vyvyan, *Marconi and Wireless* (London, 1974).

THE 1990S: *The Final Chapter*

For late twentieth-century British history see A. Marwick, *British Society since 1945* (London, new edn 1996); J. Bartlett, *A History of Post-War Britain, 1945–74* (London, 1977); and A. Sked and C. Cook, *Post-War Britain: A Political History* (London, 1984).

On Margaret Thatcher and Thatcherism see M. Thatcher, *The Revival of Britain* (London, 1989); H. Young, *One of Us* (London, rev. edn 1992); P. Riddell, *The Thatcher Government* (London, 1985) and R. Skidelsky (ed.), *Thatcherism* (London, 1989).

For more detailed studies of particular aspects of late twentieth-century British experience and argument see S. Pollard, *The Waning of the British Economy* (London, 1977); R. R. Jewell, *The UK Economy and Europe* (London, 1993); I. Reid, *Social Class Differences in Britain: A Sourcebook* (London, 1989); R. Lowe, *the Welfare State in Britain since 1945* (London, 1993); M. Adeney and J. Lloyd, *The Miners' Strike, 1984–5: Loss Without Limit* (London, 1986); R. Klein, *The New*

Politics of the National Health Service (London, 1995); R. Skellington and P. Morris, *Race in Britain Today* (London, 1992); P. A. Helsby, *How the Church of England Works* (London, 1985); Y. M. Graham, *The Church Hesitant* (London, 1993); A. Holden, *The Tarnished Crown* (London, 1993); and C. Seymour Ure, *The British Press and Broadcasting since 1945* (London, 1991).

For meditations on the 1990s see A. Danchev (ed.), *Fin de Siècle: The Meaning of the Twentieth Century* (London, 1996) and H. Schwartz, *Century's End: An Orientation Manual Toward the Year 2000* (New York, 1996). See also J. Naisbit and P. Aburdeen, *Megatrends 2000* (New York, 1990); D. Bell, *The Coming of Post Industrial Society* (New York, 1973); F. Fukuyama, *The End of History and the Last Man* (Harmondsworth, 1992); I. Hassan, *The Postmodern Turn* (Columbus, Ohio, 1987); C. Newman, *The Post-Modern Aura* (Evanston, Ill., 1985); S. Bukatman, *Terminal Identity* (Durham, North Carolina, 1993); S. Connor, *Postmodernist Culture* (Oxford, 1989); V. Sobchack (ed.), *The Persistence of History: Cinema, Television and the Modern Event* (New York and London, 1996). For Baudrillard see J. Baudrillard, 'The Year 2000 has already happened' in A. and M. Kroker (eds), *Body Invaders* (New York, 1987). See also M. Poster (ed.), *Jean Baudrillard, Selected Writings* (Stanford, 1988). Compare J. F. Lyotard, *The Postmodern Condition* (Minneapolis, 1983).

On time see S. W. Hawking, *A Brief History of Time* (London, 1988); G. J. Whitrow, *Time in History: The Evolution of our General Awareness of Time and Temporal Perspective* (New York, 1988); D. Wilcox, *The Measures of Times Past* (Chicago, 1987); G. Piel, *The Acceleration of History* (London, 1972); A. Aveni, *Empires of Time* (New York, 1989); J. Rifkin, *Time Wars: The Primary Conflict in Human History* (New York, 1987); D. S. Landes, *Revolution in Time: Clocks and the Making of the Modern World* (New York, 1983); and E. D. Manches Ermath, *Sequel to History: Post-Modernism and the Crisis of Representational Time* (Princeton, 1992).

For versions of the last millennium and the first half of the next see F. Fernandez-Armesto, *Millennium* (London, 1995) and A. Berry, *The Next Five Hundred Years* (London, 1995); and for the millennium and prophecy see G. Duby, *L'An Mil* (Paris, 1967); M. Reeves, *The Influence of Prophecy in the later Middle Ages* (London, 1969); N. Cohn, *The Pursuit of the Millennium* (New York and London, rev. edn 1970); A. Williams, *Prophecy and Millenarism* (Harlow, 1980); E. Leoni, *Nostradamus: Life and Literature* (New York, 1961); P. Boyer, *When Time Shall Be No More: Prophecy Belief in Modern American Culture* (Cambridge, Mass., 1992); S. D. O'Leary, *Arguing the Apocalypse: A Thing of Millennial Rhetoric* (New York, 1994); A. T. Mann, *Millennium Prophecies* (London, 1992) and W. H. G. Armytage, *Yesterday's Tomorrows* (London, 1968). For futurology see D. Bell, *Towards the Year 2000* (Cambridge, Mass., 1968); D. Gabor, *Inventing the Future* (London, 1963); The Club of Rome, *Limits to Growth* (London, 1972); C. Freeman (ed.), *Are There Limits to Growth?* (Brighton, 1973); and K. Kumar, *Prophecy and Progress: The Sociology of Industrial and Post-Industrial Society* (London, 1973). See also C. Sagan, *The Demon-haunted World: Science as a Candle in the Dark* (New York, 1996).

On risk, chance and global survival, see M. Douglas and A. Wildavsky, *Risk and Culture* (New York, 1982); I. Hacking, *The Taming of Chance* (London, 1990); R.

Falk, *This Endangered Planet* (New York, 1972); and J. Ellul, *The Technological Society* (English translation, London, 1964).

On the space age see W. A. McDougall, *The Heavens and the Earth: A Political History of the Space Age* (New York, 1989) and for what lay behind it J. D. Bolter, *Turing's Man: Western Culture in the Computer Age* (North Carolina, 1984); L. Bagrit, *The Age of Automation* (London, 1964); H. Hopkins, *The Numbers Game* (London, 1973); D. Burnham, *The Rise of the Computer State* (London, 1984); H. Pagels, *The Dream of Reason: The Computer and the Rise of the Sciences of Complexity* (New York, 1989); P. Coveney and R. Highfield, *Frontiers of Complexity – the Search for Order in a Chaotic World* (London, 1996); and S. Levy, *Artificial Life: The Quest for a New Creation* (New York, 1992).

Compare N. Annan, *Our Age* (London, 1990) with J. Adolph, 'What is New Age?' in the *New Age Journal* (1988); and for one fascinating new age phenomenon see J. E. Mack, *Abduction: Human Encounters with Aliens* (Harvard, 1994). See also K. Pimental and H. Teixeira, *Virtual Reality* (New York, 1993). For other cultural phenomena and the role of the media see J. Seaton and B. Pimlott (eds), *The Media in British Politics* (London, 1987); and G. J. Mulgan, *Networks and the New Economics of Communication* (London, 1991). See also R. Bright, *Disneyland Inside Story* (New York, 1987). For consumer culture see G. Cross, *Time . . . Money: The Making of Consumer Culture* (London, 1993) and D. Miller (ed.), *Acknowledging Consumption: A Review of New Studies* (London, 1995).

Index